*A Cause We
Believe In!*

A Cause We Believe In!

Living through 21 years of Sudan Civil war

Bul Nyuop

A CAUSE WE BELIEVE IN!
LIVING THROUGH 21 YEARS OF SUDAN CIVIL WAR

iUniverse books may be ordered through booksellers or by contacting:

iUniverse
1663 Liberty Drive
Bloomington, IN 47403
www.iuniverse.com
1-800-Authors (1-800-288-4677)

ISBN: 978-1-5320-8134-7 (sc)
ISBN: 978-1-5320-8135-4 (e)

Library of Congress Control Number: 2019912718

Print information available on the last page.

iUniverse rev. date: 01/31/2020

"Some of us were born during the wars, grew up in wars, went to school in wars, and grew gray hair in wars"

By Dr John Garang de Mabior

In loving Memory of my parents.

Of mother Akon Mayom Bol and father Reec Nyuop Bul whose last breaths were all about me, how they missed me so much, their most regrets. To my mother who escorted me as I started my journey out of her motherhood, and painfully as she regretted one thing just before she passed that "dying while not knowing what ever happened to my Bul-Manyuon". Also, to my father who loved me so much, so much that he accidentally felt dead in a heart break upon wrongly misinformation that after so many decades of separation, I was only few miles away from him and the message that I wasn't coming home to him was unimaginable. I love you and will always carry on your love.

Contents

The Prologue

A cause we believed In is a memoire, an account of my young life, of a personal story that include; the tender age, the few steps leading to the millions of steps over the long journeys as a refugee across four countries to the ultimate answer; South Sudan independent in 2011. The memories and experiences are from personal knowledge acquired over the years including those that have altogether shaped Southern Sudanese history, particularly those related to the very reason of my journey. It's a very painful story, sometime amusing and emotional upon rehearsal, but it worth telling and continuing it. This writing is a vital reminder of my life and the challenges, ultimately how I ended with, *the cause we believe in*, and the birth of the Republic of South Sudan. As mention in the first line, it's a personal memoire, but one intertwined in the greater Southern Sudanese armed struggled for freedom against the inhumane and oppression of the Southern Sudanese people in the hand of a religious Islamic government of Khartoum. For those reasons and many, this is our journey, a Southern Sudanese journey through personal account and in part representing the voices of many who wouldn't speak for their own and the millions of heroes; deceased, veterans and those still leading the very cause of the struggle.

The historical content of this book is only from a personal expression, perspective and experiences, hence should not be use formally. Nevertheless, it's an account of the life I lived in relation to the history, the very cause that had impacted my young life. This writing is in addition to other published stories and in no contraction. It's part of collective struggle that covers generations of Sudanese life, and generations of wars that recently ended in the utmost achievement, the secession of southern region of Sudan, leading to the formation a country, the Republic of South Sudan. This is a life learning experience, part of what has changed my understanding of things, part of how I had come to accept the foreign life as my own, and unfortunately part of the negatively impacts that had affected my being including the physical or emotional attributes. Southern Sudan history is an emotional one, especially when foretold by those who had direct experiences and I am one of those who get emotional about it.

I was very young in 1987 when my first footsteps out of my family and village took a turn that was hard to look back decades later. This mean, some of my own memories and experiences may not be crystal to capture the journey or rethink the stories that led to not only our long match to Pinyudo, Ethiopia but what our whole story became; a refugee, and the long journey that followed over the next decades. Nevertheless, we need to continue shaping this journey, continue digging and awaken our minds and share this piece with those who could do better or speak well about it. We are the raw data for our stories hence personally obligated to share in the reconstruction of the whole. The source of the history is well shared among many boys who had become part of my life and luckily, they had shared their knowledge with me over those decades, about how the story began, the reasons behind the long epic story and it impacts. The truth is, this journey had cost the life of many, and had impacted many families negatively, however for those who lived to see the victory and the promised land, I tip my hat in a tribute to those challenges, and those who experienced more than some of us. This writing is also a response to so many requests especially during my college years when so many college mates, teammates, coworkers and professionals all wanted me to share my story with them. To me, telling my story while a college student would have impacted me negatively and I hope those fellow students could still have their question answered from this much content.

Special thanks

I want to extend my special thanks to those who had contributed to the development of this book, especially my sister Ahou Reec Nyuop, who in fact is the source for all the cultural knowledge included in this book. My thanks also go to my former Red Army, later named lost boys of Sudan, particularly those whose contributions have shaped my life, those who had helped me in so many ways though those tough times. As mentioned directly in the book, the first thank goes to my cousin Ajang Bul Nyuop who help me survived the early harsh years of Pinyudo. Without him, my story wouldn't be here.

Another thanks go to the warriors, the SPLA fighters including its inspirational leader, Dr John whose reasons of the war was a sooth for some young like me to understand that it was a just cause and despite our own suffering, liberated us from the bondage of the Khartoum and it's supporting mass. Much more thanks goes to my education, those who had aided me with all the resources, scholarships and grants. Thank you, Mr. DeBord, Miss Edwards, my foster mom Guadalupe Dildine and Mary Deans among others. Your relationship and guidance really helped me transitioned into the American life. Last but not least, I also want to acknowledge the contribution of organizations and institutions including the UN, Western Washington University and Governor Scholarships foundation.

The unexpected Turn!

It was 1987, just passed mid-year, when I returned from the cattle camp that my life was about to change, and drastically in a way we never saw coming. In the few weeks before I quickly return home, I was very excited of the opportunity to be at the cattle camp. This was my 2nd time being at the cattle camp. I had been to *Pageek* cattle camp, and there I was in *Payaar*, two of the Kongor many cattle camps. For most of my boyhood to that point, I have been a home boy, helping mam and dad with the few cattle, goat, sheep at the home front.

This opportunity came because my uncle's two sons were on their way to Ethiopia in the first wave of the recruitment, hence there was a need for me to help in taking care of both my father and uncle Bul Nyuop's cattle. My dad and uncle were always together. The vacuum was also widened by my sister who had returned home, leaving only my elder brother and cousin Nyuop-Gardit in charge of dozens herd of cattle. The two needed a boy. My brother Nyuop and cousin Gardit were young men, much responsible in the cattle camp affairs than taking care of the cattle. My brother was emerging as an unchallengeable wrestler and cousin Gaar-Aluel as he was also call was a very tall handsome singer. My present as a boy was very dearly needed and welcomed. Both could use me a lot.

As a dinka boy, particularly in the dinka section I came from; Twi, being at the cattle camp was a golden opportunity for a boy and I had missed that for too long prior to that

1

opportunity. A boyhood in the dinka was not a complete one without having to experience the life of a cattle camp. A life of so much challenges, yet what most boys longed for. This was a life of nearly no solid food, but completely of fresh cow milk day in day and day out. A life where people slept outside in the open during shine and rain, shill or warm. A life of hard work not only tending the large herd of cattle, but also cleaning after them, and leading them to the pastures and water areas over far distances. This was a life of competing boys. The life of which boys had to make themselves tough else face mistreatments of bullying both by peers, girls, and older men. A life of many challenges, yet the hurdle without which you would be of less regarded in the community. An educational life for future leadership. And despite how hard it sounds; it was ironically the life the dinka boys always long for. In another word, the road to our own *dinkanism*.

Cattle camp was where boys developed into wrestlers, to brave leaders, into warriors and yes into the future leaders of the communities. Boyhood was the base of the cultural education and leadership; you can't stand the challenges that the life will later present if you couldn't stand the life of cattle camp and that of boyhood. Either at the cattle or at the home front, a good start of personal life in the dinka began with a strong boyhood understanding of the community and its structure. As communities that passes on community history verbally, boys had to understand that role from their early years. And despite my young age at the time, that was the life I had missed for a long time. That was what boys want and my want at the time. I was mentally ready for it to be a dinka boy. I was finally in for a challenge.

My first two weeks at the camp went as expected. I started with great excitement, thanks to a warm welcoming by the peers. Many kids knew me, but also of my brother who at the time was making his name for their cattle camp. Already a hard worker, I was ready for the tedious work. Though I was a little too young and inexperienced, that didn't pardon me from many of the challenges. And despite the cherish welcome, I was the boy to be send for all the needs, a boy the other boys were testing their cattle camp skills on, the freshmen boy. Thankfully, my brother knew better to take care of me. He knew I was experiencing all those challenges of a newcomer, in term of how I was being treated or home sick challenges of non-solid food. He didn't step in to help in keeping me away from other boys' bullies, something that if he did, would have done me no favor especially my future.

However, the real challenge at the camp was not the work, but what comes with the cattle camp's live. The new life was overwhelming especially on my health. The sickness got the worse of me even while I tried to hide it. This was something other boys could bully me you for, at least they could think I missed home, mother and worse of all, food. I didn't want them to know it, but it became serious, not concealable. My brother had noticed the severity of it, so he asked me to return home for few days, a week or so. Though I was internally hesitating to accept, I was not helping and no medication to help me recover. I agreed, ok with the hope of quick recovery and returning. I wasn't running from the cattle camp's living, at least I didn't know what was awaiting me. I told my friends that my father wanted me to come back and that I was returning in just couple of days.

Bul Nyuop

One day, shortly after the cattle were milked and released for the pastures, there was a distance cousin going back home that day, my brother told me to leave for home with him. We took off at around 9 am, shortly after the cattle were released to the pastures. We dazzled for hours of long walk with few rest stops under the shades. I reached home that same evening, very tired and looking forward for a nice solid dinner, shower, and a long deep warm sleep under the cover of a building.

My mother and sister were surprise to see me since there was no way to communicate my return prior to my actual arrival or that I had been sick, nevertheless, they were excited. My father and younger brother were not outside at the time; my younger brother had been the boy; he was after the cattle. He had a hand full of all our goats, sheep, and cattle and of course chicken, he was very busy. He too had missed me. I had never been away that long from them, only few times when I had gone to our aunt Yaar Mayom's house and short time at Pageek. My sister was preparing dinner when I arrived home. They were overjoyed seeing me, at the same time there was still a question in their heart especially my sister about why I had left elder brother alone with the cattle. As my father return home that night, he was surprise to hear I was back after only few weeks. He was not pleased but I was lying down shaking with shivering cold and he couldn't help but to keep it inside him. I had always been home, and my father loved that because not only was I a good herder at home front, I was too a big reliable helper in the farm and hunting.

My sister and I never try to understand why we switched places, why she had to come home when she was needed the most to milk the cattle. We both should have been at the camp. However, we became aware of our father's plan soon just before it became official that indeed there was a phase II need for children to go to school. He was trying his best to take me out of the community eyes, to hide me and to placed me where I always wanted.

At that point the war and its ripples had reached most villages, at least those communities that were backing up the SPLA. There was no secret, the war was going to need more than just volunteering, there was going to be another call for men. At the time, the Sudan government had turned Southern communities against each other, arming communities, fueling tribal hatred against the SPLA/M main sympathizers, the dinka. In my part of the dinka, Murle was among the communities the Khartoum government had armed against their neighbors, us in particular because of our backing of the SPLA, or because of the SPLA chairman, Dr John Garang. Against the Bar-el Ghazel and Ngok dinka, Missirya or Murahilliin as they were also called were made more hostile and they too were armed to participate in cutting down the dinka.

In all cases, the well-equipped communities were told the dinka was their enemy and at the same time their source of wealth. As they often raid, they burn houses, take animals and other livelihood properties, abducting children mostly girls and women while killing men and of course all who resist their actions. Many people chose to send away their young boys to relative who live in much safer communities or to the inner cities. People were angered by such acts. This anger caused many to set their own defense, to acquire weapons to defense their own home and properties. Those were among the reasons the thousands volunteered to acquire arm, thinking they would come back to defense their land and stand against all the raids. Many of the young ones were also into this quest as they looked to be the future of their communities.

The raids were frequent. In my area of Kongor, there was a famous one called Ber-Majuang, named after their leader, Majuang. *Beer* in extended pronunciation is the local name for the Murle. It happened the very place I was born, Payoom. On that raid, the Murle came as a community. They organized in big number, not only strong men, they came with women and children. In their thinking, the women and children were going to get the cattle, sheep, goat, chicken, children, women and the men to fight the few dinka or chase them away. They had the impression or the information that the dinka youth have gone for the SPLA and their communities were defenseless. Of course, my community stood its ground before an armed reinforcement arrived and defeat them including killing its leader. That raid left a long-lasting memory but at the time also motivated many men to seek arms. The scene of that battle remained special years after the incident and before I left the village. Such frequent attacks forced some areas to be evacuated including some villages of Kongor.

As the second phase of that 1987 recruitment came around, SPLA was not only asking for volunteers of grown up men, but also for children who might go to school in places like Ethiopia, away from South Sudan in search of quality and un disturb education. In this regard, the SPLA/M request a certain number of children from a community and it was then decided at the community levels whose kid(s) would go and who will remain for the next turn and as required number is submitted. Of course, so many kids ended up joining voluntarily even those whose names were not submitted by their communities, especially because of the need for defense. As I later learned from my fellow boys, many who had been evacuated from their communities because of frequent random attacks also joined the journey voluntarily.

As my father heard the rumors of the second round, the chance was likely to be his son; and it was going to be my brother or me. His attempt was to hide me, took me away from the community view, to the cattle camp. At the early going, my mother and sister except father knew nothing about this going to Ethiopia. And after only few days away from the village, things had rapidly changed. As my parents received me back from the cattle camp, they confronted me with numerous talks about the ongoing recruitment, shouldn't have returned home at that time and I should not agree to going. Although I was ready for the cattle camp, I was not ready to go far away as that recruitment was concern. I was young, never been away and really lucked the aspiration that many had about Guns or any other life beside that of the village. However, my friends and peers' willingness to joining this recruitment made the reason for me to accept that opportunity too. Most kids at the time influenced one another and the same time bully those who though to remain at home.

My parents, especially my mother was very concern. She knew me very well. I had always been on her side, a favorable lovely boy, but had also known me personal and what I can do. She had seen my relationship with others and a lot on how I would treat others. I was a very humble and forgiving boy. A very lay back, shy boy, who could never take something in a wrong way, a boy who could not open or take the lid off a food container even when starving to death. As a boy who could avoid encounters, but not fight his way out of danger, someone who could be slap at once check and stand ready to turn the other cheek, a boy who could be taken advantage of. For her, I was a boy not ready for such a life, especially one witnessed from with many who had returned from the SPLA training camps. My mother and sister were recalling a life they had seen among soldiers who had passed through our village, soldiers who looks really malnourish, too skinny like they had been denied food for long. This was my parents' understanding of what the journey would be like for me.

She tried to discourage me, and for me to return to the cattle camp. Nevertheless, and regardless of how it sounds or whatever the parents were saying to dissuade me from going, there was no way I was remaining with many of my friends and age mates going. I had made my mine, it was done. I was enlisted, the one going, and it was sad for my family. After all, it was my father's turn to give his son. His brother's nieces went in the first round.

This recruitment was clearly promised as schooling intent; therefore, the young were preferred or ok. The process went quickly. We had only few weeks to prepare and day by day as we neared that last day, reality was kicking in, there were excitements, fear, horror, and doubts. Perhaps my brother was told that I wasn't coming back to the cattle camp, they had to find another option including my sister returning. However, that was a no for her until the finale of the process. While my sister was preparing my food for the journey, my mother had optioned herself to escort me out and my younger brother was not taking a second away from me. We were every day going to Pawel, the Kongor court center for our preparation and rehearsals. As I left that last morning, my younger brother was not ready to say the last bye to me. As my mother, father and I were walking toward Pawel on the main road, he was running behind us. He has been saying "if Bul go, then I am also going". It was neither him nor me, but a die together rises together sort of option. We were very close.

We arrived at Pawel for the final gathering. All the kids from other municipal centers; Wernyol and Duken or the communities of Duk County were there on the day of our departure. Pawel was very crowded, but only a matter of few hours and last greeting before it was emptied out. It was a very emotional day, with some excitements and reservations of inner thoughts. We were leaving the village, unlike the previous days, there was no returning back to the village on that day. It was a great day for those who were anxious for it, and a sad day for others; families, friends and for siblings who had to separate that day with one of their love ones. It was a day full of final farewell speeches, of words of encouragements and words of advice as always with the dinka culture when someone travels far away.

At around 2pm, it was a go time, we started southbound toward Wangulei, the next municipal center. It was chaotic, loud and noisy as we fought for the path. We departed by municipalities, i.e. Kongor, Wernyol, Duken and Wangulei. We were singing some emotional songs; about leaving the village, peers and love ones for the last time. As I later recalled, there was a long line of very little kids and few escorting adults. We didn't have much to carry, just food and cans of water. We were very fast at that onset. My mother was carrying my stuffs and I was along with the peers' chanting and singing bye-bye songs. As we went from town to town, and municipal to the other and through villages, we met more and more kids and we both marched toward the unknown direction, at least we didn't know but this was our journey to Panyido, Ethiopia.

We stopped for days in Manydeng as we awaited the final speech by then SPLA commander and assigned governor, Kuol Manyang Juuk. He was a feared man many of us heard of him. His speech was not only motivational, empowering, but also scaring the shit out of weaker ones among us. He was confrontable in scaring some to return to the villages, which is kind of ironic because as a commander, he would be leading the chant for recruitment. He never made it near me, but I never showed sign of weakness as my parent wanted me to portray so I could be spared. After few days there and having gained some rest and more foods, we were on our way again. We matched southward, parallel Madingbor, at the time occupied by the SAF. We run by quickly while maintaining minimum noise including footing. We were trying to avoid behind heard as that could have cause attack not only on us, but perhaps more on the communities. After weeks, nights and long days of walks, we finally made it to the end of dinka land, we made it to Anyidi, and just ahead of an inhabited territory; the Ajak Ageer dessert.

The desert, with its center as Kachtong was a wide-open territory between the two waring communities or tribes: the dinka and Murle. As the name Kachtong implies in dinka, this place was perhaps an historical place, a point where a certain fight was ended. As for our sake, the desert later became the area the boys encountered their first disaster, the taste of the journey a head. As with most deserts, there were many challenges expected, not only limited to hot sun, sandy wind but also thirst. We had limited water. More importantly, the area was possibly infested with Murle raiders from or to the dinka land roaming about. With the conditions in mind, the plan was to get on the journey during the early hours of the day so much distance is covered before the potential headwind, scotching sun and thirst.

On the morning of our journey, we got up, started out well. The sun came up very unfriendly. As we matched toward Kachtong, our age, along with the dusty head wind slowed our movement. We were unexpectedly caught by the sun before we reached Kachtong. At around eleven o'clock, with the sun already hot, the line stretched, we stopped for water break. We drank directly from the tanker, by hose. As we proceed, it got hotter and windy, the front batch was forced to rest at Kachtong. There was a hope for water there, but nothing to be found.

From Kachtong, the next destination was Machabol. However, with the dry windy and lack of water, the strategy to avoid thirst didn't help; we were urgently forced on the road before the sun cooled. The journey was again set, people to precede in the order of municipalities as we had prior to that point. This organized way didn't take long as everyone was long for water. Immediately out of Kachtong, we were running in all direct, no one was following a path, and the SPLA soldiers who escorted us including the very person in charged led the way. Thankfully, we were still young, healthy and energetic to run most of that distance. We kept up with the gun men as they run shooting into the air to see were birds would flight out, an indication of water source. There was no stream or river known, but we anticipated pools of dirty water, the ones the wilds drink from. It was obvious that birds and wild animals were always near the waters, so the locations the birds might flight out from upon hearing the gun shot was a hope of the water pool.

The man in-charged of us, Chol Aruai-Machar, also known as Chol-Mapath, now a brother-in-law was an SPLA rank. He was tasked with a very risky mission to lead us safely to Ethiopia with a personal consequent should any kid die on the way. With the incident of Ajak Ageer as he just witnessed and much of the journey ahead, there was a high possibility. No doubt he prayed hard throughout that journey and particularly at that instant. He was not the only one crying or praying hard, the few adults including my mother were praying for God help. Thankfully, God came to his and all our rescue, we found water, after some scary long runs. As I later learned from others, some boys were infamously saved by their own urine. The first to run to the water got some in their jars and run back to help the young and slow ones. I was lucky to be among the first who came to the water. At first, the soldiers warned people to make sure no one mess up the already dirty water. But as more and more came to the water, many jumped into the dirty and muddy waters to cool themselves off.

This was our early exposure to the road ahead. For many adults including my mother who was to return shortly, it was a tough moment to envision the journey a head. We set around the pool to rest as others filled their cans for the journey ahead. Soon, it was getting dark and we had to get going before it totally dark out in the mid of nowhere. We started out slowly again; people were tired after that scary first disaster encounter. I was young to notice if we had people who didn't make it, but clearly some were caught almost giving up.

As we neared the outskirt of Machabol, it was getting dark and scary again. There were a lot of thick bushes, possibly hiding places for the wild animals and attackers of any kind. It was also possible to go astray. The adults cautioned that we walk together and a little away from the bushes. We finally made it to Machabol at around eight o'clock PM. This post was a little situated some meters above the sea level. At least we felt an upward gradient as we walked. The night went quickly. It was here at this post that I and my mother parted. She had to return home with few other people who were returning. This was the last time I saw her, the last picture I remembered, and the last time we exchanged words as we chartered our road to Pinyudo, Ethiopia evening before they left.

The journey a head of us was scarier, not only with another possible thirst, but in much fear of attacks by the local bandits as we headed toward the Murle land; the Gumrua and Pibor area. In Pibor many of the locals tries to snatch away the young ones, others attempted to buy kids or lure them to their houses with food and milk. However, there were a lot of soldiers at Pibor to keep the security of the new arrival against the suspected abductors. In addition, we were warned of all the possibilities especially those that could be dangerous. We had few days of well-deserved rest at Pibor before the next journey. Our day and time of departure were kept secret to avoid possible ambush by Murle against us.

The next stretch of our journey took us through the Anyuak land; from Ajuara and Pochalla all the way to inside Ethiopia. After several days of walks, of sleepless dark and scary nights through a very dense forest, we crossed the speedy flowing Ajuara River to Pochalla and denser grassy narrow road; we were trending toward the Sudan & Ethiopia border. The forest was so dark and thick with tall grass that we heard the noise of the boys from far, but it took us a while before we got there. As I could recall, there was no perfect road, we were cutting through the thick forest. The echoes from the boys by the river dragged our tired bodies toward them with hopeful anticipation of final stop.

Finally, we emerged from a heavy thick wet forest, very tired and dumpy but with a growing excitement. As we stood just across the water, they were in Ethiopia and we were still in Sudan. These were group of boys that came months before us, and they look very happy seeing us as they were told prior to our arrival. Their present on the bank and their excitement to see us and seeing them was a relief, a signal that we had come to the destination, Pinyudo. There were so many boys by the river. Some boys started to recognize one another, started calling each other across from the river and with the roaring water of the hundred plus feet Wide River, it was like chaos, it was noisy, and acquaintances barely heard one another. As I later recalled this experience, it was our own lord of the flies' story. We found ourselves at the beach, very young and seem un organize and random, but it was a reunion.

Soon after the reunion, we started crossing, some on little canons, others jumped in the waters testing their swimming skill. We dispersed into their arms, into their residencies and many of them fed us with little that they had. As we felt at home, it was just the beginning of our long journey. We later stayed for four years in Pinyudo and rest became history.

Before 1987

It was in Kakuma Refugee Camp, in 1997, the first time since the early nineties that I was reminded of my age or birth in details. In Pinyudo while I was at my primary two, during school registration, our biography was taken along with half upper body photo. Underneath the picture frames, we spelled our names, year and place of birth. There were no ID issued out of those photos, and we never used the pictures for any reasons. Since Ethiopia, age was never a factor in our daily life. We never categorized or grouped ourselves by age in doing anything, we only chose who to do what job base on our physical looks and ability to do the job. Coincidentally, it was again at school registration, a decade plus and in another country, Kakuma Kenya, when another short biography was taken for the second time. In that second time, the registration was for Kenya Certificate for Primary Education, or locally known in Kenya as KCPE. I was a candidate, having passed my entry to eighth grade. We were only two months into our final year of our Primary education, or as the eighth-grade Kenyan curriculum English book titled it well; "the stepping out". During our first registration in Pinyudo, our minds were fresh, and many had recorded their ages as were told by their parents. Ten years after that first registration and a decade since we separated with parents, many had not kept those memories, especially through the hard challenges that have wiped out needed memories.

For some early years, the stories surrounding my birth were very vivid in my memory just as my mother uses to tell me, but as the challenging years of my refugee live added up, many of those great memories faded with time. Thanks to agemates, local events and the communities that we were raised in, some of those memories were shared. Again, I was reminded of the stories surrounding my birth and my agemates. Over the years in addition to Kakuma years where I regained some of the lost awareness, my sister came to much of what my mother use to narrate about us, the people and in this case my birth story.

According to my family and relatives, I was born in a village call Payoom, Kongor County, Jonglei State, South Sudan, the former southern region of the old Sudan. I was born at my parent's house, not at any medical facility, like nearly everyone in my village and in most cases the Southern region at the time. Home delivery was the normal way and doctors were traditional midwives, non-educated but experienced in their own ways. The year and date of my birth were never written anywhere. My parents, particularly my mother, used to narrate my birth verbally. According to that same narration, I was born during a locally known rainy events call *Adoot*. Many people were educated about their birth details, the events and places. Those times were very Stone Age for the Southern Sudanese, there were no recording of many things let alone births. In addition, there were no significant reasons for record keeping and even hard because of the illiteracy. However, the dinka like other African communities kept all their past and ancestral history on their memories and passed on verbally during the upbringing.

During my KCPE registration, I guessed my age and put it on the record book as May 25th, 1978. This was a total estimate but with no person or reason to dispute it otherwise. May and 25th were just my favored numbers, and 1978 as an estimate to keep myself relevant to others, in a sense keeping a similar age group. Being seen or perceived as the youngest among many competing boys was something of no favor. We often wanted to make ourselves big. I tried to make myself recognizable. Those estimated ages were left on that candidacy record book and nowhere else. There were no IDs issued showing the ages, and we were never asked about our ages since the day we record them on the book. Despite my effort to pretend, my classmates from that primary class to years of my secondary school in the camp, those colleagues still referred to me as "small-man", and physically I was.

At the eve of the millennium, with the opportunity of resettlement to the United States, we were reminded of our ages once more time and this time with restriction and understanding that they may remain in the book possibly forever. We were asked to think about our ages and specifically to mention the date, month and the year of birth, and to write them on paper, possibly permanently. This was an awakening and too a reminding of our parents and what they use to say about our period of birth. Many boys me included did not want to write down on paper a date we couldn't remember or that could be questionable or possibly causing the process. Many of us left the dates and months to the authorities, including the case workers who suggested January first for almost everyone. We then added the year. I chose 1984 because at that point, it placed me in the minor age and reasonable satisfying my then physical appearance. This was 2000. I was a 3rd year high school student and January 1ˢᵗ, 2001 turning seventeen. Coincidently, the age in most cases matched an American high School junior though I didn't have that knowledge at that point. During that resettlement registration, the starving refugee life of Kakuma had thinned many of the boys and our physical looks at that point and guested age were unquestionable. Mostly, January first was assigned to many of us.

In my attempt to reconstruct my life and lost memories, I consulted my sister in 2009 for more information. She, just like my mother was very good in remembering the verbal history, specifically about my birth, and once again she confirmed what my mother used to say, that I was born during *Adoot*. My elder brother was different, he suggested an event that was earlier than my sister and he had a reasonable point. Per his suggestion, I was born during the celebration of Mayom de Kongor. His suggestion narrowed the age to the boy born before me, whom I was told was born around 1975-74. The two suggestions were not far apart. In addition, the events surrounding our birth were never distinguished especially with no record at the time of the events, some could have been during the same year. In my quest, I sided with my sister's in confirmation of my mother's narrative.

With my birth year fixed traditionally at *Adoot*, my next quest was to trace it to the modern calendar year, and possibility to a month. As previously mentioned, this was a local event and only limited to people from my area. Over the years, people had tried to trace the years starting with obvious references such as the 1983 when the civil war resumed in Sudan. At the time of the publication, I am yet to find someone knowledgeable. As for the birth month, Adoot was named in according to the rainy situation at the time. It was a rainy season and land was so saturated with water that animals use to stuck in the mud or in dinka, *hoc aa ke ye dot* during grazing. As the name implies, a wet season, which narrows the time of my birth to rainy months. For sure, I wasn't born on a rainy day, else I would have been named Deng, meaning rain.

In other significances, my 2008 reunion with my sister and many of my birth relatives, also brought to light another significant truth regarding my birth. Many of my family members and extended family relatives often refer to me by my childhood nickname, Bul-Manyuon. Bul of course is my family given name (first name), named after my father's grandfather. Manyuon on the other hand is the family baby nick name and many members of my whole extended family widely call me by it. They often hyphenated the two names. Over many years of my young life, I never got the clear meaning behind the naming especially because of my early separation from the family. In addition, I never used this nickname during my life away from relative, hence it never been known by friends. During this reunion, twenty years later, my sister elaborated the meaning behind my childhood nickname, and I was very interest to learn.

Growing up, I knew less of what existed beyond my neighborhood and what I use to hear. For me, my community was my world and there was less exposure to know more. Our younghood stories and education was from home, through our parents and extended family members. In most cases, grandparents were the source of most knowledge. The taught us much about our ancestral genealogy, our relationship with others, history, folklore and of course wise sayings. We had no access to what we today call the modern education. As we came to learn, lack of access was in part due to the isolation which the southerners fought for. Traditionally, my grandparents died before my birth, hence they were less in that role. I only knew about my maternal grandmother. She lived in a separate village from us, and we rarely went to her house, but she always enjoyed our visit.

I learned the history of our people from my parents and relatives. In my area of Kongor, the verbal history dictated that the dinka have tilled the soil for subsistence over centuries and the forefathers migrated into our territory over varied periods and from various routes. According to Kenyan history regarding the people of Kenya as I later learned during our refugee life in Kenya, most of the Nilotic groups including the Luo, in fact came from Sudan and were often referred as distance cousins of the dinka and shilluk. This reference solidified many ties including the ways of life we both shared and cultural resemblances among many others. Both communities have their life in rearing huge herd of cattle & flock of chicken, sheep, and lived in traditional houses and cattle huts for centuries prior to my birth.

As farmers and animal keepers, we defended on the products of our own production. We grew a lot of sorghum, corn/maize, nuts, etc., all of which were pure, naturally grown, and organic. We often produce a lot to last the entire year. Our harvest times were time of great joy, not only with the produces but celebration of an occasion that brought many relative together. As kid, we enjoyed the fresh products. We had two big farms, one was around our home, and the other far from our house; we called that distanced farm *xoor* in the dialect.

Our animal products were vital supplement to our agricultural produces. We kept cattle, goal, sheep and chicken. We often move about with our cattle, practicing zero gracing, meaning, the land was publicly shared by everyone and all the neighboring animals graze unlimitedly. Our animals were never confined or lived on grown pastures. They pastured where grass was adequate and anywhere, they could reach. And when grass dried out due to season changes, we had plenty of swampy and Nile tributaries that brought waters and wetted our soil for year around pastures growth.

Singings, hunting and expeditionary fishing were among other hobbies that young grew up in and part taking to aspire the next generation. This was always the dream of a dinka man, to be superior or inspiring to the next generation. Those aspirations and dreams were taken away from me as I launched the first journey that separated me from my parents, my village, my dinka culture, and yes, my own dinka aspirations during the 1980s to Ethiopia before my age unfold for those activities. But the cause of the civil war didn't last with me in my family; it also terminated the future of my brother as a wrestler. Few years while I was in Pinyudo, he enlisted in the army and he went to the training camp and became an SPLA soldier till he was injured.

The boys' dream among the dinka was always to grow up and be like his father or to exceed the life of their parents; to be a farmer, to own a big herd of livestock, to be married to several wives and be vital member in the society. At my short years with them, I was always on my duty especially in tending the cattle, sheep, and goats at the home front and in farming. Those characters and lessons were keys during my young years away from them. But there was no boyhood in the dinka like getting involves in the youth activities and dreams.

My brother was already making his young life known among the best of Kongor and the neighboring community's youth's right before I left for Ethiopia. He was coming up as a strong wrestler and there is one of his wrestling matches that have stuck in the memory of Kongor community and neighbors. That wrestling match nicknamed after Kuol Manyang, the SPLA and the acting governor for the SPLM at the time was a unique match. For the first time, it was wrestling with no draw. There was to be a winner. One of the wrestlers must bring down the other; one was to defeat the other. My brother and his competitor were very young upcoming future stars of their cattle camps and they wrestled so strongly and equally that no one manages to bring the other down. It took minutes and they were very tired that several times, they attempted to sit back but they were brought back to the feud every second it happens. After so much impatience and sympathetic end, my brother surged the last power to bring down his competitor and falling over him that both were conscious to the point they were carded off the field to the nearby clinic, this became the end of the match and it became memorable. Unlike regular match in which several competitors from each side wrestle one after the other, this match ended at my brother wrestling.

We lived in perfect weather zone with no surprises. There were no incremental weathers, snow and chills, storms, hurricanes etc. Even during rainy seasons, which usually came between March and June and again between September and December, the breeze never gets cold; it was always warm enough for kids to play in the rain. Unlike most countries especially in the west where sun has a seasonal or un daily appearance, sun was visible from dawn to dusk year in year out in our world. At time due to the glazing sun and high temperatures, shades were always youthful in my village and there was always a need to plant trees around the family to provide not only fruits and seedling but also for shading.

The nights were warm and glittering above even without an artificial lighting. At sun fall, some natural glowing insects, adding blinking to the dark nights. We often stayed outside until it was time for bed, which was usually late. Above at sky high, we enjoyed the beauty of our sky and its contents. Stars, and other heavenly bodies, and at rear occasions airplanes from distance land above us were always visible to make our sitting outside exciting. As in most traditional African communities, we use to follow stars as their moves around the sky were also used in forecasting the weather and in turn use to foretell farming times and harvest. We were taught the significant of the heavenly bodies including the traditional histories behind them and how crucial they were in the life of the dinka. Moon was the big player in our nightly lights. Yes, the dinka had a story behind the dark spots on the moon. We observed the move from crescent to full moon. Among the dinka, every month was counted as thirty days with evenly divided fifteen days of moon and fifteen days of no moon. Verbally, the first day of the new moon appearance was always perfectly predicted.

With the prediction by the elders, we use to keep our eyes to the sky at sun dawn just to be the first to catch the new moon. Sometime, traditionally, there were beating of drums, blowing of horns and other sounds for the exciting welcoming of the new moon. There were many traditional beliefs associated with the new moon; so many celebrations were held at those times.

Our world was very remote but the only one we knew. We were comfortable and never wish for a better one otherwise. We lived with what we could afford and longed less for what we couldn't produce. In most cases, only women had few clothes, and we only afford them through barter trade. I.e. exchanging produces with clothes. The modern process would be selling a cow or farm produce and sent over the money to buy clothes. The common places at the time were far away mostly in the far north from our village, and far south. We used to hear about Malakal in the north and Tali in the South. We children, mostly boy didn't wear or need clothes. Sometimes you would only have a short and many other times, you just walk as nude as you came out from the womb of your mother. The weather was never terrible, never cold, and never hot, it was always perfect, hence less need for purposes related to weather. After all, we children never envy what we didn't know exist. Nakedness was obvious and universal; no one laugh at any. In fact, boys who were lucky enough to wear clothes were often bullied as if they were hiding something under their covers.

Our house was near the main road, very vulnerable for strangers and guests seeking basic needs and sleepovers but was also great in other situations. At a distance in front of our home toward the open forest and along the main road, there were two stranded old vehicles, a lorry and a big yellow truck. We used to play childhood games include the game of tag on those vehicles. I attributed a lot of my early scars especially around my legs to those vehicles. On the good side, we often climb on those vehicles to spot or track down our cattle. The old vehicles were also hiding places that sheltered us from the rain while herding. Finally, but not the least, we earned our first driving lessons by messing around with their steering wheels. Advantageously, we used to extract some useful parts of the vehicles for our own use. I remembered extracting all the wire mesh, melting it and make marbles out from it. However, the rustier vehicles were obviously disadvantageous too. As we often run around and over those rusted parts chasing one another, we often fall off, got cuts and got our limbs stuck, yet we were just young boys to even regard the disadvantages or to stop playing.

As a remote area, we had no access to not only clothing, but basic need that we could produce at our society label. Yes, our people defended for centuries on traditional medicines and healing, but there was much that went untreated. Thankfully our disconnection with the outside world also protected us from foreign diseases. As mentioned early, I was born at home and nearly everyone was born at home traditionally midwifed traditionally. Till the years prior to my departure from the village, I never knew any hospital, clinic or pharmacy in my village.

The dream of a boy was in most cases to be strong, be more competitive and to be most feared. As we grew up in my neighborhood, I was blessed to always be in the company of strong boys who not only were by friends, but blood relatives. We were living our dream, to be one-day important young men of our communities and societies. I never saw what was soon to change my life or specifically that that our boyhood life was and responsibilities as cattle herder would one day be even unimaginable or sound and feel so foreign. However, the choice, and the reasons that compelled to the Sudan 2nd civil war and our brothers picking up arms, leaving the villages, love ones and the cultures was a pressure that we could not ignore and was still coming for us.

From the time the war broke out in 1983 till we were later forced to leave our only known world, as children, we never knew there was anything wrong in that small world we only knew. We never knew what we lack or what we should have as human. As mentioned earlier, I was born in the village, at my mother house and not because there was no time to run to the hospital, there were no clinics or pharmacies let alone hospital. This was in part the reason of our struggle because in the same country, there was a modernize world, with healthcare system, with industrialized food production, with better way of transportation or movement from place to place and with all kind of envy that we lacked in the south. The rising against that injustice was right and bounced to happen.

The evidence of revolve increases in the early 1980s. It was around the 80th that we saw increases in soldiers with their guns. Our older brothers, cousins, icons, and acquaintances were leaving and joining the recruitment to be soldiers. We were young to comprehends the story but being a soldier was always a wish for us. It was like something to be proud about, yet we were still weak and young to hold or use guns. We used to follow the band of soldiers when they pass bye. Sometimes, we offered ourselves to carry their luggage for them. We didn't even know or dare to question why they had guns and why our brothers were joining. However, guns were always needed for personal use, including hunting and protection against the raiders or against wild animals. We knew nothing about the war. After all, there was no other source of information besides the parents and the soldiers themselves.

As, we later learned this round of the civil war, was a renewed or 2nd civil war, so called because the first civil war, called the Anyanya war ended in 1972, some years before I was born. During most of my refugee life and with no excess to historical books, we had known vocally that we had always been in war from prior to Sudan independence; from the condominium of Egypt and British in 1956 to the early seventies. However, and prior to when we left our village for Panyido, I knew nothing of the first war and even the beginning of the second, the SPLA/M war.

The first incident that was so not obvious was my brother's education. This was early 80s. My brother was secretly schooling at that time at Payoom center, the only school serving Payoom villages and surrounding. Secretly to say because we used to hide his school materials to deny that he was going to school. I didn't understand why we did that then and against whom. I am sure my parents were aware of their world and why or whom they were hiding my brother schooling from. I am also sure the sixties were fresh in their mine, because just before the end to that first civil war, toward the end of the sixties, the leaders of our community were massacred by the enemy, the Khartoum regime of Sudan. This killing happened at my court center, at Pawel. My district's paramount chief along with associate's chiefs were massacred in present of our own population, particularly their kin. This killing was not isolate incident; it was a series that Southerners had endured. They had massacred many people in Juba and Wau, two of the major towns in the South prior to that incident. My brother was born in that year, and I later learned because the kids were named after that massacre event.

During the Anglo-Egyptian rule, South Sudan was mostly left to govern it communities by way of indirect rule, that is via their own elders. However, after Sudan independent in 1956; the uprising that gave way to first civil war and south dissents were often blamed on the leaders, the community leaders and the young men who became the soldiers. Because of the civil war, the Khartoum regimes thought that our community leaders were not doing their will and that they were organizing the youth against them, hence justifying these series of intimidations.

Southerners educations were often limited, and their rise tracked. There were no government sponsored schools in most of the Southern urban and rural areas. Dating back to possibly 60s, Khartoum regimes was notoriously kicking out missionaries who sponsored most of the Southern educations. Many Christian missionaries were tortured, jailed and their school closed. Kids whose parents really wanted their kids to go to school had to go distance including other cities far away. Many of the students who later became the foundation of the SPLA never had smooth education at areas like Wau, Rumbek and across the Southern region. English was limited to sixth grade. Again, this was another way of keeping the Southerners in check and not getting to learn the Khartoum from the outside.

Following the culmination of the hostilities of the first civil war, the northerners resumed their business exploration of the southern regions, yet again violating the closed district ordinance. A provision adopted by the English early in the pre-independent as a mean to expel the Arabs dominances and their activities from the southern regions. With this violation and many others including the abrogation of the accord itself, there was further doubt but the invitation of war.

Inside the Khartoum, southerners were played again one another, and their leaders switches to suite their trust. In this regard, Abel Alier, the first executive council of the autonomous Southern Regional assembly was reinstated by Numeri in 1980 when he dismissed Lagu even though Southern Regional Assembly was dissatisfied with his first six-year term following the accord. In the same contact, Numeri forced Abel Alier to fire Bona Malual, the former central minister of information, and at the time Abel Alier's regional minister of industry and mining, a man who was the key voice against the central government on the issue of oil.

Khartoum did not stick to the agreement of the accord. Another violation and much an exploitation of the area and resources was the digging of the so call Jonglei canal. This was a long drainage system just at a visible distance from our home, planned to extract water from the Southern Sudd. At the time we didn't know what was going on or what it was for. Our educated and the world knew. For Khartoum, this project was mean for Southern development, for economic development, however, the regional assembly was never given an option to debate or rejected, the issue was tied to their political future and there were no more consultations. Protestors were crashed in 1974 upon the possibility of the canal. This was another cause for reaction and the world had all the inside reasons for the canal and together with our well-informed fellow Southerners in Khartoum, there were demonstrations and protested the construction. Southerners were infuriated and upon the resumption of the war, the project was quickly stopped by the SPLA Jamus Battalion.

There were also other projects that came as reward for Southern development, many never saw the light of day and for few that got started, Khartoum over the years quickly ate them away, stalled and in part transferred back to Northern region. These projects include the agricultural plantations, the Melut and Mongala sugar irrigation schemes, the Kapoeta iron ore and higher educational institutions such as the University of Wau were discontinued, not funded and transferred back north.

The other major issue leading to the war includes the mistreatment of the southern men in the army. At the time, the Sudan army comprised of all the Sudanese, yet most of the southerners were service men, files with only few holding lower ranks. And although history referred to seventies as the peaceful times that demonstrated the unity of Sudan, some of our local soldiers that were supposed to integrate in the Sudan army never saw the period in that contact, they reserve their stay in the bush following the integration. They were not watch dogs for the Southern communities, but many incidents were getting into the minds of million Southerners and war was eminent. The oppression and increased harassments against both the civilians and Southern men in uniform across the country were evidences of what later sparked the outrage that broke into the 2nd civil war.

Historians together with our verbal history stated the mutiny in which the Southern militia resisted being transferred to the north, and in so doing escalated disloyalty that quickly broke out as the second civil war. At the time, there was Sudan Army force (SAF) base in Madingbor, the most SAF occupied closer to my village. Upon the mutiny, the Southerners in the 105 and 104 battalions in Pibor, Pochalla, and Bor were the forces to be quelled, but in the fail process and under estimation by the Khartoum regime, they were attacked. Fortunately for them, they saw that coming and in the shameful face of Numeri, his ill trained forces according to Dr Garang, was destroyed to the point Numeri acknowledge the intensity of lost that he thought the counter attacked was reinforced by either Russian, Ethiopian or Libya as he miscalculated the strength of the Southerner forces. It was on this attack on the night of May 16th, that the subsequent events were inspired to happen. The next was Ayod revolt on June 6th, followed by the official birth of the SPLA/M in July that same year. This May, the 16th 1983 became historically the beginning of the revolution and the only day the Southerners would celebrate till January 9th day of 2005 when the Comprehensive Peace Agreement (CPA) paved the road to independent six years later.

The reasons leading to the civil war resumption was not due to the mutiny, it was the reasons of the mutiny. The president of Sudan when the war broke was Jaffrey Numeri, the man who ended the first civil war shortly after taking office in the Khartoum May 5th coup of 1969. Upon that invitation of war, the Khartoum administration took on some acts to quell the mutiny that included the sending of then John Garang, to come down south to quell his brothers and restore the clamminess. According to history, Garang was secretly working for that mutiny inside the Khartoum administration. He was in communication with some key leaders of the Anyanya II who never joined the SAF integration or those who pulled out after the 1972 agreement, smuggling arms to them and upon coming south. Upon this delegation, he knew everything was working out as planned. As he came to the South with the president mission, to calm the mutiny, Cornel John Garang joined the mutiny and along with the leaders of Anyanya II, they found their way to Ethiopia where they finally found and named the revolution as Sudan People Liberation Army/Movement later that July 1983. It was here after the founding of the SPLA/MA in July that the war official began.

As Khartoum loss that option of the massagers, it quickly turned to another. In September that same 1983, Khartoum tried to disrupt the unity of the South, it was meant to gratify the vast Arab north with the introduction of the September law. This was the tipping point for the Southerners, the move understood as the ultimate declaration of war. The September laws pronounced the re-division of then call *closed district* to disrupt the unity of Southern provinces, the pronouncement of Sharia law added to numerous irritations among those numbered in the SPLA manifesto got the southerners more aggravated, and this act by the Khartoum instead created a cause of unity among the Southerners. Other responses by the Khartoum government didn't help but in fact infuriated the south much. The next was the sending of the famous unit locally known as *hashara halif*, or ten thousand men due to their number, to formerly start the crackdown of the rebel units. These ten thousand armed men were responding to the surprise defection of John Garang and the restless of the Southern Units in many garrisons and the communities that were supporting the defected southern units.

At that time, still as kids we knew not much of what was happening. However, the call to raise arm and repudiate the massacre of our leaders had reach us to retaliate. For years following that 1983, our older brothers and parents were pouring in their support to the new liberation unit. It was not obvious in our young eyes during the days, but at nights, the youth were collecting one another, the recruitment to join the army was on. As young cattle keepers, many of my friends were delegated responsibilities that were formerly handled by their older brothers, sisters or parents and those responsibilities were taking them far to the cattle camps. While much was kept secret by the elder men, especially for the little ones, our mothers and sisters always tried to fill us in, to tell us where our older brothers were going and to explain why my friends were going to the cattle camps. At community events such as wrestling matches, some of the famous were never available and it started to make sense where they had gone or what was previously said.

As time passed, some of the first recruits started to return from their military training, they used to pass by, and we often help them with their luggage. Often when someone returned to the village, it was often an expected arrival and usually he will fire to the air some rounds of bullets and this was very alarming. As kids, we would run toward it. It was very fascinating to see someone from our village in military attires. We used to love holding guns, take that style walks and just pretend to be a soldier. It was the only foreign dream that we long for, to be a soldier. We never realize that the call to serve or fight the Khartoum and it military, or to hold our own guns was for war or yet to come. I was young, just living a happy normal life, not knowing that decades to come it would not only be called decades of Civil war, but personally as decades of separation from my parents and the village of my birth. We were young to the future when we eventually were compelled by the impacts of the young war to leave our land for the far away world.

Just before my call for the revolutionary and our fled to Ethiopia, the war was reaching my own village. I was now witnessing what was often hidden from us. Obviously, the war areas like Ayod, Poktap and Madding were distanced but we were hearing the rumbling of the heavy artilleries. Some people had overflown or had passed by as they run for shelters.

On one morning day, early before cattle were release to the pastures, while I was at my neighbor's house trying to get a fire, it happened so suddenly that something so unfamiliar passed overhead above our airspace. It was an airplane. In my young years, there was never anything I ever heard like that. I never witnessed a jet airplane or any military fighter jet, a boomer or MiG. The day was young, quite enough that the noise of the normal day was still at minimum, that even the sound of the small plane would vibrate the air above and be easily noticeable. As I kneed on the floor to place some cow dung's ball of fire into the scrape fire plate I was carrying, I heard an aircraft passing overhead. I was facing south, as the sun casted it rays to form my shadow in the west direction. At the sound of the plane, I turned my head sideway like a bird looking up. I saw the little aircraft coming in the North direction. It was a small plane, not that high, unlike the big ones that we were used to seeing. This was a different day and a different aircraft. It passed by quickly that I shortly resumed my business to collect fire. Before long, as started to head home, the sound returned, a little different I noticed, and from the east, at the direction of the rising sun, like it was coming inside the sun. I stopped, looked toward the sun. In a matter of seconds, the sound quickly changed, rattling and cracking I heard. I was so scared that I threw away the fire and dashed toward the house in no time. Everything was so quick. I did not know what had just happened and soon my normal day resume. As I later heard, we were boomed, the enemy tried to kill us. The bombs landed on the sorghums' field, fortunately, the field was soft they did not bust open. There were no serious injuries reported, only one woman was injured in the arm.

My call came in 1987. I was still a young boy, but had grown strong because of the life we lived, of daily wonders with cattle and hard farm work. However, this next job was taking us far away, we will grow away from the culture if we survive, and we would have our own guns and be soldiers instead of cattle herders. As boys, our only dream as we grew up was what our culture and community willed on us. There was no other cultural pride growing up then through the dinka's rite of passage. The boyhood to adulthood was marked by series of upscale developments and community participation and it was often exciting for a boy to be part of. Obviously, this process increases participation in the cultural activities such as the wrestling matches and recognitions. At the rite of passage, a boy gives up boy's role such as milking or being a mother boy etc. We were being weaned from our young boyhood to directly join the league of then call men, and many of us were not ready for it. However, it was something our communities or most individuals could resist.

Desperation beyond reach!

As we quickly found comfort in the hands and welcoming of the first group of boys we met at the new home, in Pinyudo, we only short lived the memories of the tough journey. We for the first time in over a week of living on meat and continuous worries of what was a head, were finally at the last stop and greeted by the warm welcome. We were settled in separate zones from the first groups, but so many had taken us in, providing us when we needed the most their help especially with the exhaustion of the journey. We had a lot to talk about, including our encounters with the locals on the way, the sleepless long nights, and of course our near thirst at Ajak Ageer. The first group passed through the same route, but with their own stories to tell.

We caught up for few days while we were trying to rest and recovering from exhaustions. Some of us had blisters, had pains all over their joins and of course first thoughts of depressions. I felt sick and got hospitalized shortly after our arrival, in part due to hunger, poor nutrition, weather and of course due to depression of continuous thoughts about parents and the life of abundance that we had. This was the first time many of us had been separated from our parents or the communities that we were born into and now desperate for so much with nearly nothing. It was the first time I felt the story my mother use to say, including the days when she tried to discourage me from joining. We arrived in Panyido not ready to live our own life and Panyido was not ready for us either.

Prior to our arrival, Panyido was nothing but an empty jungle, just inside Ethiopia and bordering the river that marked the border between Sudan and Ethiopia on the eastern and western borders for Sudan and Ethiopia respectively. I came with the second group, three months after the first wave, but still at our arrival, they had no shelters. The few locals, Anuak who lived a cheap life along the river were very randomly scattered, like they were not much connected, evidenced by the lack of communication centers such as market or administration centers. They were also disconnected with the rest of Ethiopia as history narrated them as recent immigrants from Sudan.

At that point of our long journey, we had exhausted the very less food we carried and world organizations who helps the refugees had not yet heard of us. Therefore, we were in dire need of the basic needs. However, our struggles were not only luck of basic needs, there were many challenges. The weather was different, and with our settlement next to the river, there were cooler breezes nights and without warm covering in our lack of blankets and clothes amid our weak bony bodies that could not generate enough heat to keep us warm, some of us caught cold and cough and other diseases. In addition, there were so many of us squeezed to live under tiny poor roofs, which created a situation that was too unhealthy. In that crowed atmosphere, sanitation and even ventilation we exposed ourselves to so much diseases. This situation got worse when diseases broke out shortly afterward. The diseases spread among us wildly and exponentially. And with no healthcare facilities, doctors and no medicines, it got worse. We were so young but faced with so much adults' world that we never had an opportunity to be prepared for.

The food we had, and its preparation might have also contributed to health problem. We were only getting so little, raw corns without supplement. For the first time, we would cook our own food and especially without prior knowledge in food preparation, our finished food was good enough for our stomachs. Obviously, we came from cultures where women had the sole responsibility in food preparation and there we were learning.

We felt disowned, lonely and in the middle of nowhere, out of touch with the world besides the land of Ethiopia that heard our echoes. Those conditions left some of us to no choice but to return home unknowingly. Many died.

I was hospitalized in that early going of Pinyudo. I came down with severe dysentery and diarrhea in no time without medicine to stop it or minimize the impact. We were so new to the crowded and un sanitized environment, with few doctors and luck of right medications. We also lacked the knowledge of prevention and because of the sanitation problem, flies and rats were spreading diseases from person to person and from one part of the camp to the other. With water diarrhea, we were supposed to keep ourselves dehydrated, drinking a lot of water to replace so much fluid we were losing, but instead many of the sick though the only way to stop diarrhea was avoid drinking or taking as little water, and in so doing, many dehydrated and passed. Nursing skills among us was also lucking. Many young sick boys like me were even picky at eating and with such limited food, once you skip a meal with the ongoing high stomach clearing dysentery, we made ourselves much sicker too and much sustainable. I lost so much weight that I felt so much weak to walk and even to take a bath. The area we occupied was so overcrowded; so many people were sleeping under small tents sharing very few utilities including the thin stunk air we defend on. We were so innocent and unknowledgeable in diseases prevention, especially with our waste disposal. There were no latrines or toilets available and mostly we were defecating in the open and not even far from our residents. This was so easy for flies and rats etc. to spreading the diseases among us. In addition, our water sources were not clean. We used river's water for all purposes. This was water full of harmful materials, not save for human consumption. In fact, there was often bright gold like sparkling running in the water.

People talks of deserted island, this was probably one, and one we never prepared for. Live was so hard and lonely early on. Clothing and shelters were very inadequate. Foods often came long way to get us, mostly taking long due to poor roads, and when it comes, it wasn't enough. At first, the assistant came from Ethiopian government, but later as the United Nation High Commissioner for Refugees heard of us, they started coming. Mostly, they were doubtful that refugees had come from somewhere to a place call Pinyudo near the Sudan Ethiopia border. But even when they heard us, they had to witness our present before food supply was shipped to us. That witnessing, took time, and that cost us, but even after the first supply of food and clothes, they were not convince enough of our number and the legitimacy of us mostly boys as refugees. In the Bible, it says in according to Jonah that the people of Nineveh that upon hearing the message from God that they had sinned against God, they immediately threw themselves on the sands put on rags clothes and sacks as they presented their repentance before God. That was our situation every time the UN representative comes to Pinyudo at our early days. Our leaders often try to explain to them how desperate for needs we were. We had to do a visual demonstration to validate our needs. We would put on sack clothes and sing songs that show our needy. Other times we would just cry following them as they collect their evidences and yes, pictures of crying desperate skeletons. At many other times we would try to fight over little food and other supplies to show our desperations.

Again, later when we started schools, we didn't have stationeries so had to write on the floor. We learned our alphabets and 123 in that manner. When the UN representatives start showing up in the camp and visiting our schools, they watched us and at the end they didn't have to be told why we were writing on the dirt. And for them as they watch us, they took pictures and life videos of us. Unlike the biblical story of Nineveh, those people who cried to Almighty God got forgiveness at instant response; we didn't get our basic needs fast as we cried in the present of those UN representatives. After all we were crying in front of human being who may not easily understand. No surprise to most of us, as we were knowledgeable of the dinka saying that "Someone else gift could never satisfied you"

The hard life of Pinyudo attacked us from all corners. In addition to the basic life struggle needs, the locals added a notch to our misery; we lost some lives in their hand. The good thing was, historically, the so call locals of Pinyudo were our own Sudanese and we knew better how to handle our own challenges, we encounter their aggression and from there on, we became good neighbors. In fact, some of them became refugees in their own land, they joined our communities and the feud was turn to friendship. As for ourselves, the refugees or particularly us the boys, we all came from different background and tribes and that include feuding communities of cultural and social differences. Even among the dinka themselves who were then the majority, there were differences in our language; we couldn't understand one another clearly; there were differences on the types of food and how to cook the similar ones. Sometime two boys would fight, but then that fighting extended as it became tribal.

However, we overcame many challenges. We thrived and overcame challenges in many ways. Foremost, thank to our elder brothers at the time, they took good care of us and good coexistent approaches were easily and foremost adapted. When we arrived in Pinyudo, we were settled by tribes and sub-tribes and further in clans. The administration initiated the system of integration. We were mixed or integrated, so boys from different background were grouped and they became the keepers of one another. With the integration, we could learn more about one another and finally clarifying some misunderstood stereotypes. Because of integration, we became in peace with people we didn't know, people we didn't trust and lack sense of friendship across tribal lines. With integration, as mentioned earlier, we were mixed, assigned leaders to oversee us and people who would otherwise be enemies became one another backer/keeper. Integration was in part a solution and an enforcement of coexistent.

Besides integration, church especially its teaching at the time also played a part in planting peace among us. While integration applied to all of us in achieving sense of knowing each other, the new Christian life also helped a lot in enforcing that relationship, in creating peace among us. Church was new, and its teaching were the opposite of what some of us knew or were raise in. Every time a touching word from the bible was taught, we tried to content ourselves within those words, especially the teaching such as loving one another and leaving in peace. I remember so many times when I felt the need to revenge against someone who might have kicked me at soccer field, or against a boy who knocked me down as we fought for food, at swimming, at the class or even against a leader who solely picked me among many others to do something for him. In such situations, my anger was only hold down by the world of love or peace heard that week from the church.

We started our refugee life very hard. I owed my life to my cousin Ajang Bul Nyuop. He did whatever God helped him with to show his present with me. He cared for me tirelessly. He was there all the time, sleepless in a nasty infectious surrounding. He went extra miles every day to make a better and tastier food from home and brought it to me. He clothed me and fed me on the time of those dire needs. There were feedings at the hospital, but it was not prepared to any standard that was helpful for sick people. There was much lacking at that early days, with UN yet to provide fully. I owe my cousin Ajang my very being.

As we felt challenges and distance from home, the lack of parental love for the first time in our young life also caused some lives. For the first time, you had no immediate family to take care of you, comfort you and turn to for any other need. We felt disowned, and many felt depressed. There were many incidents we even daydreamed about our cows and overall the love of home. On my case, at every time the thoughts came into my mind, I would just sing a song to watch it out or get engaged in something else. This cost a lot.

For others, returning home was an option, despite the fresh memories we just experienced, especially the distance and the wilderness of the road. There were numerous attempts by children to return to the warring Sudan, to their villages, and to their parents or relatives. Several plots & attempts were discovered and stopped by the adults.

In my period of hospitalization, a lot went on in the camp, so many people lost their lives, and this includes so many close boyhood friends. Later when my sickness got better, I would walk back to the camp to see my colleague. Often, I would not ask where some of my friends were, even after staying there for hours and no one updated me about the absence friends. At the same time, I never expect a death response or conclude that someone was probably dead. So, in many instances, I would keep my silent and just return to the hospital. Although I wasn't prepared to give up hope for the status of those friends that is what becomes the reality years later when I then had the courage to ask and finally learned about my childhood friend.

I sadly lost Aweech Bul while I was hospitalized. He was a cousin, but more of a dearly brother to me. He was perhaps a year or some months older, hence a keeper. We grew up side by side with a lot of influences from him. In fact, without him, maybe I wouldn't have been to Pinyudo, at least at the time. At that time, it wasn't neither very confidential anymore to reveal the death of a friend or acquaintance nor was it mournful as it usually was in the communities we came from. Many deaths had dried the eyes of so many young ones, and perhaps everyone was waiting their own fate. Nevertheless, we had been shaped adults only to swallow our own griefs.

After a long period of hospitalization in the Pinyudo dispensary hospital, I was progressively getting better and stronger, but of course with the passage of time. I was ok to move about, to run to the line to get my food, to walk to the river some kilometers away to take a bath, and to get out of the smelly hospital at times. However, even with the past of time, my physical look was not compromising to get me discharge according to the doctor. What happen in the hospital was, if the doctor sees your progress, not only just how you're recovering, but if you weren't getting stronger enough to meet the demand and physical strength needed to join the hard days the other boys were experiencing outside the hospital. The doctor never recommends my discharge and I was left in the hospital for a long time. As time went and my healthy showing very slow improvement, with the dynamic changes outside the hospital, there was a compelling need for me to make an urgent personal decision, to discharge myself. Obviously, I was waiting my time to be discharge by the doctor; however, that had taken months.

Outside the hospital, the children were integrated, and schools were already underway, i.e. groups were formed, children from various tribes mixed so the group comprise of people from different tribes, un acquaintances. Instantly when we came to Pinyudo, people from same tribes and those more closely related were living together or at proximity. The integration was done so boys from any community would peacefully live with others, hence sponsoring a future enduring peaceful refugee camp.

After my eight months tenure at the hospital, I discharged myself from the hospital, left and came to find my cousin Deng Reec Ajang. He was trying to convince his group administration, so I would be placed with him permanently. His requests were not accepted by the authorities of his group, he was told that I had to report myself to the camp administration, so I would be placed in a group that was not full. We didn't take that option, instead he told me to go to Ajang Bul, hoping I could get accepted there. Ajang was in group number nine. At that time, some groups were referred to after the name of the leaders. Group number seven, group eight, and group number nine were side by side in a cluster and they were called group de Anyuat, group de Makuei, and group de Kiir respectively after their leaders. In addition, within each of those groups were mostly boys from one region of the dinka. Many of my cousins including my uncle's son were in group nine and ten.

I left the hospital before I told Ajang, so it was going to be surprising for him to see me. The fact was, since he was integrated, it has been hard for him to visit me at the hospital as he used to do. As I came to find him, he was very pleased that I was finally discharged. Being discharge was not a bad thing at that time, it was a promise that the person was recovering, after all, the hospital itself was a very easy place to contract more sickness, and it was smelly and unsanitary. As Deng Reec tried to get me located with him, Ajang tried too, but there was nowhere, the sub-groups were full, and it was hard to keep track of people. Luckily group nine and ten were bordering each other, and there were subdivisions with spots vacated by children who had gone to live with close acquaintance in the other groups. I was placed in group 10. I became the new guy; many of the boys had already established friendship and acquaintance. Acquaintance was especially very important because there were a lot of times when a fight break out and if you had no friends or relative nearby, you could easily get beaten up and no one backing you up.

Shortly, I got my school enrollment opportunity. I was taken to school number 1, the 1st school to enroll the first group of students. School number one besides its great naming of being formed first, was also unique in that early formation and later in its history. All the boys who had a little educational background back from Sudan were enrolled into school number 1. There were not many teachers and classes were not enough for the students, therefore there were sessions, morning and afternoon classes. There were no desks inside our classrooms; the insides were dustier with very loose soil. We just had to laid down some wood or bring empty oil cans to sit on, later we built mud desk.

School started up very hard. There were only two subjects taught; math or arithmetic as it was called and English. Unlike learning in the developed countries at the time of this publication, back then we learned our alphabets in a hard way. The teacher shows how a letter is written or pronounces in the class on the blackboard. However, we had to practice writings outside on the sand. Every morning at both English and arithmetic sessions, we would come out of the classes, lined up outside in circles, kneel with the teacher standing at center of the circle and as he calls out a letter or a figure, we repeat it after him and then write it on the sand. The teacher then walks around, checking everyone's writing. Teachers were not nice especially in their approach to teaching. Mistake or incorrect answering were punishable. They would beat or step on student's fingers or beat their heads with a ruler till you get it and even then, you remain as the target. Sometime, the teacher could just make you so embarrass, sometime throwing some nasty words at you. Such incidents were discouraging and reasons that forced some to avoid the class altogether. As for little ones like me, it was not easy, but often resulted in frequent emotional experiences.

My first few lessons did not go well. In addition to lack of interest in education just because of my own understanding, I had challenges pronouncing some letters and figures in what was assumed ordinary way. This was not just me, but everyone who were purely from Twi; the Nilotic habitant of the former Twi east county of South Sudan. Our mother tongue had a unique way of pronouncing some letters and figures but not often welcomed and considered abnormal. My big hurdles were pronouncing L, 1 and 9 and of course in all the words such letters appear. People made fun of us and particularly on young one like me. Some teachers directly contributed in making you repeat or saying it in a way he wanted, which at turn created embarrassment and bullying as some kids laugh at us. Some teachers had the mind set on targeting those of us whom they knew were going to miss the question or in my case pronounce something wrong.

There were no choices; not going to school was not an option. In the group, it was known well who should be at school and who should be at home. If you didn't go to the school, you would explain. In addition, it was consequential, you would get water and help cook the food for the boys who went to school. I remember several times that I left in the morning like everyone, pretend to be going to school but then just roam about between schools or outside the class till it was time to go home, usually noted by the 3rd bell of the day.

I was in a very special class, a very competitive one with many bright kids. In fact, most of those kids later skipped some grades, i.e., jumping over some grades, like from 3rd grade to fifth grade in the same year. Many later graduated from high school at least a year before me. I was always among the quite kids in the class; my hands were never up, always counting on others to answer the question the teacher asked the class. I avoided the teachers by pretending to be following him and writing what he was saying. Nevertheless, most teachers were very keen of people who didn't want to participate, and they often punished those who missed the question. Such conditions fostered us to avoid attending the classes, exactly what I did that first term. However, as I could avoid the class, and the possibility of punishment, I couldn't avoid the quizzes at most cases. At my first exam, I found myself "chewing the pen" and left to look at the sky during the exam. I placed second to last on the first examination. The last was a cook. It was not something to be please with, not something to smile about and for sure not something to see again. My position as second to last was not just because everyone was brighter than me, I had written nothing. I did not know what I was doing.

That spot was awful and embarrassing as it came with a lot of stereotypes. It was the turning point for me. I realized at that instance to not guard myself against punishment anymore, but to protect the corrosion of my dignity. For days, I sat lonely and doing all things with no pride including avoiding people while contemplating many decisions. I was left to remind myself of the challenges and reason that brought me to Pinyudo.

As the second half of the year started, I switched to another class and from there on, my view of education and my position in the class, my willing to learn and my fear of punishment and embarrassment evaporated and positively and progressively everything changed. Since that second semester of that first year, my goal to be among the top students was always the leading force that drove me to class all the time. I went to a class headed by the most feared teacher. A medium height guy, curved, much thinner than most students, yet known for his red eyes and intimidating look, a guy who rarely show sign of happiness, and often beating up students. Sometime his intimation could just send fear through your veins and you ended up missing something you clearly knew. His name was Agou Alier, teacher Agou as we referred to him. I wasn't ready for him, and no one couldn't be intimidated by him, yet I had no choice better than being last of the class, a very not so me position by any mean. This was a big class of at least fifty students. At least there was a chance of hiding out, but unlike my former class, there weren't a lot distinguish students, there was chance to compete. When the exam came by and the results released, I felt to 42nd place, fifth places better than the cut offline. I was promoted to 2nd year.

In the first term of the second year, I jumped to fifteen place and later swing back to thirties as we went to 3rd grade. The school became interested from there on.

Our school supplies were very limited, usually pencils and exercise books were distributed once and incase of any lost, you had to explain it well. The class head student, also called the class monitor would take you to the teacher for you to get supplies. It was always a threatening process and sometimes it was rather convenience to not complain even if you didn't know where to get needed supplies. There were no markets where such things as stationeries were sold and even if there were, we had no money and lacked source of income. We didn't have school bags either, so pencils often get lost and theft was another reason. Most of us placed school supplies next to the bed and sometime just underneath, much in the visibility of those who had lost theirs.

Life was very hard during those first years of the Pinyudo refugee camp. While the caring elder boys at the time could be recognized, there were also cases were many young one felt taken advantage of. The older boys chose the best for themselves; the best clothes, best food, less work, best place to sleep and yes getting a lot of the young one to work for them. At the distribution of clothes or food or lines at the clinic, we often fought for the opportunities, stumbling over one another all for the chance of those limited resources. At these situations, the weak and many young ones could either chose to sideline and remain naked and unserved or otherwise join and get trembled on and suffered injuries in the process. It was survival of the pettiest if you will. If you chose to avoid one thing, then you could either remain naked or with no food and the impact from any of it was depressing.

As UN present started to be witnessed around the Pinyudo camp, demonstrations were organized so to exposed and our needs. And in addition to our luck of basic needs, we also demonstrated our need for school materials a year or so later when we started school. The coming of the UN was shortly followed by the construction of some big tents as food and clothes storage. Most of the time the visitors or UN representatives visited the camp, they acted around, taking pictures and sometime walking about with their long protruding nose covered, trying to avoid the smelly us or filth un sanitarily hospital environment.

Ironically, UN representative used to watch us, often taking pictures and video of us as we tackled one another down over the few non- fitting secondhand clothes or over the dietary animal feeding corns. For them, that was a good solid proof to take back to those who sent them, that indeed the skeletons were in dire need. This was the same case over the school supplies and like the UN representative, our elders also advocated for no other reason but to demonstrate to the UN. They used to say that white people some time don't believe from listening but from their eyes, and we had to intentionally fight over to sale our needy.

In the best-case scenarios, when work was shared, the sick individuals were excused from participation. In fact, a designated person was often appointed to take the sick to the clinic or to make sure they had food cooked for them. The little ones were given light duties including fetching waters for the team that went to fetch timber, grass thatch or ropes. In a way, we were our own social bees in many respects. However, there were other occasions and moments when compassion and care was not considered.

Diseases, especially communicable diseases were very predominant in the camp. Early on, many people died from luck of treatment, medicine and knowledgeable care. There were no knowledgeable doctors but the few were overwhelmed by the sick population. So many diseases were never treated but left to blend into our blood. And due to this susceptibility to diseases, simple diseases such as rickets, malaria, typhoid, ringworms, etc. were common elements among us. Fungus, ringworm, and lice's attack were among those that we could prevent, but due to other factors such as the luck of clothing, hard work etc. we left ourselves vulnerable to many illnesses. The conditions of the refugee camps in all the three camps we later visited all contributed to our health deficiencies decade later. Some kids never recovered to gain healthy growth, some experienced irregularities in their growth and others were later assumed mentally sick appearing in their act and long-term health. For a while in Kakuma, many were surprised that I grew to be over six feet ten years later when I first reunited with them after my return to South Sudan.

However, the big impacting part of our Panyidu life was not the inadequate basic needs especially after that first year; it was the endless tiresome hard labor. As a very young boy at the time, I was supposed to be among those who would remain close to home or boys of lighter choir; to fetch water, to pick firewood nearby or even staying idle, but that wasn't always the case for me. I was an industrious boy since before I left my father's house and I took that with me to my living in the refugee camp. My determination to do work launched me some nicknames. They called me "Small man" or "young man" describing me as someone who had swallowed a big man. I participated in most of the work especially around the camp. And due to my capabilities and participation in work that were often allocated to older boys, I didn't only get nick named, I was once appointed a leadership post of my squat.

It was not always best to put yourself out there as a capable person especially a younger boy because you ended up carrying a big stick or heavy load. And this almost cost me during our journey from Pochalla to Nairus. At two occasions when the younger and weak boys were transported by vans, I almost missed the first opportunity and of course missed the 2nd one. In Koor Agrep, just in the middle of the desert between Kapoeta and Buma, I boarded the truck the last day when all my age mates were already transported to the next destination, Magoos and just before the rest of the older boys continued the journey on foot that night. This was a dangerous trek, but we were running out of options and we couldn't wait for the trucks to get us all. The food we carried from Pochalla was running out. We were obviously in the middle of nowhere and luck of water of course was another situation. The water tankers were going back and forth between Koor Agrep and Buma, a military post we left 4-5 hours behind toward Pochalla. The final threat was of course the enemy locating us in the middle of the desert with nowhere to hide. As we were about to leave for Magoos, the young and the weak boys again got the opportunity and were transported by the limited vans and I again, I was left to walk that dangerous road.

The tedious hard work was the worst thing our life would always remember about Pinyudo. These works weren't always for our own good, but most for others including teachers or Pinyudo administrators and other key elites who often find affordable labor in our blood. We often help our teachers, I know they were not getting paid for leading or teaching us, but sometime especially when the situation was not considered, sometimes it didn't matter that we were paying them back, our bodies were weaker than our minds could comprehend. Our building materials in Pinyudo were nondurable materials; hence we annually rebuilt our own residents, our own schools, our fences etc. We were always worn out that at the end of every hard work. Most people would fell no appetite to eat or refurnish any exhausted energy. Most of the places the boys went to the building material were very far away, people stayed out there for weeks, staying and sleeping under the trees.

I never made it to Marol and Kuetachuol – the two distanced places where they boys went to cut timbers for construction and grass thatch for roofing respectively. I went to *Pan John Umot* - a distance place the boys went to gather ropes for building. This was a very faraway place and we had to go and return at that same day, unlike the other two. Later, another placed was found and that much closer. We called it chamlung. For clarification of those names, the boys created the names, pretty much describing them. They might have different names locally.

The most we remembered about those places was not the hard work or perhaps how far they were. Marol is remembered vividly by many because of it dark and thick forest of tall trees. We lost some of our own friends from that dark forest. *KuetAchuol,* a little closer compare to the avenues mentioned earlier, but too was unforgettable. Most of those mentioned places; people were out there for extended period of days and weeks for work. I only went to three of those places only for a day to pick up the finished products. Except *KuetAchuol,* a dinka name for accumulation of dirty, a body dirty in this case, was named as such because people would take days before taking any shower, hence accumulating body dirt. There was no source of water nearby. The drinking or cooking water came by tanks and that was often not enough let a lot showering. The impact of not showering was too visible. Most of the returning boys had scratches and cuts all over their bodies. Too, other sickness even the minor elements such as ringworms, malaria, severe headache from the head etc. were inevitable. And at times when the work was close to home such as regular going to the forest for building material or cooking firewood, we had to leave very early in the morning hours like three-four-five in the morning.

Pinyudo's work was tedious and continuous year around. School seemed to go year around in Pinyudo. There were not many days off. Even Sundays mostly started with church services and few hours of social and friendly visits, however they ended with work in the evenings. Obviously, we had no holidays except 16th May and Christmas, the rest of the time, it was work and school. There were no incremental weathers either, so there were no chances of works being postponed. Sometime, kids would try to run away from the minor group, but it was more consequential. There were always organized ways to bring them back from the communities and with punishments. The other cities were far away and of course there were no means available travel between the cities. We were very isolate and nowhere close by to run to, we were trapped or in another word, at a desperation beyond reach.

The few good days although not relaxing, were more of morale rejuvenations. The only notably were whenever our Pinyudo administrators expect special guests; the UN representative or SPLA dignitaries such as Dr. John Garang himself. At those days, we were often informed to remain around the camp. The UN visitors had to see our present, they had to see us showing those signs of miss fortunate and they had to take pictures that showed our attendant and needy as refugees.

As for the SPLA leaders, their visits were very soothing to us, not only did we get at least not work at those days, but their visits were rejuvenation of immerse moral among us. Openly to say that their speeches reminded us more about why we were in Pinyudo and why they were fighting, and again whom they were fighting against. Their speeches were often educational, encouraging and energizing us with the news of their current offensive and victories against the enemy. At the same time, they spoke more on trying to sooth the broken hearts of the little one like me. We often saw their coming as hopeful and time of joys and that always meant good news. They were our well spent times. Their messages were always optimistic of the SPLA success and that we boys will go home or will have the education that would make us leaders of our future country. As for those among us who really wished to get out of the challenging and hopeless life of the refugee and be enlisted or to join the SPLA sooner, Garang speeches were openly disappointing to them, because Garang often said to us that we were fighting the war with our pen and we were going to be future leaders of new Sudan, not mentioning joining the front. Their main message was often to persuade us to take education well and seriously, so we would be like them and to be teachers, and future leaders of new Sudan, we were often referred to as "seeds" for the new Sudan. At the end of his visits, he often left us completely hopefully about our future and with something to talk about.

SPLA was very appealing to all of us and many of us at those times were in crave to join the SPLA despite our reserve as "future seeds" of new Sudan. Of course, we were denied joining, at least openly. The SPLA training camps were mainly inside Ethiopia, at Bilpam and Bongo, very far from our refugee camp and our means to get there were very hard for those who were tied of our life and prefers to be soldiers than refugees. But even in our indirect participation in the struggle, SPLA representatives visit made us felt as if we were SPLA special reserved units. We did not have guns, nor did we get significant trainings, but we were organized in groups and sub just like the military units. Over time, some knowledgeable kids among us composed so many revolutionary songs that kept us in touch to the movement and our own inspiration. Every time whether at school or in our group or during our match to work, we sang the songs and they created intense morale for us. In fact, when Sadiq al Mahdi regime felt in 1989, we though our songs contributed much pressure in addition to the SPLA offensives. Every time we had visitors such as the SPLA/M Chairman, the camp was always busted in celebrations and our songs got chances to the radio wave that was often intercepted by the Khartoum, so they might have learned what was in the pocket for the SPLA.

Those days were better and more hopeful news that gave us engine and strength in the hard days of Pinyudo. In 1988 and part of 1989 just before the Khartoum regime changed leadership via a coup of June 30th that took Al Bashir to power, SPLA was winning a lot of key towns and posts and news were always rejuvenating the camps. Most nights we would hear this or that city or posts that felt into the hands and control of the SPLA. Although those difficult days had sucked so much out of our tender life, we were motivated by the SPLA victories. I remember the noisy nights when we heard the SPLA captured Madingbor, Akobo, Torit and many others. Madingbor was the suite where the war broke out, but in addition, that was the closest Khartoum controlled town to my village.

As the world turns:
The Exodus to Sudan

As our years added up, then in our 4th years, Pinyudo was getting better, we were getting the hang of living by our own and life was improving in many dimensions. We were getting stronger physically, spiritually and had far forgone our thoughts of home. We were used to our routine, that is, school, work and any spare time at the church and sport entertainments.

Food and other basic supplies were improving in quantity and quality. At least we were getting some flour alongside the regular maize grain. There was a yellow flour, known to be rich in protein and carbohydrate that was also being supplied. While the nutrition helped us much in regaining most of our lost energy, the flour was cooked during the heavy workdays and unlike a year or so earlier, now there was food for those who return from long hot day of work. We also had been growing our own vegetables; cabbages, tomatoes, fresh corns, and legumes, which added much fresh nutrition to our food supply.

The population at that point had increased, and our relationship with Sudanese in other Ethiopian towns was getting easy. People were travelling between Pinyudo and other towns. There were more that came to Pinyudo.

We were into organized competitive sports matches among groups. Our group # 1 was the football powerhouse, the one to beat. We had many of the best players going to school number one, therefore they played for group one.

But those competitions were not just between our groups, the games were also organized between and against the local teams, and with fellow Sudanese from other towns including Itang. While the common sport around the camp was the international football, other organized competitions were being introduced. I still remember the hot tea drinking competition, the running around the chairs and filling the buckets with water games. The venue where most of the local football competitions and other sport events were hosted was near my group, I always attended. They were always amusingly exciting times. In addition, night parties were growing, and I recalled attending few them, particularly the one near my group.

With the improvement in our standard of living and progress in our education, there was just at the corner, the rays of the world turning. As per common saying "when there is prosperity, disaster is not too far behind". The betterment of Pinyudo in the fourth year was an alert to last days of our camp. This finally came with the fall of Ethiopian government under Mengistu who had backed up the SPLA and associates. 1991 was the turn of the new world; series of world events had happened and continued to that point, not just in Ethiopia. The allies of Mengistu had collapsed; the fall of Soviet Union and the Berlin wall, the gulf war, and beyond his fall; the rays to SPLA split. We were in most cases disconnected with the world and we didn't see this development coming, but it soon came to our urgency.

Few months prior to the May 21st, 1991, Mengistu Haile Mariam overthrow, the SPLA/M has been under his mercy, both in the original formation, perhaps advise, and in provision of training bases. For long since taking power in the early seventies, Mengistu had been unshakeable leader, he had crashed his enemies and those who showed opposition to him. He too helped in crashing the early opponents of the SPLA leadership. As a result, his enemies had only got bitter and united under one goal, to get rid of him militarily. When the Ethiopian People Revolutionary Democratic Front, with the backing of the Sudan Government and perhaps some western world finally got their fists against Mengistu and the communist system, his government was overrun in a shame defeat. He was overthrown and casted out of Ethiopia along with his friends; the SPLA and refugees; both at Itang, Dimo and Panyido camps. Just like Mengistu himself, we had to run out of Ethiopia quickly.

Our fled from Panyido in some sense was a relieve from the never-ending hard work of Panyido. The message came very quick and we left like we were going to return. No one saw it and we run out unprepared. I remembered finishing my fourth-grade first term examination. The results were announced at a gathering just before the nights of our departure. It was a very urgent evacuation. We were heading back to Sudan, just inside at the border town of Pochalla at least that was all we knew. It was spring, but very wet and more like winter season. The road toward Pochalla had to go through the longer route, along the river and via the Gilo post. We didn't have much luggage but had to carry loads of foods and other basic needs. It took us couple of days wading the mud from Panyido to Gilo. We first settled on the Ethiopian side, Gilo one while waiting to cross to the Sudan side, at Gilo II. We had at least two weeks at Gilo before we finally made our two days walk toward Pochalla.

Despite the fled of Megistu and most of the refugees far inside Ethiopia, EPRD chase the Sudanese and perhaps any of their resistance all the way to Pinyudo and to the border at Gilo. There was constant warning that Oromo was coming. On the way, SPLA was destroying any equipment and arms they couldn't get out on time. Kiir was among the last to cross Gilo and he too urged the refugees to rush out. However, people ignored the calls, denying heading to Pochalla where hunger was widely unavoidable, and some intentionally discredited the warnings; interpreting them as intentions to drive them out of Gilo. Nevertheless, the attack indeed surprised Gilo and swiftly everyone was caught not ready. The Ethiopian People Revolutionary Democratic Front or EPRD army as they called themselves came from the rear, flanked Panyido and emerged at Gilo, catching many and creating ciaos with no help. People were drove toward the roaring river as they run away from the guns. There were those who could not swim, many with little children, and the sick. It was chaotic. People didn't know what to do. Many jumped into the overflown river totally in no plan & fear, only to drawn. Some were jumped over by the heavy non-swimmers both to die helplessly. For many who run away from gun points, along the river not knowing where they were heading only to get lost in the think mountainous wild. Others got caught and were taken as prisoners. This was historically an awful incident.

Starvation & war;
the years of Pochalla

My group was already in Pochalla when the attack of Gilo happened and only few of my group mates who had returned to get some food and those we left sick were caught in the middle of the attack. I lost one brave friend during the Gilo attack; a boy called Deng Aliei. We never knew what happened to him; killed or lost. Some of the returnees who might have seen him during that fled said they saw him with the group that run along the river toward Raad, an SPLA border post just inside the Sudan, east of Pochalla.

We were settled some four miles from the town center, just in the open forest along the Sobat River's tributary at a place called Golkur. This was a spot we were told to make as home. There no known prior settlement, just an open forest that we ended up clearing and construct our small shelters and later lived there till we left in early 1992.

As we worried much about the attack at Gilo and where about our friends caught in the attack, we were still in the prevailing enemy that forced many of those friends to return to Gilo and Panyido. At that point, we had exhausted every little food we had brought even our worthy belongings. I was young, and not determined to return to Pinyudo or Gilo amid that intense hunger prior to Gilo attack. But as some people return to Gilo and Pinyudo, there were some boys among us who entered a barter trade with locals of Pochalla, the Anyuak. We used to accumulate our valuable items and some boys among us would travel to the Anyuak village and trade the items for corns. This was also a terrifying option, because Anyuak were very tricky, at time they would enter the exchange but then they would run around to ambush and kill the very people they exchanged with and then take the corn back. However, fear had no choice but to "die trying" as 50 cents, the rapper had composed. That never stopped us, they boys developed their ways out.

At that point, I had my school uniforms from Pinyudo, all tagged under my bag pack. It was my favored belonging, but it was at this desperate point that I took it out at last sold it for a meal. We often share our luck and altogether pushes our days longer. These locals or tribe in general were known of excluding themselves from the movement, sometime portraying the dinka as foreigners, or specifically as people who travel aimlessly, or lucking permanent home. They were very primitive, knowing only their own little world. Their children had clothes and they were eager to get modern property in exchange with what they had, either being farm grown or animals' products. Their life depends on fishing and growing crops such as corns. They were never near the civilized cities where they could do real modern trade, but sometime only barter trade was available with the people from the towns. Pochalla was a military post, inhabitant by the SPLA who only possess few civilian clothes and other belongings.

As for few of us who remains around the camp, we scraped by on few helps from the UNICEF and some weekly distribution of meat by the camp administration and of course our own hopes. The UN could only afford to land a small aircraft on the Pochalla small lending strip. We were getting cups of beans and maize grain.

But as the Gilo attack closed us out of Pinyudo and all our tradable belongings running out, we turned to the God given resources around us. Thankfully, South Sudan, the former southern region of old Sudan indeed is a breadbasket as it has been frequently noted; with both above and under the soil endowed resources. It was time to have curiosity kill the cats. We were pushing one another to try thing we had never ate before. With familiar trees at wrong season of bearing fruits at the time, trees like willow, we started our adventure with the willow's leave. We used to feel the leave off, cooked it, and when the leave turned yellowish, it was done. We then drained the water and ate the leaves. Yes, it tasted awful, sometime very bitter but taste was bearable. We were selective because some leaves were better than the other and often, the fresh young leaves were preferred. They were less bitter plus once the water was drained from the cooked leaves, bitterness was also drained out. There was also a kind of really soured crawling plants called *anyiwac* according to the dinka dialect, named as such per it tastes. The best meal of this was when mixed with a small corn flour. Such a meal was complete, at least enhanced us to drink water and of course much filled stomach.

We knew and believe God was with us through all those times. As God was with the children of Israel during their wandering at the Sinai, providing them water from the rock and dropping bead and flock of quails, we too believed He was with us, helping us in one way or the other. At our starving hours, when there was no regular food supply, God provided as he did with the children of Israel, He provided fruits. There was one kind of fruit that many of us would ever remember. *Waak*, as some of us came to know the tree first time was like God sent. *Waak* was in abundance especially around Golkur, producing berries kinds of fruits. Most of the time, we were often scattered in the forest scavenging for these fruits. Although there was not much from it, it kept us reaches the next supply. What was amazing is how plenty it was and the time this became available, probably a good supply just like God provided bread to the Israelites children.

As wild fruits diminish and getting farther away from our reach, thanks to the biweekly meat ration, curtesy of the SPLM leadership. There was a biweekly ration of cow's meat distributed to us. Every week, we would wait in expectation immediately after we received that weekly supply. The meat was not enough, but we used to cook it in plenty of water, so we would have a lot of juice to share. Such a supply pushed us a head.

Passing time was the goal of our survival. One non-food action that kept our survival was the bonded among the boys. We kept our company strong and if one seems more hopeless, we all would gather to motivate one another. We also kept ourselves occupied by playing games. We had dominoes and another game we call *"tok ku row"*, unlike football and other energy exhausting games, these games were just played while seated. No energy waist, of course we didn't have energy. Our participation and gaming relaxed and occupied our minds from the worries. It was not until you try to get up that you may feel dizzy and no that you were too hungry. At this point, you would stand your ground for few minutes to regain some sight before starting a step. At the end of the game, you will realize that the sun has gone down, another day is almost gone. For anyone who had what to wait for, like counting for someone to come back from Ajuara or Gilo or even hopeful for Saturday, all we had to do is counting down the days and hours. At this point, many had stopped playing football because our legs were now very weak and no energy to exhaust. Our football fields were starting to re-grow some weeds in them.

As starvation took a toll and hurting us during the daytime, we barely slept well either due to constant fears at nights. There were many odds against us. We were located along the banks and before we came to Golkur, that location we later call home was a forest, thick jungle where not only animals roam about but also the home of mosquitoes. Mosquitoes' bites were the starvation that bothered us night in night out. The mosquito bites didn't only suck the less blood left in our protruded veins; it kept us up at nights, unfortunately keeping us reminded of the hunger. And then there were the rival locals. Anyuak was the biggest threats of all.

Amid the mounting challenges, we had our hope. We understood our situation and all we could do was to just live it, hope for the best days ahead. We knew what brought those challenges upon us and we were determined to the cause. At our time in Golkur, the promising courage of a good leader kept us hopeful. I remember the days when Ajang Alaak, the UN coordinator at the time, took frequently visits through the muddy on-foot narrow road between Pochalla and Golkur to see us and to bring UN Visitors to show the white people that in fact the minors were in Pochalla. There was one unforgettable moment when he visited the camp quite early with a white lady. Both arrived in Golkur very early with their sleeves and trousers pulled up as both emerged from the dense forest. They were wet, looked exhausted and with some mud spattered on their clothes. Together with other action taken, such demonstration of leadership comforted us, often promised good hope.

Even for people who didn't want to return to Gilo to fetch food, there were other reasons to go back to Gilo. During the fled, when Gilo was suddenly attacked, people were caught off guard and many run just to save their lives. In the process, a lot of belongings were discarded as gun rang from all ears. My friend Maker Dier Atem lost one of his vital personal property and he wanted to return there. He requested me to accompany him. We prepared for our return and two days later we left for Gilo. The walk was much scarier than when we initial passed through that road. First, we had to go to the main town of Pochalla and there on the riverbank, waited for people who were going back. Many people were going back and forth that road to find food in Gilo and to get back to Pinyudo.

We were lucky to find people right when we got to the river at Pochalla and after a day of wondering the swamp and densely forest of mosquitoes and wild animals, we reached Gilo II just before the sun set. There were so many people on the bank of the Gilo River. There were no families, all were young adult males and they had recreated Gilo 2 as their home. Obviously, there were no houses not even tents, they only slept just flat in the open, rain or shine. It was raining often there at least we experienced that during our few nights, yet those hungry bunch of people had nothing to worry about but their stomachs and hopes to find loads of maize that were thrown into the forest during the fled. On our first night, we got served by some friends; it was a great meal of soaked mixed of maize and beans. We didn't wait that much, the next day; we started our search for my friends lost. The perimeter of our search was not very narrow or specific, obviously he didn't know exactly where he had thrown it, but he knew only one side of the road. The forest was very dense and wet to make things worse and on top of that was that so many had searched through the area already. After a day and half, we lost our mojo, we believed that someone had found and took it. During the search however, we were lucky to recover some thrown away bags of beans. We did not get his bag, but our return was a success in some ways.

Un successful in finding his secrete item, we decided to head back to Pochalla. The return was much better; at least we had eaten enough food the days prior, we felt a little stronger. Upon returning while we were about 20 kilometers away, we saw a much bigger airplane circling overhead in Pochalla. This placed a little smile of hope on our faces as we approach. We didn't really want to feel optimistic that it was food supply, but we though at least the plane looks bigger than the small ones that have been coming. We kept our doubt and as we got closer. We were making a lot of guesses in our heads that it could be enemy plane or in the best way possible, perhaps food being drop. In the case of enemy plane, we had to keep our ears and eyes attentive for a bomb's sound. At the time of our departure from Pochalla, the field for hopeful food drop was being cleared and promises were that the big planes were first going to come and survey the field. Our best hope was the later guess. Upon our arrival we instantly approached people who were washing their clothes along the riverbank for the updates regarding the plane we saw circling the town. Someone responded that it was Manute Bol, from America. Of course, many of us have heard Manute prior, never knew he was in America.

I guessed that was not food, I murmured to myself and I felt disappointed. As I later learned, his visit was much welcomed by many of the dinka especially from the Bar al Ghazel region, where he belongs, who had composed songs about him. In the verbal history that many dinkas learned about Manute Bol, it's believed that Manute was taken to Wau from the village, the capital of Bar el Ghazel province, one of the famous towns of old Sudan, now in South Sudan. In addition to those verbal words, the familiar song that mentioned Manute as the tallest Sudanese, according to the song goes *"Yii Manute ke Majok Dengdit areer Wau"* meaning Manute and Majok, were still in Wau. His visit as he came from America probably made the song as thing of the past, a proof that he was not residing in Wau as was song proclaimed. That night when we came, he was already gone back, never seen him till I had another chance when he paid another visit some two years later while we had moved to Kakuma Refugee camp in Kenya, in which case I missed him again. In Pochalla, many including me noted that his visit was the turn of hunger struggle, because few weeks later, the leader of the camp Ajang Alaak started talking about some food dropping. We were told that the UN should drop some food, but first we had to clear a field where food would be dropped from the plane. The small airstrip we had in Pochalla was not paved; it was a normal mud floor and too small for a bigger plane to land on. We were very excited that eventually we were talking about food drop or food in the process of coming, we just had to wonder how long that would take till the words become a reality.

On our soils, inside the war territory Southern region and at the very place were the first mutiny that ignited the war happened, food was not the only challenge. We were always in a constant fear or warning of any possible attack and bombardment from the enemy. That finally came at the end of the first year, we were warned of a possible attack. This came during our Christmas celebration; we were halted from matching to Pochalla town when the threat became eminent and clearer that it was the Anuak. Anuak? A threat that was previously ignored was at the time taken seriously. The expectation could be that the Anuak were leading the enemy to our camp, from Ethiopia now that Ethiopia could be a backdoor. It wasn't clear how that would happen especially via Ethiopia, or the massive of the approaching enemy, but every night till that early morning, our ears were open for any crack and our bag pack on our side were equipped and ready to run. There were few approaches taken in the camp, which include being always on the high alert, to be always ready. Night curfew especially the travelling between Pochalla and among our groups was also enforced. In addition, the noise level was also to be kept low in the camp especially pass dawn. Finally, the SPLA forces also took some measures to safeguard against the expected enemy. There was some patrolling especially along the river. The few teachers who had guns were armed and reinforced with some older & experienced boys among us. Some older boys among us were told to be ready and to back up the few teachers who happened to be our guidance.

The enemy was expected to attack both the main Pochalla and our minor camp that was few miles in the outskirt of the main town. There were few patrols that were often done during the day along the long Pochalla river. Few nights later, at the dawn of one Saturday morning at around 4.45 am amid our sleep, we heard the first shot. We had been attacked. As for many who heard it, the sound of that shot was known by the experienced as a deadly one. Someone has been shot, and indeed as we came to learn in the morning, the first shot the first victim, one of the well-known teachers in our camp. Shortly, there was a pierce fire fight, the gun rained. We tried to dig and cover, but we had no holes or trenches to hide out. We lied focus, attentive to the windows, and of any voice that would prompt or command us to run.

We were residing a long one of the Sobat tributaries. There were groups very adjust to the river, a shot could easily kill someone from the other side of the bank of the river. My group, #1 was about quarter of a mile from the nearest bank. The enemy came from the opposite side of the tributary, across from our settlement, they were trying to cross to the camp. We too expect it from our side, the open forest. There were only few armed teachers and the main town of Pochalla was very far and we couldn't be rescued if the enemy breaks through the weak front that we had. Our hope was that the few gun men including our own teachers who had guns would stand their ground in defeating the enemy, the "live or die" believe from our militants. Beside the hopes, there were also bad scenarios diluting our hopes. There was also another fear that if the enemy faces a tough challenge from us, they could retreat to cross the river somewhere and again re-attack us. Luckily, in addition to us strengthen hearts and commitment, God was also on our side and our gun men stood their ground for several hours and finally the enemy was defeated after hours of fierce fight. At the end, we had casualties, less than could be anticipated, but we were victorious.

As that attack was now spoiled, the enemy has been defeated and although it has taken some lives from us, and the expectation that they might return, they suffered good defeat and this worry was off for a little. We resumed our food shortage worries and we were looking forward to the food dropping that was yet to come. We never saw food dropping before and how it works, all we had experienced was bombs drop by the enemy. In fact, later when food was dropped, some of us were scared that it could be bombs. In not long, the project to clear a field to drop food reached us, we were called to clear the field. Some of the boys among us were selected from our minor groups to go to Pochalla and try to clear the area for the food drop. Of course, this was a very exhausting task, but it was the only glint of hope. The Pochalla administration was also relocating people who had settled in the presumptive area to be cleared. There were no tractors or any kind of machines to clear the field off the big trees or tall grass. The boys had to use their last energy for the hope to exchange it with the hope of food if that was the case. In the speed of hunger urgency, the area was ready in matter of few days. After that, it was just the eyes and ears that paid attention to see and hear the plane coming with food. We expected big planes.

At the time, there were small planes that supplied condiments, like oil, salt and few bags of beans and sometime

UN personnel visitors. While we waited and waited, seeing and hearing no updates after the field was cleared, we were losing hope and patience, gratefully the preparation for food drops was underway in Lokichogio, Kenya. After a long period of patience, the wait seems over. On one morning, we woke up like any other day, keeping our ears open and eyes in the sky in the hope of food coming. There were no pre-signs that this day was going to be the end of hunger. This day eventually came. At around nine-ten o'clock one morning, we eventually heard a different sound of the plane, a loud one, a much bigger one; at least we could notice that unique sound before we finally allocated it as just above our tall trees as we emerged from our small huts. At the same time, while we hope for the big planes to bring food, we knew the big planes could also be our enemy that would boom us. So, there was always that concern of what if the plane is an enemy. However, some of us didn't really want to have such a though, the worse scenario. We were embracing hope. We came outside and we saw it as it went toward Pochalla, where the field was ready to receive its function. Just before it would drop anything, it had to fly some few times to see the target and acquaint itself with the field location, dimension and the surrounding.

Pochalla was a distance from us, the trees blocking our view, but we were so interested to see whether the plane was food plane, or enemy one and what it was about to drop. Some of us run to open areas free from trees to follow what was going on with the plane. As it went around and around, some people suggested that it was only surveying the field, that it wasn't probably dropping anything. That was disappointing to hear, and that is what ended up happened on that first visit. After several rounds, we all were looking at the sky and at last we saw it leaving. Truly, it was just a surveying plane, it had nothing to drop. We were all disappointed, but at the same time, we reasoned why it came, to view the field, it was about time.

Few days later, it came again, this time prepared to drop some food. It flies once a little higher, then came back much lower, and then third, it started low and goes up as we saw some white pallets rolling down from it. At our distance, the drops were like little white papers, you could see the sack and pallet flying in the air just like papers, and some people thought they were school supplies. But as the drop contacted the ground, there was a loud sound just like heavy object being dropped. Some of us paid close attention just in case the drops were boom. However, there were some kids from Golkur who started to make their way to Pochalla and later in the evening, they came with affirmative answer, that yes, confirming the food drop. Some boys in fact came with some physical proof, with some maize grains to solidify the good news.

The other not so interesting story was the plane missing the target and drops fell on the nearby residents. At this early round of drops, starvation was high that people were impatient with the law and how the food was supposed to be distributed. Even knowing that the plane was going to make at least two drops in one visit people were waiting nearby in the forest with anticipation to crawl toward the field to steal some before the food is collected for distribution. As the plane come around for the second or third drop, some of those hiding out were injured by the pallets.

We got the official confirmation that evening with some people being selected among us to go and get some ration for us. Everyone wanted to go, but we were organized enough to appoint some among us. It was a much-awaited evening. It became a routine for the plane to come drop food in Pochalla and the small planes landed with additive such as oil, salt, sugar, soap and beans. After a while, we were getting tired of walking from Golkur to Pochalla carrying heavy food on a wet swampy narrow road through a four-mile-thick forest. I know one time, the bees broke out, or perhaps someone destroyed its hive and many who travelled that road, not aware surprised by the sudden attack. In addition, people were spreading the news that the Anyuak were hiding near the road to kill and loots from people who were walking by themselves. Now we were realizing the fear that we had disregarded during the starvation time. Or perhaps, we were indirectly advocating the opportunity to get our own food drops at Golkur.

Despite the promising Pochalla with continuous food drop, school resumption, the bad time had left memories and stories. People were still looking to exit Pochalla. People were travelling back and forth between nearby garrisons including Pakook, Pibor and of course Pinyudo and Gilo. Others wanted to go all the way home. The other hopeful destinations were Kapoeta, and Kenya. Many attempts were made to exit Pochalla. There was a story of a man known to have shot his foot with a gun, so he could be airlifted to Kenya for treatment and eventually to a better place after discharged from the Loki hospital. This was "when there is a will, there is a way" curiosity.

The small aircraft that use to lend in Pochalla with few basic needs such as salts, beans, soft and sugar uses to take people along as it returned to Lokichogio. Many of the people who got the chances to Kenya via these small aircrafts got the chance through known dignitaries, or as people say, through "who you know". This was scrutinized further by tribe and sub-tribe. There were two main sub-tribes of dinka widely heard as the beneficiaries of those flights; the people from Bor with no specificity and the Bar el Ghazel tribe, sub-tribe of Agaar community. The facts were so clear that many nicks named the aircraft as Majak Agar (people from Agaar) or Majak Buor (people from Bor). The aircraft itself was nicked named Majak base on it all white body with some red strips colors.

As we started to resume our normal life, many of the boys finally came back to the group. We were again looking forward to restarting our school, sports and just being independent as was the case in Pinyudo. We were clearing of our playing fields that had been left unused for the duration of the starvation. The schools were underway, and very fashionable for me, we resumed fourth grade. Our classes were some ten - twenty seconds walk from our residents. Our teachers also lived with us. And with the food drop near us, we couldn't be happier. We didn't have much work after school hours as was the case in Pinyudo, so things were going much hopeful. Nevertheless, we were still inside the warring Sudan, civil war was raging, and anything could happen. Un fortunately, it was the next story, our own that became our enemy and that indirectly led to our urgent evacuation.

The House Divided!

Since its founding in the summer of 1983, the SPLA/M has confronted great challenges internally and externally; starting with the internal power struggle between the initial leaders and those of Anyanya two (un integrated Anyanya), then with the fall of Mengistu, the SPLA strong supporter, and ultimately, the numerous defeats. They all came at their own times, posting different challenges and each was handled separate and accordingly. While I had no history or details of each impacts to the SPLA, the fall of Mengistu was more than just impacting to the SPLA, we too run out of Ethiopia and in a hurry when Mengistu and his government were overthrown. For the SPLA, that was the toughest impact. Mengistu and his government have supported the SPLA from the very beginning. The SPLA founding and foundation was laid in Ethiopia, the training camps and all the assistance came through Ethiopia at the help of Mengistu. The early struggle between the SPLA against its brothers of the Anyanya remnants was ended perhaps courtesy of Mengistu as was told. With the sudden changes, the SPLA suddenly lose all those supports. The enemy felt energized and though the SPLA was done, and that they will deny it any start up in the South or at any other country and that they will rush in to crush the remnants.

But like those other challenging times, the movement recollected itself, kept the focus on the ultimate enemy and learns from the impacts. The movement quickly set its training camps inside its territories and supplies through other ways. The SPLA was moving forward. Perhaps in their own perspective, felt stronger than before. However, the tougher test was yet in the making against the movement. The inside enemy knew well the keys to SPLA success and its weakness. The disgruntled, many who felt against the movement or against its chairman, wanted to capitalize on the SPLA weakness, particularly those brought about by the fall of Mengistu. For the leading voices, they saw the fall of Mengistu and perhaps the fall of Berlin and communism and other circumstances as reasons and opportunity to convince the entire SPLA for change in the top leadership.

We were in Golkur, Pochalla, just emerging out of our toughest starvation when we suddenly heard of the call against John Garang, the chairman of the SPLA/M. The announcement came over the BBC news. We were puzzled and with less access to information, we were thrown into another deep worry. For weeks, people were crowding around the few radios while others constantly visiting Pochalla to find more information. We were worry about our fate.

For the SPLA, there was a lot to make of the call, whether it's had a link or influence from outside, Khartoum or just internal dissidence and obviously where the mass stands with the call. The obvious was, it was a distraction. Nobody not even Lam himself knew where such agitation would take the movement or the communities that were backing up or the source of movement. However, the split as it was later called occurred at a very bad time for the Southerners and the SPLA itself, for both internally displaced and those outside the country such as the refugees. This was an expected, or perhaps at the wrong time. Since its founding, one of the SPLA strength was its stand behind one leader.

As I later learn about the story or the proclamation, this call was spearheaded by Lam Akol, the former foreign minister for the SPLA/M. During his short time planning to overthrow Garang, he had posted contact with many of the leaders and by the time of the declaration, he had along with him commanders Dr. Riek Machar, and Gordon Kong Chuol among other ranks and files. For those who saw it coming or those who later recall the timing, there was no surprise. That plan came shortly after Lam was fired and reassigned. On the other hand, Dr Riek Machar, Kong Chuol among others had their own grievances or perhaps easily convinced by the argument. They accused Garang as a "dictator" and call the rest of the SPLA units and leadership to align with them in the new vision for "Southern Sudan independent".

After many consultants and assurance, Garang called the SPLA meeting of the high commands, those left on his side. By the autumn of 1991, he had learned who was with him and what to make of the call for that leadership change. Soon, many came to learn that the defectors have declared themselves as SPLA/M Nasir with their base in Nasir. Although there no knowledge of defectors next move, the naming of the defected branch and it site created an understanding that was worry some, an expectation that the army may aligns on tribal lines. The split posted worries among the multi-tribal movement and not only the Nuer who were left in the SPLA, but also for those dinka who were with Riek and those deployed in the Nasir area. The news of the split was quickly circulating.

For many of us who came from Pinyudo, we knew Riek Machar. He was one of the most heard commanders of the SPLA. During the SPLA/M victorious years of 1989-1990, we heard his name a lot and when he finally visited, we welcomed him with full celebrations. The news of his defection however resurfaced quote from his Pinyudo speech, especially the meaning when he said, and I paraphrase "the little person's gun can kill a grown man". Others thought of his arrogant and education as a possible reason that made him always look down on the uneducated commanders before him. However, he was too from the South Sudan's 2nd biggest tribe, the always proudest Nuer. Others have noted his background as a son of once Nuer leader. Perhaps the main force behind the move was the Ngundeng, a Nuer claimed prophets who proclaimed some prophecies in favor of the Nuer and Riek as many came to learn over time.

In late September 1991, about a month after the declaration, SPLA Nasir came out of its stronghold, matching toward the Kongor, the home area of John Garang as it was written at the time. The attached started from the present day Duk County all the way to area near the present Bor town with pursued toward Juba. This tactic was to post off Garang by killing his people. The SPLA Nasir ironically turn itself against what they formerly denounced Garang for, and the vision of their movement, the independence of South Sudan. The call had turned tribal, the very consequential impact the SPLA main or SPLA Torit as the Garang SPLA came to be call had feared and it was the unthinkable. The SPLA Nasir by that time had recruited the army called "white army" among the Nuer tribe with the help of a great false prophet whose calls gave an inspiring but wrong message of support to the army.

Many civilians run in all directions and separately for safety. The civilians who underestimate the attack and of course many who were caught unprepared run toward the swamps for hideout. The other group run following the main road toward present day Bor town and the area toward then equatorial province. For my father and others who tries to run with their cattle knowing not where they were heading, they were faced with so much challenge including slow escape. This was a very scary fled. Thousands were killed, abducted, loot and livelihood burned, and the rest drove toward Juba and beyond in a long chase. According to the relief organization individuals who runs toward the attack to help as was later published in the *Emma war*, as the SPLA came to nick named the conflict after Riek's English wife, and as the title of the aid worker book, the entire path was covered with dead bodies every short distance, with some hanging and other mutilated unthinkably. As Scott Paterson later wrote in his documentary "me against my brother" the Nuer went after any dinka that had life in it, a kid or older person. Many women were caught, raped and taken as wives along with young girls with all males killed. Others got lost and some fell on the hands of wilderness and of those barbaric communities who sympathized against the dinka. After days of chaotic run, so many people who seem to have escaped didn't have anything to eat and it cost the life of some especially the young.

It was over a decade later, when then little girl who later became my wife would tearfully recall the hard to belief story of her own experience when she got separated from parent during that sudden and dreadful fled. For three months, she was a lone with her cousin, also young at the time. The two made it through many jungles, walking along side soldiers, sleeping wherever they were prompt to stop for rest as they kept asking about their parents. However, they were not alone, so many families lost their love ones with no way to communicate or share some information. Three months later when she luckily found her parents, they were overwhelmed by her sudden unexpected appearance. At that point, the family had already presumed her dead and some of the traditional rituals had been performed in that anticipation.

They later run further from displaced camp to the other, running from the main enemy and terror of the lord resistance army. Like my memories of our starving days in Pochalla, she recalls the starvation that hit them in the camps and vividly the stories of them eating rats and selling all pieces of their belonging for a bit of meal. The fact that such memory stuck in the mind of such a young girl speak much of the severity of the struggle. My father and many extended family members collaborate same experiences.

The SPLA Torit respond was a little too late but also consequential. The first response however was to put on hold the offensive planned against the enemy and to divide its already thinned forces among the fronts; keeping eyes on the main enemy and rushing into the rescue civilians from within enemy. The confrontation between the two divisions of the SPLA ended the attack on the dinka as SPLA Nasir was pushed back, but the consequents of that war went beyond and several years after. The Nuer civil war was born from that conflict between the communities who felt the cause had impacts their land and people for no benefit to them. For the SPLA, the split was the turn of the movement, the turn of progress, the downfall to state the fact. The guerrilla lost a lot of territory as it found itself fighting two or more fronts. At that point, the movement was only on the defensive as more fallout continued. Nyuon, the very respectable and brave SPLA commander, at the time only second behind the chairman defected from the SPLA Main, only to hunted down and die shamefully against the moment years later.

Other conflicts were also born from or during the split including Karbino Kuanyin, another commander who defected and ended up waging a war against his own people. Nyuon, one of the bravest SPLA high command also spoiled his reputation when he too deserted the SPLA and fire his gun against the movement he helps found. At the end, as Garang later expressed, and I paraphrased "the split or Dr Riek stabbed the SPLA at the back" at a dire time, a period when the movement needed such a unity to not only reestablish training base inside the South, but focusing its main goal on attacking Juba. In fact, that reputation has never left Riek and it could be traced to the 2013 conflict that sparked the new country crisis and continuous divisions/hatred among the Southern Sudanese.

The journey of a thousand miles

On the opposite side from Bor, at Pochalla, the eastern corner of now South Sudan, our fear was constantly rising. We did not know what to expect especially on the side of the main enemy. However, we anticipate it was taking every option to attack us over in Pochalla. We were in Golkur, a few miles from Pochalla town center, less armed, and with no mean of quick communication with Pochalla or the outside world in that matter. While most of the news were reaching us through BBC and radio SPLA, the prospect of enemy attack wouldn't never go through such means.

Thankfully the SPLA always kept us on high alert, our safety was too a priority. On the 27th of Jan 1992, the move out of Pochalla came instantly, and quickly we were launched on the longest journey, as we heard at the time, to Nairus. At the time, we didn't know how far this was going to be, or how hard or challenging, but there was no option and no planning, the enemy was eminent. We were heading toward the Kenyan- South Sudan's border. We had no maps to see where Kenya was in relation to our journey, and all of us boys with few adults knew nothing of the area we were travelling to, only few accompanying soldiers had experienced of that road.

Like our fled from Panyidu, we never look forward for another. The memories and challenging aftermath of the Pinyudo fled were still fresh in mind, in fact less than a year. We had no choice especially when the enemy was around the corner. As we started off our long journey that one evening from Golkur, we experienced the test of this journey in not too long. We were going toward Pakook and this is the only distance we heard before. From there, Buma was our next stop and there onward, we knew less but have heard of tougher journey through wild and long desert. This journey, going through the many local habitats, was going to be a test for us to see our own local's communities as enemies against us and the SPLA at large. We were warned however not to ever stop alone or accepted being lured by the locals who could promised to give us water or food on the way. As we seem to run away from the known enemy of all the Southern Sudanese, the local enemy was too threatening.

However, our weak bodies were not ready for such a journey, and immediately into the journey, everyone felt tired, felt weak and soared. My body was telling me to rest, my feet were getting blister, my knee joints were very soar, my luggage and neck were giving up the heavy load on my back and head, but I had to keep going, in fact, I could not afford to give up my spot on the long line form. But there was no place to rest, the Anyuak were ever hostile that it was even riskier to relax behind or take an individual rest stop.

As mentioned, we were not ready, not even for the shoes to ware. Many didn't have good shoes; only sandals and our own made call *Mutikeli* mostly from car tires. And there was no sympathy from the heat and terrain. Many had blisters at the early going and throughout the journey. But more important, we were very unfit for this journey. Despite all those conditions, we kept fear in our head and the fear that drove us on that journey, we urged one another, and we kept encouraging one another and the thought to not put others in dire situation.

Our first rest from Pochalla was a most waited rest; unfortunately, it came after at least 3 hours of walk, let alone that it was only a rest meant for people larking behind to catch up. We had to find a good place, i.e. past the village of the Anyuak or were their hidings were not expected. It was always a good feeling when you had to wait for other because in the process, you were taking rest of your own body near security. But after every rest, it was worse to restart again, to reenergize, and to re-engine the body. The knees, the feet and all the joints were always volatile.

The journey that used to take four days was only two-three days even for our weak skeleton bodies. We arrived in Buma, settled on side of the hill. At that point and despite other challenges, we felt far away and very safe. Obviously, we only settled in the open, among the rocks and by few short un leafy acacia trees. Buma was not far from Pochalla, still inside the waring region of Sudan and the ultimately not out of reach of Khartoum. However, Buma had a reputation as one of the SPLA posts that was un though to pursue by the Sudan Army Force. It was the SPLA strong, in fact had been so since the resumption of the civil war. We didn't know how much of the SPLA was available at the post, but at least we hope they had big artilleries on the hills that would shell and destroyed the enemy before it got to exchange fire with the SPLA forces.

Our sense of safety however did not last, the news of Pochalla attack and falling into the hand of the enemy invigorated us only after a day plus at Buma. The survivors out of Pochalla came running the same distance in a day and half. Where the enemy came from, we had no quick idea, many of us felt puzzled, but to only imagine how spared we felt. As we later learn, this was one of the many 1992 victories the SPLA split had handed to Khartoum. Not only was there no SPLA present around the Malakal and most of the major cities in the Nuer land, but the SPAF had taken advantage of the split, supplied the Nasir faction with their military needs and money and in doing so bought their free passage to Pochalla.

The Pochalla was not totally evacuated at our departure, there were a lot of people behind; the communities with little children, the disables and severely sick people who were all waiting for luck to be lifted by planes to Lokichogio, Kenya or those who were waiting to catch any SPLA vehicles to Pibor. Many were affected in the attack of Pochalla. Beside those who lost their lives, some were captured and taken to Khartoum and of course the resources including SPLA properties that were taken over.

The SPLA response was to split their smaller units over so many fronts including some who run toward Pochalla or in the rescue of the dispersed defenseless refugees. At Buma, the enemy could shell us, it could bomb us. This situation became an immediate threat. The enemy could avoid the path we took and instead could disperse into the desert in their expectation of our next move and path or they could keep their satellite in that direction, so they could destroy us with bombardments. In addition, Buma could not sustain our present for long especially with no access to basic needs. The next journey out of Buma was also expected as more dangerous. This was a journey toward a very long desert. The next destination was Kapoeta, but that would be after days if not weeks of walk. We did not know the distance to be exact. However, this journey from Buma to Kapoeta was a long one with known reputation according to the SPLA history.

The plan was that most of our travelling would be at nights not only to avoid the enemy radar, but also to minimize a chance of thirst. Unlike few years earlier as we passed through Aja Ageer, we had more reasons to be more strategically careful here. My group started out from Buma between 2-3 pm one afternoon at expected warm hours, however it was sunny and good enough. Our first planned stop was after 5-6 hours from Buma, at a small post before Koor Agrep. We had been rested for days in Buma, now more energize, were ready if that was the safest way out. At early dawn, we arrived in Koor Bew, rested, fueled and shortly got on the road again till we arrived at Koor- Agrep. I arrived there at around 9pm and many came later. We were to settle in the middle of that Sahara for few days while we await the next move. We ended up taking couple a week there.

That place was Koor Agrep, not habited by people and not even animals, only small desert adapted animals. The adults who knew why the place was called Agrep said, it was renamed after the military battalion of the SPLA, a battalion called Agrep, who happen to have passed at the place before and had memorable experience that left the place so named. In those few days, we were once more reminded of the Kuet Achuol days of Panyidu. It was very hot, with unbearable dried wind and of course with no water for bath. The drinking and cooking water were brought from a far by tanks. The foods we carried were running out.

Bul Nyuop

We waited at Koor Agrep while seeking Red Cross and other UN agencies to arrange some transportation to the next post, Magoos. While resting was deserved, hunger was not very imminent. At the end, we were again set to continue the journey. We received few trucks to transport people over the long desert, but we had to take turns or at least starting with our little ones, the weak, sick, and women to the next destination. The ride was across some six plus hours to Magoos, another military garrison on the way to Kapoeta and Nairus. I was young among my colleagues, but because I had always been like an adult in my life, never remain behind in any long walks, never pretend to be sick, and never fail to do what was requested of me, I was remained with the older boys as I could humanize myself with dignity that I was honored. Over the days, the round came and went continuously, and as the number left in the desert grew smaller, I found myself looking much younger among my elder's mates. Just before the rest of the boys would start out on foot across the desert, I got my chance.

On one windy and cloudless morning, I was again up for my opportunity. The trucks had come back the previous night and were parked as our leaders screened us for the few opportunities, thinning out those who should board among the rest. I was the youngest, at least we could physically tell among my group and although many had believed in me all those times, they gave me the opportunity to finally take that last chance. I was called to the dock and soon we were on our way. The trucks were loaded to maximum, with barely any space to turn or sit. We stood most of the way. Amid the windy desert, the vehicles dazzled all day long, all you could hear was the whistling of the wind through short shrubs. We stopped several times for the vehicles to cool down, for the drivers to eat their readymade foods, and as our drivers meet other trucks returning to Koor Agrep.

It was a long steamy ride. The trucks were covered on all sides with plastic and it made it so hot as we drove. Obviously, this was not a paved road, just a human foot marked narrow sketches. After a long day, we finally saw signs of the of the destination. We arrived at Magoos, dusty, tied and yes, hungry. We were greeted by earlier arrivals and again warmly.

As for my fellows left at Koor-Agrep, they started out on foot. It was a scaring option, but we were running out of options. After hours of walk, streaming across the desert not knowing where they were heading, not knowing the fate of their safety, very weak physically, mentally; they were the strongest people. They relied in many prior experiences and God. They had made a long trek when they finally were met by the trucks and by the following night, everyone had come, and the place was so crowded and so noisy. As I later learned, this journey was almost fateful for my cousin Gabriel. His best friend realized his absence in the group midway in the walk. He was carrying too much load, mostly other people properties.

Luckily, this was better garrison compare to Koor Agrep, at least water wise. There were boreholes to sip water from, and most of us finally got a chance to shower first time in a long time. Like all the posts that we had passed through, they were not towns, no shelters; people just sit and slept out in the open. Magoos had a wide empty like field of crops, which was where we all slept at night. However, as we felt safe again just after the long journey, the most expected challenging walk, Magoos and their locals also had their hidden agenda. As was the case with the Anyuak out of Pochalla, there was a similar fear throughout the journey and at Magoos. The Magoos locals were too against the movement and of us, mostly the dinka. It was all in the mid of our well deserve slept when all over sudden, our own fellow Southerners, the local Taposa tribes armed themselves and awoke us with pierce quick gun shorts in to the crowded. We rose up and started running in all directions, stamping on one another and the luggage on the ground. We didn't know the direction we were heading to and many didn't know where the shots came from. It was quite a chaos. I run toward the small compound that was the center of the post, somehow saw a dugout and jumped into it to hide. The few soldiers run toward the outer of the field, only to find the shooters already gone, had loots some.

The following morning, we came to learn of the injuries and fatalities. Over the years, I came to know some of the victim of that shot and they include my friend Simon Dau, who got bullet into his neck. The other victim was my fellow Kongor community member. The next few days to the last day we left Magoos and during the trip out there, there was always fear and we tried all kind of security including curfew. The decision to get us out of Magoos was not quick either because the SPLA, the UNICEF and all the parties involved had to be wise in making sure the road at least is safe from both know enemy and other bribe locals and that we had the basic needs. We spent few more days there, trying to rest before another short and dangerous walk, beside we didn't want to show the local enemies that we feared them, or their attack set us on the road quickly, they shouldn't know when we were to resume our journey.

When all our journey recipes were ready, we were set to depart again and in the same manner as we left Koor Agrep with the sick, the weak, and some individuals with children taking the first few opportunities via convoys to Kapoeta. Again, I was left to walk. The last day came, and we took off one late evening during a drizzling chilly night. This was one of the scariest walks of all we took to that point. It was a lot of running to dash away from danger, through a very dark night on a narrow and wet slippery road. The road was not far from the locals, in fact we could see the rays of fire at their houses and the commotion in a distance. Anyone with a cloth on or shinny object was in no time covered with something dark. It was dangerous to get left behind, and regardless how painful or awful you felt, you could not make any sound, nor could you let your personal belongings make any noise at all. Thanks to many of the adults, they quickly noticed when the lines were stretched, they stopped the front to sit and make everyone wait quietly for the rest. As we sat quiet, breathing hard but gently, they extended their security perimeter at all directions. That night felt very long, we felt so scared. By the early dawn, we felt the grim of safety as we felt the danger zone was behind us.

We reached Nairijil, an old post just at the outskirt of Kapoeta. We rested there as we waited for everyone. We scrabbled around empty half-collapsed huts. It was hot, and wind just like Aja Ageer However, we were tired, sleepy and many of us felt to sleep the instant we heard that we were staying there till the evening. By noon, everyone had finally made it to the post, we had arrived safely. We proceed to

Kapoeta later that evening. It was a short and relaxing walk with no imminent threat at that distance from Kapoeta. It was there, on that road that we met then commander Kiir with his SPLA units, loaded in trucks and heading to Pochalla.

As we neared Kapoeta, I was much hopeful not only because we felt safe and expectation of some deserved rest, there was prospect to meet some of my immediate families who also had fled home in the impact of the Nuer attack on the dinka Bor. Along with my group, we arrived at Kapoeta shortly after the sun set. Already dark and curfew in place, we slept again on empty stomachs.

Early the next morning, I worked up and looked forward for that day and so were most of the boys in my group. My cousins came, and they took me with them. I was disappointed to find no immediate family of mine. I returned to the group at ten am, only to find the group relocated to the outskirt of the town toward the road to Nairus. We were on our next destination, to Nairus. I almost missed it.

Our journey to Nairus was a smooth ride; at least we were not walking. On one of our stops at the SPLA/M post, I met my immediate cousin, Dau Riak, aka Dau Yaar Mayom. He left Pinyudo few years before we fled in the fall of Mengistu and I did not even know he was already a soldier. It was a surprise, and we spend short good minutes. In fact, he brought me some food. I was very excited to see him. He later lost his life in the fight for Kapoeta when the town was retaken by the Sudan army forces.

We arrived in Nairus that night. It was already dark and again just like our arrival to Kapoeta, we knew nowhere to find water or to get ourselves food. The inadequate water brought to us was not even appropriate for drinking, it tasted salty. Again, as we arrived in Kapoeta, we slept on our empty stomach on our first night in Nairus. Thankfully, this was our destination, we had made it home. Unlike our previous settlements, Nairus was not a jungle, at least. We started our life, quickly by establishing our residencies and soon toward schools. However, we were in Sudan, inside the war and not from the reach of Khartoum army. In not long, we were forced to flee Nairus in the attack of Kapoeta, having spent only about 3 months. We run to Lokichioggio, the Kenyan north most city right at the border with South Sudan.

Loki as was also called, was a place we heard so well, particularly while in Pochalla. All the airplanes that brought food to Pochalla and many South Sudan displace camps flew out from Lokichogio airport. We quickly found freedom in Lokichioggio. Although the town was at the border with Sudan, it was a Kenyan town and we found it safe from Sudan bombardment just like when we were inside Ethiopia. We were enjoying drinking clean water, participating in buying and selling to and from Kenyan and of course the privilege of a developed town.

Nevertheless, Lokichioggio gave us a preview of what was yet to come, the future life in Kakuma and that of other Kenyan cities. It was there at Lokichioggio that we had the taste of Kakuma endless dusty wind, and the unfriendly of the Kakuma locals. We were also introduced to high stake robbery as a common standard of life in Kenyan cities.

Life of a refugee.
Kakuma Years

While in Lokichogio, the debated was proceeding to relocate the refugees further inside Kenya, to the heart land of the Turkana district, between Lokichogio and Lowdar, a place called Kakuma. The deal came to our realization in July 1992 between the Kenya government, the UN and possibly the unnoticed voices of the SPLA that Kakuma would be the site of the Sudanese Refugees. While that was a welcoming news for the refugees especially in anticipation of a safer place inside Kenya, the process and order of moving was instantly disagreeable within the Sudanese communities. Most communities were neither willing to be the first to board the trucks and hence sleep among the hostile local Turkanas around the Kakuma nor did any community wanted to be the last to sleep in Lokichogio. There were legitimate concerns. We knew the hostility of the Taposa; particularly between Kapoeta and Nairus, we anticipated the same with the Turkana. Historically, the Turkana and Taposa of Sudan were one people and share similar kind of life. At Loki, we experienced a lot of their raid on one another. Their fights often flared over to the town and near our residencies. A long with other experienced including our own attack at Magoos, people didn't want to be last in Loki and not first in Kakuma soil.

With the relocation to the Turkana heartland secured, the next hurdle was the relocation itself, i.e. who is going first and probably last. Many communities were reluctant to be the first in Kakuma, sleep in that open land, and with no security, or to be the last out of Lokichioggio. A side from the fear of Turkana at both ends, there was also a theory about a possibility that people may end up in Khartoum, in the hand of main enemy. Many people still had the memories such as the shooting in Magoos or other places when people were abruptly attacked or raided. Perhaps the later was an SPLA tactic to keep us at its grip, particularly the youths back into the south to join the movement. Those concerns however placed the leaders and all the parties in some limbo. The camp leader at the time was a man called Ajang Alaak, a dinka Bor in the subtribe Kongor. I do not know how the decision was reach, but due to that disagreement on which group to set its foot in Kakuma, he along with his immediate relatives of what became group eight accept the risk to lead the refugees to Kakuma. Coincidently, Kongor community which literally mean lead led the way.

My group turn came in mid-September, we were loaded on trucks and arrived in Kakuma, I believed on the 27th 1992. Though the ride from Lokichogio to Kakuma was two hours to nowhere, it was the first smooth ride of our experience. It was the first paved road we drove on. After the short ride, the paved road ended as we got off down on to the dusty and into the grove forest habited by the local Turkanas. We continue two-three miles away from the road and into a narrow piece of land that lied between two seasonal rivers. As went farther away from the road, southward, we bypass many people who came before us, scattered and every time we approach such people residencies, people would run to us to see if their friends and family members were on the trucks. It was so dusty that when we got off the trucks, we were already covered in the red sandy dusk. Our trucks finally came to a stop and we unloaded and shortly the trucks left. We had nothing; all we carried with us were our personal luggage, some food, and empty canes for water. For a short while, we didn't know where to go, so we just put together our belonging and we started playing while other start wondering how the night fall will go about. As we thought about our first night there, a guy came, asked us to follow him as he led us away from the dusk road into a darker forest. He finally came to a haul and said; you guys sit here till further notice or otherwise make yourself at home, that was home!

As the evening rolled in, we circled our luggage, thought of our security. As anticipated coming into Kakuma, we were concern about the locals attacking us. That first night, we went worry much about our safety than food, shower or the luck of comfortable sleeping place, hence we didn't lid any fire. Like we went to Pinyudo, Pochalla, Nairus and Lokichogio, we were used to making any jungle home. For the next nine years, that very spot became my group and where my school. We were not going further inside Kenya. As refugees, we had always been skewed distance from cities. In Panyido, we were settled some four-six hours away from the next town. Same as Pochalla and Pinyudo, at the outskirt of the town.

As time went by; days into weeks, into months and into years, Kakuma would become our home for the next ten years for me and long for others. As a very remote middle of nowhere, locally habited by Turkana, Kakuma was also the route of the dry nonstop sandy wind that blows through the entire Africa. As we felt the fear of the unfriendly locals every night, the days were neither fearless either, the winds were just life threatening as the people who called these nowhere their sweet home. The strong wind kept us intact throughout. As we tried to build the small huts using the twigs and leaves, the leave dries up quickly, then the wind shakes and chipped off the leaves leaving the structures just open and un protective. Sometime during the day, we would just prefer to climb up the trees and find a good wind breaker branches to hide around and sleep. However, it was always cautious not to sleep deeply up on the trees. During the day, it was often windy that visibility was just some meters. You could not see a person from just two hundred meters, sometime the cars will keep their honking and light on while driving slowly through empty roads. For many of us it became a custom to tie a piece of cloth on your head as a cover for yours eyes and hair from the sand the wind was blowing. However, if you could cover your hair and face, you would not resist breathing in the dusk, eventually evidenced when you blow your nose. In addition to our bodies, the gushy wind was making our food and water dirty and unhealthy to take in. At time we had to put off most of our activities when the wind became unbearable. At other times we had to do all we had to do what we can. As days became months and months into years, we eventually came to accept the challenges of Kakuma as permanent. Kakuma became a real refugee camp.

Our refugee life was well captured in Kakuma than Ethiopia and other displace camps we recited during our travel to Kakuma. It was there, Kakuma we lived the longest number of years, and realized what the life of a refugee was really like. Unlike Ethiopia, this was semi-arid desert, with both high intensity wind blowing all the years, often causing health issues. However, we came with luck as the locals themselves acknowledged. Before our arrival, rain was never something that the local have to consider when they built their huts or to keep animals around, it was rarely. The longs narrow seasonal streams which bordered the long strip of the main camp were known as dry gullies, but that changed upon our arrival. At my years there, they often flooded, often cutting off people from the camp and so many people were displaced because of continue eroding that wiped out much of the land & structures. We also planted a lot of trees that by the time I left Kakuma, the camp looked a lot greener than when we first landed on it. The town economic status was a boom with our arrival, many Kenyan moved in from other part of Kenya to take opportunities at the camp and to open high demanded business for the refugees. The services including education indeed were more prosperous in Kakuma.

But as I as reflected on the peaceful memory of Kakuma, there were too many inflicting years of challenges, of feeling abandon and what it meant to be a refugee that overshadowed the few good time or good memories of the camp. Unlike the progressing years of Pinyudo, we started Kakuma hard and never left behind those years. Our life in Kakuma defined the real life of a refugee. Whether the unwelcoming of the locals or the people of Kenya in general or just an accumulation of long years, Kakuma defined a lot of our refugee hood and a lot of what it meant to be on someone else soil or in the care of another. This is not to underscore the giving by millions or the UN help of the refugees in that camp for decades. We always lived to see a future a head; it was more of about hope that kept us in tack. In my evaluation of Kakuma years, this was the camp that really defines the refugee life in my experience and knowledge. Yes, in one way or another, we acknowledge the stability from the main enemy, however there is much negativity of Kakuma refugee camp. We had experiences and challenges that made Kakuma memories as high of a pillar than other refugee camps including my short refugee life in the United States. We encountered all the same challenges as from the previous places of our settlement and more.

The locals were more unwelcoming, and many lives were lost in their hands. Yes, we cannot forget the continuous attacks and looting at gunpoint by the locals Turkana, how they chase us when we went to the forest to collect our building materials and attacks on women collecting firewood. I can't forget the fearful nights of 1995 when food shortage kept us silent mostly during the days and Turkana keeping us locked indoor at hot nights. Many of us students couldn't light a lamp at night to read at our houses or at school for the fear of Turkana. Night parties were limited. A little Turkana boy or a dirty and stinky animal-skin clothed woman can spit at you and you must hold your temper for the fear of consequences either to oneself or others. For few of us who try to exit Kakuma and return to Sudan during our decade, maybe to join the war, it was not easy traveling back as police brutality and robberies on the road to Loki were unbearable. We were stuck in the camp. We had few ways out, we had no choices, and we lived as we kept hoping for best years. As for the local, we didn't invade their territory; we were on their land due to the contract signed by their government and the UN. Kenya in fact was not often friendly, there were always torturing when travelling through Kenya by Kenyan polices or what appeared as planned robbery every time we go to shop at the towns. At our time and it has continued after my departure from Kenya, the number of police posts increases, and it seem tactically to benefit from travelling refugees. There were no laws that were to pin down the refugees from travelling and the police never those laws, but they were often vocal about refugees not to travel. However, once they were paid, they would let people travel only for the travelers to get into same trouble at the next station. I can however acknowledge the wide belief that Brutalities subsided during Kibaki and Sudanese were treated better until the next Kenyatta took power.

As for the local Turkana around Kakuma, they never realized the benefits they earned off the refugees. Many of the local earned enough food and clothes freely as many refugees felt the need and friendship to share with the starved looking Turkana. In fact, some of their small kids often roamed around the camp, slept in the camp and the rest at the end the day left the camp with their stomach full and bring home some souvenir. In fact, some of them went to the refugee schools for free. They benefited much, but still they were not considered and showed cruel to us. We came to learn too that if you give much to Turkana, they become so happy that they turn against you, that they were not good when they were happy. At those times, we mostly feared Turkana and Kenya police brutalities than the struggling life of the refugee itself. At so often there was a widely belief that the police were law enforcement during the day and were Turkanas and part of the gangs at nights.

We may have been welcome politically to stay in Kenya, but really with the police brutality we experienced. For anyone who looks at the economic benefits, there is no doubt how much the refugees had contributed to Kenya economy, but still we couldn't even travel safely without harassments and imprisonments.

We had a lot working against us in Kakuma. The gushy wind and starvation kept people in doors most part of days and at nights the fear of the locals, Turkanas terrorizing the community with surreptitiously killings simultaneously kept us squeezed at nights. Every night at those days was darker as the darkness itself. We student could not go to our night studies anymore; individually it was scary to light a lame at night to read in your own house. However, that didn't limit many schools addicted like me, plus the stake of passing the KCPE was high; this was the road to continue education. I always shot my doors, sealed my windows at night and then study. Yes, with sealing the windows and every crack in which the light and oxygen could exit and enter, it was always steaming with bad carbon dioxide. But to succeed educationally in Kakuma Refugee camp, you had to be fearless and hope that God walks in front and behind and through challenges and that is what motivated me the most. During the days, people could not go far out of the camp borders; you could not relax behind if you went out with a group of people in search of building materials in the forest. We felt confined in Kakuma, our freedom was limited as if we were in cages.

As a boy at the time, my choices were even narrowed, either to live and pursue education despite the hardships of the refugee camp and the unfriendly life of Kakuma or to exit Kakuma for Sudan and join the SPLA or just drop out and turn bad. A lot of choices were made; some friends chose to expatriate to Sudan; others went into small business to support themselves and others dropped out of school with no alternative agenda. I remained footed and despite all the challenges, committed to school, and remained faithful and hopeful for God delivery as He did in Pinyudo and Pochalla. Like in my situation and belief and amid those awful days and years, faith grew in Kakuma and so many people turned to God, worshipping days and nights. In so believing, live changed drastically after years later, food supply increased, the relationship between Kenyan police and refugees either near Kakuma or on the road improved. As for the fear of Turkana, Kenyan Police were brought to tour at nights, and we resumed our normal live and our night studies slowly. From 1995 to 2000 when I left, live was stable despite inadequate refugee life we can't run away from. It was also between this period that many of the immigration to the United States was shaping itself and the local Turkanas were seeing Sudanese leaving, a thing they didn't want to let go despite their never-ending assaults on us.

However, those good times didn't last as family members and friends whom I left in Kakuma later retell their stories years after my departure. The bad years resumed and intensely between 2003-2006. For three memorable nights, the locals invaded the camp, openly firing their guns from group to group and as people run away, abandoning their belongings including the rare food, they collected those rare belonging. Like 1995, nights were sleepless. As some of my brothers and relatives later told me, every cable person was missioned to equip him/herself with spears, arrows, bows, and stones to guard their families against the well-armed Turkanas and criminals who were taking advantage of the terror. At those days, people didn't know their chances of survival.

During my years, I remembered the many times a Turkana boy would spit, kick you behind, curse at you, throw stone or sprinkle some soil in the air as a sign of curse or by cutting a line in the soil and vetting on you to dare crossing it. They demonstrated a proudness in their country, in a land they were regarded less. Those incidents reminded us of our early years in Panyido, when the local Anuak who most of them were in fact Sudanese immigrants would called us "*ajuil* or personalized us as "deer", meaning someone with no homes, as people who walk aimlessly from place to place, wonderers. All these mistreatments were in fact motivating and always rejuvenation to our commitment to the struggle to have a peaceful country. Yes, I never dreamed of a Southern Sudan as a country, however the SPLA and us in the refugee camps, displaced and people back home always felt optimistic of the cause of liberating the entire Sudan. It was not until the very early turn of the century when IGAD showed a complete commitment to achieve Sudanese peace initiative that the vision of New Sudan became achievable as a separate South Sudan. I knew the goal was to have a country, obviously Sudan in which all the citizens would be respected and in return call it their own country.

The challenges that faced Southerners or SPLA/M effort to liberate the South Sudanese were not entirely from Khartoum. We understood our fled from Ethiopia was not solely in the hand of the Ethiopian government that replaced Mengistu but backup by the regime in Khartoum. However, we expected the consequences of being a refugee and particularly in foreign land. Nevertheless some of our own communities, and individuals, were collaborating with the Khartoum government and in many cases contributed much to the struggles of the SPLA/M and death of many civilians on this road to freedom. The saying that "inside enemy is more dangerous than external" was true. Those local collaborators were obstacle in areas where the SPLA and refugees did not expect enemy present. Our suffering increased the spirit of patriotism toward the movement by individual accounts. Those incidents often motivated me and sparked a spirit of patriotism and believing in the cause of own country. These among many other factors contributed to our strengths and motivation that kept us footed during the hard challenges of the refugee life.

The commitment to the war or as in the title of the book was not only seen in the heroic SPLA soldiers who fought without pay, against old, in the unshakeable strong leadership of John Garang and many senior members, but also in the heart of struggling refugees and displaced people. In the civilians who sacrificed so much; their love ones, their insufficient food and animals, their unwavering moral support, their run from place to place without any blame on the SPLA and much more. In the refugee camps, our struggles were always sooth by the SPLA victories or momentum or directly from the fact that it was a just war. In any event of SPLA news of victory, it was always rejuvenating. We would rock the camps despite our weak shaky legs. We plowed the streets with morals; chanting revolutionary songs that remind us of our courageous leaders and the mightier of our army, and of our cause.

The bad news often doomed the camp, but sometimes downplayed or pretended untrue. One such rememberable incident came in 1994 when news spread that the leader of the SPLA was either caught or killed by the enemy. The news brought a calm atmosphere inside Kakuma. Clearly, that was the last thing the SPLA family would sacrifices. The source of the alleged could not be believed, but there was no option. It was hard for Sudanese refugees on what to make of the news. Many were pouring into the administration compounds to seek the validity of the rumors. Those were sad days for all the Southern Sudanese and affiliated brothers. People were grouping around few radios to hear how the news came and what to make of it but with the hope that the SPLA chairman, also known as C-I-C, Dr John Garang as he was well known by his comrades and Sudanese would response if he was in fact a life. That was not the first bad call about Garang and the fate of the SPLA or for Southern Sudanese enlarge, such a fateful called happened before when we were in Pochalla.

In the days following the SPLA split, there was a much sad news that Garang, the chairman of the SPLA was ceased off the power and had run for his life and no known where about he was hiding. Upon that initial threat about the SPLA and it hope in the leadership, there came immediately a deep calmness in our refugee came in Pochalla. Such calls were always tactics to find immediate where about the SPLA leader. The success the enemy was always looking was not only a victory to wipe out the SPLA, but even with the killing or capturing of its leader, of course that would be a blow to any organization and especially the SPLA and the hope of success.

However, the SPLA knows that it was fighting for the citizens dispersed around the globe including the refugees and those in displaces camp, and where about their leader especially after bad rumors was always hurting the Southerners desperately. Hence Garang quick response was always expected and he delivered on both incidents. In 1994, he responded after two quite nights. At those days, just like the case of the 1991 split, many were hiding out nears the few radios and particularly around the BBC news hour. At the end, his voice emerged one evening saying the SPLA Chairman is speaking, alive under the tree inside South Sudan and the movement is running and moving forward. As barely remembered from that radio announcement a decade later, in his well-known voice, the paraphrased was, why would I reveal my where about to my enemies, I am in Southern Sudan under the tree, the only place I could be. Prior to these announcements, the camp had been very quiet; everyone was keeping their ears open and in touch with BBC news hours that had been our source of solid and confident news broadcast. However, after his response, that night, the camp was rejuvenated, there were morals everywhere, people were gathering and singing revolutionary war songs as we had in Pinyudo and people were running and match in total excitements.

In Panyido, life was good as education was concern, though lacking a lot of the educational supplies and time to study due to hard incessant works. Education in Pinyudo had a home future and liking that became definite in Kakuma. Since I resumed my fourth grade in Kakuma all to the very glorious three years of my high school, education has never been so much enjoyable, and more promising. It was here at Kakuma that many of us got the opportunities that others especially our own SPLA combatants never had the chance and very much thanks to them. Unlike me, many of my Sudanese friends achieved dreams to study alongside the Kenyan's best. Many boys ended up in Kenyan Universities and others got scholarships to study around the world. Through tough times of Kakuma, educational spots were my caves. I could either be found at the libraries, after school group studies or night studies at school or at friends' house. Despite the enormous challenges of Kakuma, I was always in class besides the few times when I had to sneak out for a teacher I didn't like or when I had not finished my homework. I also could not forget the days when I was severely sick during the final quarter of my primary school senior year that even the very final exam day, I barely finish the exam.

We can sum up Southern Sudanese life over the decades of the wars as life of deficiency, but with optimism, life of tiredness, of hope and about believing in the cause. It's because of the just reasons that Southerners endured all the challenges that millions fought and died for, that they never faulted, that Southerners were divided and steered toward each other yet never lost the vision of the cause, that they experienced deadly defeats yet never surrendered, they were wished bad luck, yet they voted unanimously for their own destiny. It's the same believe that carried millions during the course from place to place and year to year for safety with all the burdens, lacking all the basic needs and through challenges. It's because of these reasons and many as elaborated earlier according to the SPLA/M manifesto and highlighted by the root causes of Sudan's civil wars by Johnson that we stood strong for the self-determination and individual freedom.

Unknowingly, the new millennium approached us with its secret or rewarding. For me it came early, the opportunity to get out of the Kakuma challenges. The chances for the minors as we were called and many other families who became the beneficial of the resettlement, something that started back in the late 90s finally becoming fruitful in the eve of the millennium.

For us all, history was in the making, the very reason of our cause was taking shape in the favor of the Southern Sudanese people and our struggles. These were years away, no grays view at that movement, but it was being prepared, and people were hoping that the turn of century comes with its luck.

I was a third year or junior high student, just passed my final exam to fourth and final year when we finally finished our process of resettlement on December 1st, 2000. From when this opportunity of resettlement was revealed, all to the last date that I finished the process, I never overjoyed any moment or share any glare of hope of getting out of Kakuma. Very importantly, I missed no school day in pursued of that resettlement opportunity. Prior to this opportunity, I had never known any close acquaintance that had gone to America and though I was following up the process of this resettlement, I was not very excite of the opportunity. I was also pessimistic about the chances of getting out of Kakuma in that ordinary process. We had left every refugee camp we had lived not peacefully but in urgent of fled often in fear of our life, so this peaceful walk or flight out of Kakuma especially by choice seem untrue to that point. Nevertheless, it was a given opportunity and all the kids I knew with their elders were taking the chance serious. And with such demanding chances and few opportunities and the urgency to be among the first, it was hard. The process took months for others to find success while other got their name compromised.

I made few attempts to go after my names, but with school and such, I never got the process via my own name. Luckily my cousin, Gabriel Chol Atem name called among the very first. He was underage, minor hence he was eligible to include his relative/acquaintances to accompany him along. With no hesitant, and my other cousin John Riak already on the list, he quickly consulted me with the opportunity. He informed me, and we grouped together, followed the process from initial registration till we successfully board our first flight out of Kakuma on the evening of December 3rd, 2000.

I was hesitant but pessimistic of the process. In one side, I never thought something good would ever come for us especially voluntarily given and considering all the suffering at our desperate times. On the other, there were legitimate concerns. For me, there was thought of what America would be like considering the history of slavery or Negros. Also, the resettlement was another separation between me and parents, and this time, it was happening due to my own will. I never had the opportunity to notify my father about it and I didn't know what his side would be. My brother of course loves the opportunity that had come for me. He knew it would be the best to outdo all that we had gone through.

Bul Nyuop

He told me just before I would leave that he was to let our father knows and persuade him that it was the right thing for us all as a family. I knew not any person who had been to American, hence lack the knowledge. They were rumor of not returning and even during the process you had to affirm that you were not coming back. This later point summed up a lot of worries and some people declined the opportunity. I was not over joy; but I made it to myself that I will celebrate when I return in the future.

As a result, only few relatives and friends knew that I was about to immigrate to the United State of America. I kept the process at a low profile till few days before my flight out, this was in part because of the chances of failing the interview and my whole doubt of the process. I didn't want to celebrate although I was too excited to get out of Kakuma and its life. Nevertheless, my cousins arranged a small gathering to farewell families in a traditional going away advising forum.

And even with my lack of enthusiasm in the process of resettlement, I did not want to blame myself later if in fact the opportunity becomes the chance of a better life, after all, I was still going along with my fellow brothers, all who had been the family for years. As for the many of the boys, these were golden and joyful chances, and many were not waiting to let the opportunity pass by. Kakuma and in fact the entire refugee life had been tiresome, and I remember the boys who celebrated this opportunity by throwing the few corns he had in his bag pack, a sign to cast out and leave behind Kakuma throwing celebrations, and farewell.

On the 29th of November 2000, just few days after we finished our last orientation, our names were scheduled to leave Kakuma on the 3rd. At this moment, I finally was sure that indeed, I was on my way to America, and I had to farewell my friends in that short time possible. Nevertheless, the mind was restlessly at the anxiety and worries.

Surviving for a just cause!

So, what kept you going, how do you get the courage to continue, how do you keep your mind away from that rough past? Do you experience bad dreams of the past? Who inspire you or what is your inspiration toward life? How could you afford the American dream and be blessed to come this far as college? What/Who/Why............?

Those were few of the dozen questions that often came across during my conversations with friends and those who came to learn about my past, particularly during my four years of college. Those seem as normal questions anyone could get ask especially those that had a foreign background and particularly from war and food paucity continent of Africa. I believe the questions were numerous and free flowing from the questioners because they cared and wanted to understand my life. While answering such questions could have provide needed education, for me, the answers were much troubling, more of a reminder of my tough past at time when I was trying keep memories behind me. For the cause we believed in, answering or sharing my life at the time as many were doing was a way to spread the message or a creation of an awareness of the unheard Southern Sudanese struggles, particularly as the result of the civil wars. Such education was also a vital way to understand the lost boys and their experiences in America, especially what transpired them. Our stories were never written anywhere; therefore, such communications were raw news to the world.

In my own thinking and at my situation as a college student at the time, I saw it personally favorable to focus on my education and less as an advocate. For me, such a role needed more than just answering questions. It required more campaigning; speeches, researches and travelling. I couldn't imagine any dent my campaign would add especially on a small campus and thousands of miles away from the US government. I wasn't ready and even when fellow students invited me to talk about the movie and the related book, "God Grew Tie of Us" by John Dau. My story would have been the answer. I saw the cause, but still couldn't see myself committing. Thank to many fellow Southerners who stood for all of us, particularly those who were taking routine visit to DC to spread the unrecognized suffering of the Southern Sudanese people of Sudan.

In addition, I didn't want to put my fellow students to hear or even comprehends such experiences that they couldn't do anything about. Many of them were brought up in a peaceful world that any of my own experiences could be consequential into their thinking and perhaps their studies. I chose to withhold my reality of the past, pretended like I had no such experiences or was not part of the lost boys' story. Nevertheless, there was a glimpse of my story already revealed by the WWU Western front, the school newspaper. In fact, much of the interest was awakened by the paper. The article was only the first of me on the school newspaper, but as of the top runners, my names were often on the cross country and track & field articles and websites. With that limited taste of my life, many people were really touched, and even more interested to learn more, at least many of my fellow teammates were still in desire to learn more. This is the rest of the story!

Life is like a learning curve, a lesson learned from one level provide guidance for the next level. In the same manner, the experiences and challenges of my young life have been instrumental in my later. My present life is a realization of my past. The experiences learned had shaped my life, along with God, the SPLA, and school. This chapter is the answer to those many questions and in fact is the backbone to the whole book.

As in the words of John Garang, the founder and chairman of the SPLA/M, and I paraphrase "the strength of the SPLA soldier lies not in the weapons they carry or any other advantage if any in fighting the long war, but in the believe that it was the right thing to die for", the cause we believed in. The above phrase in most cases summed up what drove me and perhaps most Southern mass during our challenging years.

During our refugee life, when our lives were so vulnerable, when there were so much odds against us, when so much challenges occupied most of our days, living day by day, and night at a time, there was always hope in each every one of us for a shiny day when our suffering will pays off, shortages turned abundance, insecurity turns into freedom, cries into laughter and tears dry up once for all. We lived with hope that our cause was a just cause and not of our own inevitable experience as many locals including our own stacked against us during the struggle.

We were always looking ahead and keeping ourselves as next or in any way supporters of the cause. While many of us were growing into their turns, others were doing their chores in the struggle in one way or another; whether it was by providing basic needs, moral support, nursing the broken, raising other generations of army, carrying on the live and future of what was to come, or passing on the history of the struggle justifying the cause and reaching out through their stories to help the cause.

There was always hope for an ultimate triumphant, of victory or and in new Sudan. As often said, people who suffered for what they believe in always surpass their challenges, those were us, that was me and my mentality. We were determined, embracing the cause or as in the political wording of the SPLA, our destiny was self-determination. We had a purpose and we understood it directly as our call.

God was our light; our strength and He was with us at those many odd moments. We called his named a lot during many of our long dark journeys when our tied skeleton tries to pull us forward. God strengthened and kept us. He fed our empty stomachs and shielded us from the rains of fire. God have not only been my guide throughout, but also my hope in the tone of disbelief and trouble in the days of Gilo, at Golkur, at Magoos, and in Nairus when we were at the mercy of his mighty hands.

From the day I set out from my father front yard to Pinyudo, my first foreign land and throughout my life, God had been in my life. I had called and hope of His almighty salvation during all those difficulties and today that it's because of Him that I was able to make it through. He too provided me many opportunities that including survival and this educational publication. Yes, there were often millions of thoughts that came to mind, thoughts of giving up, and temptations, but He alone kept my head straight and unto His guidance.

God kept peace among us especially in our early days of Pinyudo. When we met up in 1987-1989 in Pinyudo, many of us obviously were strangers. We came from different warring tribal backgrounds and many cultural differences. While many of us already understood the bigger reason that brought us to Pinyudo, many also understood the cultural background that had much conflict with each other. Even on our way to Pinyudo or SPLA recruitment in general, there were many communities that had shown so much against the cause or disproportionally suffering for the cause. I personally believed God created the very enduring atmosphere that kept us not only glued to our main goal, but peacefully. Yes, our own elders, the few grown up kept us together and I counted the integration that eventually made us one another's keeper, friends and brothers for life as in the case of the lost boys. That integration, when we were organized or forced to roommate' kids from once warring communities to live together, created a bond that not only enforced the very reason of new Sudan's vision, but one that was the recipe of our coexistent.

The churches' teachings kept us together. Somehow, every Sunday that I attended, there were always talks about love and peace among strange ones. Often, the preachers were very selective in their ministering, in the bible words that they picked, how they preached it over, and the message that we had to carry forth with us for the rest of the seven days of heavy work.

Most of the preachers at my church picked bible verses that related to our situation, to our stories as people who were wonderers just like the biblical Jews' people. Whenever we heard a chapter from the bible especially that related to the Jews or children of Israel, we took it as ours.

As the bible described the bondage of Israelites in Egypt, their exodus, their stubborn and steadfast hearts toward man made spirituals offerings, their miraculous crossing of the mighty red sea, their wondering in the Sinai deserts for forty years as God taught them His lesson, their mighty conquer of the promised land, their numerous victories, He too stood for us. He was their God and He loves them, and we felt the stories were too ours.

Over the years, many of us became acquaintance to the story according to the Old Testament book of Isaiah, chapter 18, the children in the "land of Kush". The story in the verse didn't only meet our situation, that was our story or in fact description of the Kush Kingdom which we felt were our ancestors. It showed that God love us, and always hope He would never forsake us, that He would one day turn our bad days into good days, our broken hearts to joyful hearts, and our enduring suffering be enduring peace and prosperity.

While residing in Kakuma, and in addition to having faith in God or relied on Him throughout those needy times, church as is often called the house of God was indeed a getaway place, a place of relief, a place to escape to avoid or lessen the impact of all the intricacies of the refugee life that we lived in. The many hours we spent at the church neutralized our feel of hunger. In another word, church engages us away from the Kakuma challenges. We always had dancing and worship at the church the entire weekend so frequent that most of the day went without thought of body needs.

Despite the many challenges at Kakuma, it was the much peaceful place that we lived as refugees. Our education was progressive during the Kakuma years. We never spend years without school. A lot more students were enrolled compare to Pinyudo or Pochalla. Obviously, so many refugees met up in Kenya all from many fronts. The need for education was higher and competition developed as a result. And due to the system of examination, as in many other African school curriculums, which arranged student exams score in term of order from number 1 in the class to the last student, there was always more competition in studies to avoid being last. As a result, and despite all the challenges of the refugee life, we placed education and times spend high on our priority list. There were a lot of students in each class in every level of education and competition was high. Families and student themselves want to be among the top in the class and school enlarge, that promoted seriousness and children had to study hard beyond class textbook in order accumulate knowledge and to be ready for any Exam which usually came from unknown textbooks. This didn't just increase our educational knowledge, but it kept us away from home most of the times, and in so doing we passed time. In another word, the more time we spent at our studies, the less time spent on life experiences and out of the trouble.

Life was very challenging in Kakuma, always one meal a day or many days without. Many kids went to classes in the morning and upon discharge at 1.30 pm, chose to remain behind to study and getting home late just for dinner time, some social to bedtime. Again, in this way, school plays such a role just like the church in keeping us away from the tough times or other chores that could otherwise be unfavorable.

But since our young age, particularly in Pinyudo, education took a very vital value in us. Occasionally, we were getting reminded of what brought us to far away land or the wider reason for the SPLA/M and the civil wars altogether. The leaders of the camp and SPLA/M Chairman often in Pinyudo motivated us to put our mind and mighty into schooling so we would be future leaders of new Sudan. They used to preach to us that it was due to lack of education that the Arabs were able to fool us, use our resources against us, and even marginalized our people and land. In my memory, and throughout my educational career, education was my choice infighting for our freedom. In Pinyudo, we used to sing it, chanting it;

We 're the leaders of tomorrow,
Tomorrow is our time to be the good leaders".

Other quotes about education that persuade us were much in the speeches the leaders kept preaching to us, often equating education as a supplement to a gun fight, with the expression that "pen should be in your right hand and gun in your left hand". For them, education was our way of being participant in the real war and education was as important as the fight itself.

For me, those were convincing reasons for education, ones that were not our individual dreams or aspirations. As we later came to learn about the educational experiences of the very people who were leading the movement and many who never went far in education, most of them were threatened and denied jobs despite their educational knowledge. In many attempts to deny educational opportunities, many missionary's schools that taught in English were closed, and missionaries tortured and expelled from the country. Our leaders' explanations were that the Arabs didn't want Southerners to get higher education, which in another explained why English were limited. This motivated us in seeing education as another voice in waging the war.

Those reasons motivated us, inspired my own experiences and why we left home in 1987. Those explanations brought to light why I had to hide my brother's school supplies years before 1987. The government was after those who were going to school, particularly in the South. At the time, we never understood the politic of it, but only to spare my brother from any potential problem. Such a fear was instrumental in my reasons to Pinyudo, Ethiopia.

The road to South Sudan freedom was long and consequential like any war, obviously overwhelming and costing everyone involvement in one way or another, including our early separation from our own parents at young age. However, the challenges on the way were not the circumstances that faced us, they were the very reasons that forced us to flee home. The challenges that came our way got us stronger and more determined to the cause of our flight. We never expect a smooth road to our freedom. The challenges aggravated us more and directly inspiring many to always have the reason to serve in heart. It was because of the war that we had fled our home very young, sleep in the cool rainy nights in many dangerous places, we run across deserts, we walked thousands of kilometers, we crossed crocodile infested rivers that consumed many of us, and been forced to seek for food from the international communities under the umbrella of humanitarian world food programs such as the lifeline, the United Nation, the world food program & Red Cross. Those uncountable reasons carried us and made all our suffering in the camps much bearable.

Growing up, there was always aspiration to be a soldier, to one day carry a gun, dressed in the dazzling uniform and all the pieces often under soldiers' waist. For some of us, this was a reason that took us to Pinyudo. At that early years, I was not knowledgeable of the war. I never related the attacks on our village to the war, but most of us grew up with the mind to defense our communities.

In Panyido, some older boys who were knowledgeable of the history of the war, perhaps those whose fathers, uncles, brothers etc. had participated in the first civil war or this 2nd civil war, taught us more. They along with many other adults composed some revolutionary songs that educated and energized us of the SPLA/M and all the reasons for the civil wars. For years and through our tough years past Panyido reminded us of the reasons for the struggles, and in doing so, fueled and strengthened our will and moral.

Indeed, most of the song carried secrete messages, drilling pride in the job well done and the reasons why SPLA and the community it's protect should fight to the finish or till the Khartoum accept peaceful solution. The songs were inspirational, emotional, more energetic and encouraging than anything. Every time we were in the moment singing those songs, there was nothing like it. The intensity and determination on our faces, the tone of patriotism and gifted in our voice symbolized much of the just cause for the war.

Our morals in the Refugee camp was an evidence of future SPLA and it was something the Khartoum could not ignore; in fact it was due to such believe & knowledge that Khartoum tried to attack our refugee camp of Pochalla in 1992. Such a strong believe in our cause was in part the strength that diffuse the difficulties we were facing in the camp and across the Southern region. I remained footed amid the challenges knowing that I was there for the right cause, for the sake of freedom.

Our present in the camp was also kept hopeful by the frequent visit by the SPLA representatives. While most of them visited the camp for reasons to get some of us join the frontline, the camp was often engulfed in happy festivities every time we received them. The festivities: singing some revolutionary songs and matches brought happy moods among us. Such occasions reminded us less of the challenges that were apparent but the reasons of our challenges. They often came with good news and again putting us think of the reasons that drove us to the refugee camp in the first place. The facts were the reasons for the war were beyond personal choice. What kept me or us together were not individual strengths or courage or what I participated into past time; it was the very reasons we were fighting for.

Our reasons for the struggle were not educational, were not the reasons we had to attend the class or be mentally changed, they were the reasons of the war. As captured in the SPLM/A Manifesto and many expressed verbally, they were the deep grievances encored in the experiences of Southern Sudanese lives. Ever since pre-independence

Sudan, Southerners had seen so much suffering, alienation and injustices among many. For us in the camps, they were those reasons that kept us above our own sufferings and challenges of our deficient refugee life. They were same reasons that million died for in the front lines, voluntarily going beyond calls and individual abilities. They were the same reasons that many mothers went strong to raise families by themselves.

Apart from the basic challenges of a refugee life; lack of basic needs, being a refugee taught as a lot, including who we really were. Khartoum administration played Southerners against one another, a tactic in which they armed some small tribes who were less participant in the SPLA by manipulating their beliefs and urged them that the Dinka or Nuer were the real troublemakers in the country's affairs. We suffered in the hand of our owns, the locals we found on the journey, fellow Sudanese and foreigners.

Our settlements were not welcome by many locals as in the case of Anuak in Panyidu and Pochalla, and later with Taposa/Turkana in our settlement of Nairus, Lokichogio and Kakuma. In Pinyudo, Pochalla and Nairus, many lives were lost as the SPLA pass through their land, from and to the SPLA training camp in Ethiopia. For us in Pinyudo and Pochalla, we suffered our own share in the attacks they waged against us just because many of us came from the communities that supported the SPLA or were SPLA fuel in all respect. As elaborated in my Kakuma life experience in the earlier chapter, Sudanese suffered a lot in the hand of Turkana.

This same game was evidenced in the 1991 split and aftermath that nearly devastated the SPLA and perhaps the post independent South Sudan. Though there were thousands who never got sucked into the Khartoum tactics from the major backers of the SPLA/M, many individuals and tribes were inspired and, took part in aiding Khartoum. Many lives were lost, the Shilluk kingdom was reportedly devastated and of course hatred was planted within the Southern Sudanese during those series of civil wars against the Khartoum. Such divisions spanned over to the refugee camp and at time led to fighting that were meant to revenge.

The doubtful gift:
going to America

******* Oh, look at that, over there, way in the sky, its going into the cloud, wow! What is that? I questioned my childhood friend Awe Bul.

It's America, he replied. It's an airplane he went further. That long white thing behind it is a smoke, he continued!!!

This was our childhood dialogue, when I initially heard of something call America. As per that conversation, America was not a land; it wasn't a country as we now know it. It was just a plane per our knowledge at the time. This was how we used to refer to the plane when we were young, especially the big planes that usually leave behind a long tail of smoke and usually flies high above the sky. I was only a young boy during that initial knowledge of the word America and as a dinka boy, I should have known only our own world or the culture of the dinka and only those things surrounding us. In the world I knew, we were growing up in nowhere close to experiencing what airplanes really were; leave alone, countries and many modern devices. As for many dinka parents as mine, with very limited knowledge of the world, it was that limited traditional knowledge that they all passed to their kids. Later before I left home in the late 1980s for Ethiopia, I never knew or had seen any low flying planes except the Sudan MIG that bombed our village just the year before we left. For me, all the high-flying planes were America according to my then young life and knowledge. However, with the world assistant and modern education,

129

we were finally and practically introduced to the modern world, a world wider than we knew at young. Starting in Pinyudo especially with our refugee basic supplies that had various American labels, plus few visitors who came from America, it was finally making sense that America was not a smoke, not a plane, but a land, a country far away.

At our early days of Pinyudo, when education was still about arithmetic, science of hand washing and limited English of v for village and e for elephant, we had very limited knowledge of the world. There was no geography or world history yet. But as mentioned in the previous paragraph, I quickly learned of the world from the food that was supplied to us, from the containers that read "the United States of America or simply USA". As we came to learn about the United Nations high commission for refugees, its formation, World War I and II, America as a land became clearer. Where it was on the map or its full name as United States of America or U.S in short, grew with the passage of time.

The newer lesson about the United States that I remembered the most was the history of the slavery and their freedom. This came in my first year of secondary school, also known as Form-I, according to Kenya educational curriculum. We read a small novel titled, "River without source" The book briefly mentioned how the slavery started and run through African coasts such as the Mombasa, Sierra Leon, and Ghana. In the same book, there was something about how Abraham Lincoln and John F Kennedy had contributed to the birth of freedom for the slaves. As mentioned, this was not a history book, but a novel. In the same context, I came to know about Martin Luther King Jr.

But other incidents also taught me about America. In Pinyudo, there was an American congressman who visited us while we were in Pinyudo and the song that we use to sing about it. While in Pochalla, Manute Bol, visited us and I finally came to learn where he came from. In Kakuma, we received many of our own coming back from America. By 1999, the resettlement process that I would later be part of was shaping itself and the name America was the only option we knew as the destination. I was hoping to finally travel by "America" to America.

By 2000, when the news of resettlement opportunity called, I was not yet sure about going to America. There were no immediate persons I knew who have been to the United States, I had no inside knowledge of what the process meant. Nevertheless, there was a high demand, a lot of people were jumping on the opportunity. I was very reluctant both in the desire and in pursued of the resettlement opportunity. My brother and many relatives, cousins and friends were vital to the decision, they never feared anything about going to America, unlike me. My father was in the displaced camp near Uganda at the time and I didn't have a chance to inform him about it. At the end, after series of thoughts and questions like what I got to loss, I gave a green light. I reasoned that if I passed what could be an opportunity, I may rebuke myself for the rest of my life. I reminded myself of the "never try never know" phrase.

I started to take frequent walks to the office of Radda Barnen and travel back and forth to my former group to find my names. But because everyone was doing the same, the offices were always packed and case workers hard to be allocated. In addition, people who work at the offices were

Sudanese; it's took tireless days to get through, sometime not successful altogether. Most of the officials were serving people who they knew first. I was getting impatience. It was school time and I didn't want to miss my classes, so I was coming to the Radda Barnen later in the day. Kakuma was always hot especially in the evening hours. Most of the Radda Barnen offices were inside the multipurpose centers, in this case there was one for zone one and the surrounding and one for zone and the surrounding zones. I was in zone six, one of the newly named zones, but my names were supposed to be in zone four or at the multipurpose of zone three, about 3-4 miles from my secondary school. By the time I got out of the class, headed to the Radda Barnen office, I was sweating hot and the time was also running down. After couple of weeks in despair, I was almost giving up the search for my name, just to cross my fingers and hope that they appeared.

Others had their own challenges in their decision to embrace the resettlement process. While the journey could take us to the best place ever heard of, there were concerns. The land was too far away as we anticipate it or as said by few who had been to America. Many families were skeptical of our return and so few families who had one kids orphaned didn't feel easy of letting their only one go. In fact, many girls didn't find the same opportunity to come because where we were heading was known as a good place, yet there were doubts and in traditional African communities, girls were considered more valuable and could not go were uncertainty exist. Later during the resettlement process and interviews, there were questions that increased worries of returns. There was a perception that if you were asked a question about return to Sudan and you answered yes, you would fail the process. This made it hard for others to get involved in the process especially the girls.

As for the many boys, later named lost boys, who had faced a lot of challenges since leaving home in the eighties, there was nothing bright in their future but to find opportunities where they exist, after all, they already had so much, nothing would be so worse. We were counting on one another and our history. I was not travelling to America alone; a lot of the boys who had been part of my life, who had defined me, and my inception and knowledge of the Sudanese world were also in the process of the resettlement. My cousins were going, in fact we were on the same form and we were going to live together. If everyone is going; I would be on the same bus as them, be fine, I declared to my doubt. The idea for opportunities that had never been available to us, like the dream to go to the university made my decision.

Over in zone one, my cousin Gabriel's names emerged. Gabriel was in group 12, living with my other cousin John Riak and his best friend Primo Kenyi, all under the care of our cousin Kuir Angeer Mayom. Upon receiving the good news, he kept it secret for a while but eventually made it fruitful to John and his best friend Primo. At that time, if your name were called or luckily released, people would swarm you with emotional request to add them into your form. People were very desperate for opportunity to exit Kakuma especially for America. Some went even to paying or doing anything in that matter to find such opportunities. Gabriel was good at keeping things under the table for a while. He is not a person who gets so excited about things.

He learned that he could put together a form that could include more than two people. No one was in mind but his immediate relative and friend. At some point, he told Primo and John Mayom Riak that his name came up and because of his age, he had the privilege to add a company to his name. He without hesitation made a quick decision to add my name, John and his best friend. There was no clear max, but there were also rumors that the more you had on your form, the less chance of success. Others were approaching him to have their names added.

Upon the good news, we went in to submit the four name and the rest went as anticipated. The process went on quickly than anticipated, taking us seven months till we were set to leave Kakuma on December 3rd, 2000. Of course, coming to the United States was not a free give if you didn't get your stories well or together. Thankfully, the interviewers were getting the same story for all the boys and girls. We were rooted out of our homes, lived together for so long, later understood the same cost of our separation, therefore the history was the same. As a result, the interviewers really could not see us lying. The boys narrated a unanimous history, which in turn made the process simple for everyone. The process had been speedy on our favor, we ended one step and the next step resurface in no time.

As the process took it course, you would say someone was more hopefully, but I was still skeptical. Until November 4th, no one had seen the result of the process yet, no one had yet left Kakuma for America. Some people were done, just waiting to book themselves out of Kakuma for good. And if that group was impatience with the process particularly in the desire to get out of Kakuma, we were always busy;

I never shown reluctant or slowdown in my studies at any point in my process. We were going to school at the time. I was finishing up my last semester of the 3rd year. And since I was skeptical anyway about the whole resettlement process, I was still studying hard, missing no day in pursuing the resettlement process. I was the best student in the class, ranked first place in the first two years and didn't want to let up that going to the fourth year; hence I had the motivation to continue studying hard. My final exams and my resettlement process were promising, but I continued by education like I wasn't going anywhere. We sat for our final examination, just weeks before our process concluded and when others were already flying out of Kakuma.

I kept the resettlement process to myself; not even classmate and friend knew about it. Nevertheless, it was a widely known process and nearly kids who went to Pinyudo was part of it. Many kids were often absence from classes and the impacts of the resettlement process was ultimately evidenced in our examination performances, the overall grades were down including my own. I still finished at first place, concluding my strong three years at the top.

Our resettlement final step came immediately after our final exams. We finished the orientation and immediately afterward, our names were scheduled to fly out in less than three days, I believe on the 28th of November. We were notified of the release by many who came across the posted names. The name and announcement were posted outside the UN compound and on a big tree near the Kakuma refugee camp hospital, next to my group.

On Saturday, my cousins organized a farewell celebration. Like me, they were not overjoyed to come to

America, but we were too embracing the opportunity. The celebration was a kind of way to say bye to many friends, family members and relative all at once. As usual in the dinka culture, when someone is going far away, he/she gets pre-advices on how to live in the distance land far away from the scope of the culture. At our going away farewell, the elders of our community came, all the people whom we were related and all our friends. We were the second to leave from our sub-tribe of Kongor, so it was still a new thing and many elders threw words of great advices to us. They gave us some lines that we would always remember and rethink during our time in the United States. In our own believe, we were not immigrating or for permanent resettlement in the United States, hence they urge us to go to school, get education and return home. They cautioned us a lot about America as a beautiful land with so many opportunities, better life, so many luxuries, yet so many temptations to get us astray. Many spoke about women, about drinking and driving or anything that could get as astray for that matter. Their advices were like from those who have once been to the USA. They told us a lot of "do not", especially to keep ourselves far from women, and at least not get tricked. Yes, they want us to bring back our education, of course money, but foremost, to come back and get married to our dinka girls.

As we disperse from that going away party, we had only so much time. We had yet more friends to reach and to inform about our departure for America. With little time I had, I only visited my former group; fifty and twenty-seven, plus selected friends. Scheduled to report into the fenced UN compound on Dec 3rd and no later than 8:30

in the morning, I had little time to pack up and get ready overnight.

By the time I returned home that last night, everyone was waiting for me. Everyone started pulling me aside, others throwing words of advice while seated in a group. The night turns out very short with so much to do, so many short meetings and good-bye messages. I was very nervous throughout the night, went to bed late, and never slept either. The morning felt like it would never come. At the dawn, I was already brushing my teeth, showering, groomed and ready to get on the way. It was a very good short day yet got treated so wonderful, even by those who never had, particularly my brother's wife. My breakfast and shower were ready before I knew; something I never had before.

As for my luggage, I didn't have much, just a pair of clothes. We knew that United States had a lot of all that we would need, including clothes, so we were told not to bring much. We went to bed late and woke up the first. I was ready to leave but the moment never really hit me till the morning. I felt it as I went around our compound that morning, passing on the last greeting to everyone. I was the first to leave Kakuma from my clan. Our mothers couldn't believe. My little nieces and nephew started to tear up that I was going away as they saw a lot including their dad walking me out from the compound. Everyone wanted to escort me, but it was a regular morning with kids and all the Kakuma challenges. Many had to wave me just like I was coming back.

The walk from my group to the UN compound could only take about thirty minutes, but we left an hour early. The window of extra thirty minutes was for any anticipate delays on the way as many stop us to say bye. As so many including my brother took my bag on and everyone standing, looking at me heading out, taking distance by each step, my nieces and nephew started to tear up as they heard I was going away for a long time. They didn't know where or how far I was going away from them, but they knew they were going to missed me just like I had left years back and missed my siblings. They later grew up and during my return, they were the not the little cutes that resist calling me uncle.

The walk was like a regular walk. It never hit me that I was leaving everyone till later at the door when I had to parted them as I entered the compound. Like most of my life prior to that moment, this too was another separation. However, this was a separation by choice. It was my choice to go to America. Before we headed inside, I met my cousins whom we were coming with. They were waiting me outside the fence. They could not be check in without me. There were so many people outside the gate, waiting to say by to their friends and to see who were leaving on that day. We check in at the counter inside the fence, and from that movement, if nothing interferes with the plan to flight out that day, I was not going to see my brother and his family for a while again. It was at this short separation that it started to hit me, my heart was beating, and my mind was saying a lot. It felt like a joke while we were waiting, until shortly when the process began. The officers came, and they divided us into two flights scheduled that day: the morning and evening fights to Nairobi. This was the first time two fights took the lost boys out of Kakuma. Our next wait was, who was leaving in the morning and who later that evening.

We were left with that curiosity for a while. I was schedule in the evening.

The morning group or the 1st to flight out that day had only short time to prepare and to board the buses to the airport. The other group, we were to relax there and enjoy the much cooler compound. December 3rd was the first day the double flights started. There was now a morning flight and the evening flight. The morning group was called and there we said to one another, we will see you in Nairobi. Our day at the compound felt short.

The compound was located on the bank of the dry seasonal river, surrounded by big talk trees and wind was very easily broken down by the trees. We were seated at the back of the compound but thought out the day, we were regularly visiting friends a waiting at the door. It was a regular scorching hot sun Sunday as the sun rotated across the horizon to the west. As we make assumption about the boys that left in the morning, weather they arrived in Nairobi or not. We were anxiously waiting for our turn. I knew my brother and all my friends had return home once we said by that morning, but just for curiosity about others there at the gate; I walked to the gate couple of times as we waited. There were a lot of cars and truck randomly parked inside. But it wasn't a big compound to get lost. In fact, we could not roam randomly inside.

As the sun turned toward the west, we waited for the evening and the flight to come. It was 2.30 pm when the official started showing up; a sign that our turn was up shortly. When the roll was called, we were all present. Shortly the buses came, and I don't know how many of us, but we got into two - three small vans. As we got out of the compound, there were so many friends waiting at the exit, but because the vans had windows rolled up and tied security that pushed out the friends waiting outside the gate and along the road to the Airstrip, we could not wave or receive any recognized friends. They just wave while others run along and behind the vehicle as we drove to the airport. It was a short trip, less than ten minutes. As we arrived at the airport, there were hundred more waiting to see who were leaving that day, and to say goodbye to their friends. There was a fence of people around the perimeter of the strip. The plane was already there, we just had to load on. The roll call was called as we boarded the plane. The time was too short as we tried to find our eyes contact with our friends outside the perimeter and the roll call asking us to enter the plane.

As we ascend onto the plane, there was certainty that this was the last day of Kakuma years and others want to mark it memorably. I was later told about a boy who threw away some corns, gesturing farewell to Kakuma and the years of that scotching sun and of corns as the staple food of our refugee life in Kenya. I understood why the guy swore on leaving behind, cast out and forgone the memories of Kakuma, however our Kakuma life was that of a refugee and could not be summed as worse base on what we ate, but so of many issues. The Turkana land was barren soil, the local people there seem like the outcast of Kenya, yet they were proud of themselves and so disrespectful of the refugees. People were terrified day and night in Kakuma not because of the basic needs, but much due to insecurity posted by the locals. Many refugees were accustomed to the situation of being a refugee, the life of inadequate and innutritious meal supply. However, the scary nights of the fear of a bullet into your window at night or the sense of quarantine that we could not just roam about in the outskirt of the city was something that many could not comprehend. After all, the locals roam the refugee camp day and night collecting free foods and, in an opportunity, to exchange their produces. We buckled up, first time that happened for us, in fact the first most of us sat on the plane. The engine started. It was hard to say bye to friends especially as we look at them across the fence.

While many of my friends try to wave via the glass windows, some were scared, anxious and impatient to see the plane lifting it wheels off the ground. As a first timer I had heard that flight is always awful for the first timers. I felt it right away. It felt like my body was going up, and my heart falling. That is what nausea and vomiting. It was a long-anticipated advice and we were all prepared for it. The distance from Nairobi as many people knew by car was a day and half from Kakuma. We started questioned ourselves how far it would take us to Nairobi. The plane took off at about a quarter to four and shortly Kakuma disappeared behind us. It was a great aerial view to look down from the plane. Some of the boys who had traveled the road to Nairobi were guessing the cities that lined up underneath the plane. That is Kisumu, Kitale Eldoret, Lake Nakuru and there ahead is Nairobi, they counted.

I was silently enjoying the ride. We came to Nairobi at about 6.15pm, it was still light outside. We had a taste of the flight a head, and to that point, it was a good experience, except some hiccups when the plane lifted or landed. We arrived and as we expected, our colleague from the first group were in Nairobi, at a waiting center call, Link. Many of them rushed in to welcome us. Another thing that greeted as was the cold breeze of Nairobi's weather. The officials welcome us and just like the group that came before us, we were led to a waiting area for our next trip. They told us that we were departing at midnight and it was becoming real. We were for sure about to leave Kenya and particularly, Kakuma Refugee camp. The camp had been a home, not like we were ever welcomed by the locals. But we had lived there since 1992. With that prospect it was a matter of few hours to conclude my refugee years in Kenya, an end to my seven years, three months and twenty-four days since arriving in Kakuma.

As the clock approached midnight, turning December 4th, the airport was still busy. We were scheduled for 12.05 am. Soon we were summoned to start checking in for our flight. We were excited, yet we didn't know exactly how far we had to travel or even if we were ready for the road ahead. As we walk to the plane, my heart starts another continuous beat and the mind was going crazy, yet I showed no sign of nervousness, very calm like I had flight experiences. As we boarded the plane in Nairobi that late night on the 4th of December Nairobi local time, probably 10a.m on the 3rd of October Seattle time where we were heading to, my mind started to giggle, making "if that, then that" scenarios. Prior to the airport during the orientation, we were made aware that the flight from Nairobi to America wouldn't be a straight direct flight. The planes were going to stop and refuel through many European countries. Each flight could at least be a duration of at least six hours or up to twenty plus hours to the destination. So, I was not worrying on how long the flight will take, I just couldn't imagine going into that big plane we use to see way high past the scale of cloud.

My mind was already way ahead of myself, exploring what would happen once in America. As we entered the big plane, Sabena, we were greeted by the cool air conditioner and attendants welcoming us and checking our seats. We were all wearing our IOM outfits and yes, we were very black skinny passengers who were yet to learn to flight. We went through a lot of first-time things including seat belt buckle up, using the lab aboard the plane, eating the salad "green thing", to using escalators that made us walk funny and staggering like children or drunken individuals. Our flight took us via Brussels, Belgium to New Yolk City and finally to Sea-tac airport, Seattle Washington. It was twenty plus hours totally exhausted, yet it was fun and through the entire flight, I kept my eyes through the window for the complete glance beauty of the land. Many of us puked, others ironically looked starving yet avoided. We did not look outside the airport to see beautifulness of the areas we went through such as the New York, but we were impressed with the airports.

After a short while at the JFK airport, we left for another long flight across the continental US, we were heading to Seattle. This was 6-7hour flight. As new timers, we were exhausted, tired and hungry. Most of us sat the entire trips. As we finally approached the great Seattle area, this was the first time I came seen how glittering America was, with the bright shinny beautiful lights as we trolled down at the Puget Sound. We came in December, and already Christmas colorful lights added to the beauty. Above the city, I saw so many long lines of cars as we descended toward the airport. I was too swallowed by the beauty from the sky. We landed at the airport at around nine pm, ready to end the long flight. There were many of us, the so-called lost boys of Sudan if you wish on this one plane. Most of us knew one another and it was more comfort to see all of us coming to the same destination. We didn't know weeks later that the state would be so large that we would disappear and wouldn't see one another frequently as we anticipated. As we got out of the plane, we descend into the tunnel where we got into the underground bus. The airport was so amazing, starting with the tunnel, the high escalators, and the baggage claim to the series levels of parking. At that point, my ears were plugged, and I barely could hear anything even what the people next to me were saying. Thankfully, we were at the destination.

Our foster mom was waiting, but she was clueless of how we look physically except that we were black. There was more than a dozen of us, similar looking boys coming out of that plane. My cousin John and I were allocated to live together with the host family of Guadalupe Dildine in Lacey WA. Cousin Gabriel, the head of the form together with Primo were to recite twenty miles away from us in the McCarthy's family in Yelm. We were not aware of the situation till later when we got both families waiting at the airport. Dildine was just hoping to see two black skinny boys; at least that was what she has been told of. She had with her one of her foster kid, a small chunky boy. Because the program was expecting many of us on the same flight, they had all the parents waiting each with the name of their children spelled out on the cardboard. They started waving up the names as we approached the baggage claims. We didn't have luggage, all we had were carried on. The little stunted short guy was waving and calling our name as we headed toward him. The boys were all looking toward the sign and one by one, we dispersed toward the sign boards, into the crowd and quickly into the arms of the Americans.

At that point, four of us were still in proximity, thank to both parents. My cousin Gabriel Atem as our leader wanted to know where we were going. We united both parents, exchanged the phones and shortly we farewell each other. We didn't know how far our home was or even if we would be far apart from our cousins, but we wanted to remain in contact.

Our mom's van was parked somewhere on one of the top or midway floors. We jumped in, prompted to buckle up and there we rolled. As we started out, we saw the van going down and around in a circle, from floor to floor all the way down. At the stop sign, we waited our chance and then we emerged into the American community. We had introduced ourselves to the family at the airport, but the little guy called Dylan was hardly getting them straight. As he started to teach us about America or what mom had prepared for us or where our beds were, he kept forgetting our names and every second he was asking our names repeatedly. I couldn't blame him for forgetting my name so easily because even his name was hard to pronounce. He had never heard such a name before. However, I could say he was so interested in having some elder brothers as he started to call us. We were tied, especially me. I wasn't ready for a lot of conversation but to take shower and lay my head on a comfortable bed that I thought would be my next description of the America as a comfortable place.

We finally arrived, got out of the van, and at the door, it says welcome home Bul and John. We felt welcomed seeing that, but life was way too far ahead of us. Dylan runs up and we followed him. The living room was between the basement and the bedrooms. He called us up; more stairs to our room, there were two beds awaiting us. It was late when we got home, so mom tried to get us some food quickly, but I don't remember eating anything that night. I was out of it. Dylan showed us the bathroom, located much closer to his and between mom's room and Dylan. Yes, I never slept on the mattress of my own prior to that night, and it was so comfortable to sleep on one finally. I don't know whether it was the comfort of the mattress, the long tiresome flight or that the nights were short in America, the morning rolled in quickly as Dylan rushed into our room that first morning at his house. Of course, we didn't want to get up, but the little guy never dares. We were new and we were going with any rule given.

I looked at the window, crack it and gushed in a cool winter breezy. It was foggy outside, and I could see a distance through the window. This was the morning of December 4th, 2000, our first day in America. A lot was waiting us to learn including understanding the quick talk of Dylan, but there coming from the crack of our upper room window was the breeze of chill. Yes, if the breeze could have a sense of feeling, I would say that the morning was smooth. We enjoyed that morning, trying to take a long rest in our comfort ever slept on mattress, but also, we had our first meal of the day awaiting us. I may say Dylan was morning person or maybe is used to waking up early because of school, but he could not take advantage of the no school day.

He rose up early that morning like he wanted to be the first to see us, but also to be the first to share first ever breakfast with us. Our foster mom had woken up that morning to welcome us with her scramble eggs and some toast and a choice of milk or orange juice, but it was Dylan who knocks at our door to call us down for the breakfast.

Dylan used to talk fast; we didn't understand him very well, even his name sound weird to say the least. Yes, it was the first time reading a name in which Y is next to a letter D. Sometimes we would ask mom to say what Dylan just said and other times we pretend like we understood him. However, I would learn soon later that it wasn't just Dylan that was hard to understand, but also the kids from school and Joe from the McCarthy. They had hard time understanding us too. We knew that we spoke good English, but what we spoke in Africa was more British than American or a mixed of African & British.

The next day after our first breakfast on Monday December the 5th, mom asked us if we need to go shopping for clothes. Yes, shopping was another word of that morning. In my refugee camp, I probably was used to buying a cloth or two once a year. We had no clothes from Africa; we left the few we had. I had only in my bag pack my best pant and shirt from Kakuma in addition to my immigration uniforms I had on. After twenty plus hours of travelling, those clothes were ready to get off; we needed our first American clothes in addition to the breakfast. That morning of the December 5th, we went out to the departmental store, Fred Meyer where we got our first American clothes. Fred Meyer was only two minutes from our house. Wow, they had so much of everything, I murmured to my cousin as I scanned my eyes around. Back in Kakuma, the clothes' stores were always small open-air market. I never experienced the choice that was at my view right at that moment. At the end, we got everything from school bags, stationeries, trousers, shirts, shoes to Jackets. I thought it was a lot of shopping in one time, sometimes I hesitant to pick additional shirt after the first one, we never bough such quantity in Kakuma at least not at one shopping. However, we continue to pick more as we were told. When we got home some hours later, it was pitting time and we were surprise that we could return anything that didn't fit us. That same evening, we requested to use the phone for the first in our life to talk to our cousin over in Yelm or at McCarthy. Mama Lupe showed us how to use the phone, what was to dial, how to dial it and putting our mouth close to the small opening at the bottom where the sound transmits across the thin wires over to the receiver at the other end. This was before the cordless handset and cell phone, hence we had to sit by the phone or hold it closely. They told us about their new place, that they had animals and a big wide grass garden, a farm. Their home was in the outskirt of a small new city; hence it would take them at least ten minutes to the nearby store.

For us, I was very anxious for school, wanted to start my America education quickly. Our new foster mom had secured our school admission, but first we were to get vaccinated as no one was accepted with no childhood immunization records. She had asked us if we got vaccinated, if we had immunization records. Of course, we never heard such a thing let alone being recipients. We said no, but we thought we were adults and need no vaccination anymore like children. I believe she confirmed with the office and school before the end of that December 5th day that indeed we had to get vaccinated. The next day, we visited the doctor for the first time in America; we got our first shots of the immunization series.

On the 7th, we went to school, the North Thurston High School. The school was already in secession and 1st quarter was almost over. Unlike the Kenyan school year which is like a regular year with classes starting in January or early February and end in December, the school year in America was from late August or early September to the following May or June. We were also new to the system of quarters. In the school that we enrolled in, it was almost the end of the first quarter, the fall or as we call it autumn in Africa. In Kenya or Kakuma, if a student start classes late, he/she may never get accepted or perhaps not sit for the examination. We came to North Thurston High School, got introduced to the admission and eventually to ESL most sweet & loving teachers, Miss Edwards and Miss Collins.

Miss Edward, the English teacher, was a little older physically, yet she was full of joy, energy and very passionate for all the kids in her class. I would never imagine any kids in million years that would say anything bad about her. She made us feel ease, patting you at the back as she talks with each student. She never sat at her desk for student to come to her, she was always running around to help everyone. In math and Pacific Northwest history class in the same portable next to Miss Edwards', was Mrs. Collins. She was also very nice, serious about teaching, but also opens for any help. Both teachers later remain as best friends of ours even after they retired from teaching. The next day, we were to take the placement test, so we could be allocated appropriately to the regular classes in the next quarter. That process brought us to Mr. Debord, the computer class teacher. He introduced us to sit next to the "box-like" (before the flat screen) machine, called the computer. He gave us English spelling test shortly after our initial acquaintance. The test was so simple, spellings and pronunciations, the kind of 2ⁿᵈ grade level. I felt so embarrassed considering my secondary school level background. I just passed my 3ʳᵈ year exam to four years when I left Kakuma. There and despite the test, I was again in first grade. The people back home were also outrage when they heard the demotion that I had gone through. However, my mind was fresh and completely understood that it was American law, at least from the cultural orientation we went through during the immigration process. We learned that everyone who comes to America must recertify their educational background, and that could mean repeating or taking a satisfactory test. Also, it was a difference country, and I convinced myself that you could you probably will be disadvantaged as someone not respectful of the law if you don't comply. I never showed any of my disappointment at the time and sure to no person.

At the end of that test, Mr. Debord took time to tour us around. It was during this first day at school that we got the taste of snow. There were few flakes of snow falling. The drops felt cold for our bare skin. He told us that, autumn through winter quarters were the highest seasons for snow falling, we will get bigger one later, he said. At the end of that tour, it was just amazing to see how so many classes were under the same roof, some upstairs and others down and kids swapping from class to the other. Lockers were on the way and some kids switch books as they move from class to the other. The ESL and some few regular classes were in the portable buildings outside the main building.

December 7th was just a registration and test day for us. We left immediately after the test; we went to the clinic to get our immunization done. No one could start school without immunization completion or prove of childhood immunizations. The next morning, our mom introduced us to the school bus system; she took us that early morning to where we would be waiting for the bus. She specifies the time the bus would come, and if we missed it, we should walk back home so she would drove us to school. Our bus stop was two blocks away from our house and we had to trespass to get there. In Kakuma, students and teachers use to wake up early and had to walk up to ten miles to get to the school before the school hour began, which was usually eight o'clock. It was not so surprising for us to ride the bus to school, we knew this was America, very developed and we left all possibilities, surprises and expectations as they were.

For as, everything looks undistinguishable and we could get lost on the way home easily, hence we picked a way to identify the direction toward our house. Our bus stop was some 3 minutes' walk east of our house and we had to go through a private property with the sign "no trespassing". To avoid getting lost, we placed our eyes on the "dead end" sign, just right before the private property sign board. We never got lost anyway, but I didn't know dead end was not unique, that it was everywhere to mark the no exit or an end of public access. But challenges were at every corner. At school, finding your class especially in the short time when the classes were switch was very difficult. I set my eye on one route at a time. I used to get done with lunch early, giving time to find my classes or get familiar. The portables were the easies; they were separate buildings and not many of them either.

But a lot of thing happened to get us feel comfortable. We were uniquely and warmly welcomed by the North Thurston high school, faculties and students alike. The welcoming was obvious among the faculties, from Mr. Debord representing all the teachers, the attendant's lady, upstairs at the library to Whitney at the cafeteria and of course with our portable teachers. That same spirit was also demonstrated by the student, many wanted to be friends, to share lunch table or sat next to us at the class. They used to regard me and John as brothers. In fact, one student bought for us two black caps with writing "Warner bros".

As we felt welcome into the American society and North Thurston High school in that first week in America or Lacey, we felt detached for the first time from other Sudanese and of course Kakuma. Our cousin Gabriel and Primo were in a different city, and we did not know how far away they were. And later when we were reunited again, we could not constantly see one another as we wish and despite our experiences with walk, this was not a walking distance, luckily, we had constant phone contact. There were still a lot of boys and girls coming to the U.S but we had no news of anyone who had come to our state or close to where we were. In addition, we had no contact with the very people we left in Africa and they didn't hear that we had arrived safely. We had or knew no telephone numbers for anyone in Nairobi, so there was no instant way to inform them regarding our arrival and our few days in America.

On the 18th of December 2000, just the same week when our school went on recess, Simon Dau and my cousin Elijah Chol had made it to Olympia, WA, just some miles away from us. We had no idea till Simon found us with a ring of a surprise phone call. He got our number from the sponsor or his case worker. He was resettled just few miles away from us, in the capital city of Washington State. It was just a matter of personally contact otherwise we knew someone was now near. And because we found ourselves isolated from other Sudanese for the first time in our long history, anyone who was a close by Sudanese was now a brother or sister even with no past acquaintance, and now Simon was. While he didn't know where we were, he took an effort, inquiring from his host family the direction. This was years before the GPS that later revolutionize driving. The distance was about 3 miles.

On his new acquired first bicycle; he sat tall, nicely dressed for the chilly new weather, with his backpack, he started out away from his home, and not knowing how he could really identify our house once he come close. The roads and street, the likeness of many buildings, the addresses were all the things we never use before; and everything was new even the rule of riding his bicycle on that narrow-sided road. Before he took off from his home, we told him that we were going to wait for him somewhere.

We were very anxious to meet him; we told our mom and she was ok so long she was in the house and it was the first time she was going to see another Sudanese besides Gabriel and Primo. We went outside, jump on the trail and went to the road we expected him to come from. As always when we stepped out from our house into the new weather of Washington, we threw on our jackets, then left few minutes early to wait for him, on the bridge right at the junction, keeping our eyes around in all directions to see where he was going to emerge. We were very excited, though I didn't know Simon prior to that meeting. We were soaking a little but it worth waiting. Shortly, we saw someone in a distance. He had his backpack, helmet on and well dressed. On the bike, he looked talk, so we started to believe it was him. We were on the bridge, so he couldn't see us, but he anticipated us there. As we saw him, we came down the bridge to meet him, he saw us, continued to stroll toward us, already in the mood to jump off and few slides he did. We greeted one another and again at that moment, we had our Sudanese community of three.

Mayom and Simon new each other prior to that meeting, perhaps from Kakuma. However, Simon also knew my brothers and John's late brother Dau Riak. That prior knowledge help, but regardless, we felt like brothers, we felt like we were acquaintances, and we felt complete to again talk about dinka matters. Often after that, we kept our contact very close, mostly call one another and at times come together to sing Episcopal hymnals in our dialect. Church & singing were among the few we had missed a lot in our short time in America. We luckily, we had brought with us some hymnal's books from the refugee camp and we often turn to them once bored with TV. We joined the church of living water, where we quickly learn in singing as we followed the choir with songs projected on the overhead.

After only two weeks in my American high school, the school first quarter came to an end, there were exams, quizzes and papers. We were not required to participate because according to the policy, we had missed much; class assignments, homework etc all were counted toward the final grade. We were enrolled into the ESL classes; their credits never count toward graduation. It was unfortunate for me especially because I was a high school senior when I left Kenya Refugee Camp. We were made aware of the American system of education and of the term "recertification", which explained that we might have to get tested or forced to retake some classes or altogether get demoted to take courses that are considered as prerequisites for college bounds. It didn't bother me to the point of disappointment, but I continued my appealed to the administration and finally my home credits were retrieved, and I ended up graduating in two and half years from high school.

In that first few months following our arrival, every weekend was often a much waited one for us, we often looked forward to joining our cousins for dinka or Sudanese time. Thank to both of our parents, we were often united. Our foster mom took us to McCarthy the first weekend to spend the weekend, it was a fun time together and their parents were supper excited seeing us. They often had plenty of food and bedding for all of us. The McCarthy lived in Yelm or McKenna, WA to be specific, but few minutes into the suburb. They owned a large area of farmland with few cows on it. We used the field for soccer every time we visited. In fact, it was on that field that we took our first driving lesson. Dad as we all used to call him taught us how to mow the lawn and later how to drive the real car. They own some cows and my cousins who after a decade without being goat and cattle tenders, we saw them enjoying feeding the animals during our stay at the McCarthy.

Bul Nyuop

Our first Christmas in the U.S rolled by anticipating much, but it happens, and a day passes by with less and less surprise. We had Christmas tree and we went to church for evening prayers that night and that was it. All you would see and feel around was the spirit of people saying happy holidays or happy Christmas, plus the colors of light and funny designs to welcome what we called the birth of Christ. Yes, we were overflowed with food that Christmas night unlike our years back in Kakuma when sometimes you will sleep just with the joy of the Christmas in your empty stomach. How Christmas is celebration was among the first differences we found between our new home and the refugee camp we left behind in Africa. Although we had less in our life over the years of our refugee, celebration of Christmas and Easter never showed how poor we were. Those were over super enjoyable days. Christmas in Kakuma starts with people saving little by little of Kenyan shillings to buy Christmas cloths, or had strong lunch and dinner before or after days of drain out celebrations. For Christians, there were celebrations and matches that start on the twenty fourth and end two or three days later. As for not so devoted Christians, it was a day to dedicate to God to forsake your sins. Yes, Christmas days were our happy days in the Refugee camps, even with our inadequate basic needs. They were the days we careless about our hunger and challenges of the refugee life, but excitedly celebrate ceremoniously. Especially with Christmas often falling days before the ration distribution, those few days of the month were often dark days, people would go a day or two without food. Nevertheless, at such times, we somehow had the energy if not the faith to fully participate in the festivities and matches in the spirit of Christmas.

Coming to America, we expected enjoyable days of Christmas celebrations, prayers, much then we did in our refugee camps. We went to the church on X-mass eve and then the following morning and prayers went with surprising timely services, nothing like our Kakuma services that had consumed us for seven years prior to that very moment. I never anticipated that American Christmas would be such a celebration of personal desire, and less about Christ birth. The beautiful tree decorations, the gifts, the gestures of "happy holidays", the wishes for a snowed Christmas, Santa Claus, candy cane and all the things associated with American X-mass were new things for us, and I viewed them as human desires. Yes, we took part; we decorated our Christmas trees, taken some pictures around it and of course at the receiving end of the gifts. There was much less about Christ either in the short service or in any other demonstrations.

On the X- mass morning, the twenty fifth, we were overwhelmed by another new phenomenon, the first unfamiliar weather experience; snow. The whole week, there was talk and forecast about white Christmas on the Christmas day. It never made sense till that morning when we woke up with a surprising glossy and whiteout. We were really surprised by how much snow that really fell. It was all white everywhere. As I leaned and crack open the window, the breezy cool air slowly rushes in, forcing me to close the window. The few cars were running slowly and as I came downstairs, I saw the kids playing in the front yard. I knew from my geography background that snow was very cold, but as I look at the window, there were kids playing outside, some making snow man and others throwing it at one another. Our own little Dylan was requesting us to go outside to play in that chilly weather. As days, weeks, month and years goes by, we came to learn that it was something part of American, it became frequent to see heavy snow fall during the Christmas week or on the Eve of the twenty fifth, no wonder why American call it white Christmas after the white snow. However, to mark the American Christmas, our foster mom had bought some gifts, placed them under the indoor so-called Christmas tree. She also made a big diner and her daughter was invited to celebrate with us, if not to see her new brothers. Yet to come, the New Year was no different from Christmas but the excitement we saw on TV across America including our own Seattle skyline Space needle was the countdown to the New Year.

As we welcome our first New Year celebration in America, we were only few days away from the start of our first school quarter in America. And while I felt happy for our first quarter to come upon us, I wasn't happy about going back to ESL class. Yes, our ESL teachers were the best, but just the idea of going to 3-4th grade equivalent of our primary school was a waste of time for me. We understood why ESL, English was our second language, and maybe the teaching was in a fast pace in the regular classes, but by no mean was what we finally learned in the regular classes any new to us. Our educational background in Kenya was super hard compare to the high school in America and that prepared us for the American curriculum. The curriculum was different; of course, our new studies included the American's and some Pacific Northwest history. Sciences were the same, nevertheless. In fact, I was later given full home credits on the sciences and world history. As we got our studies going, we got incorporated into the regular classes.

American history was one of the class I felt in love with. It was fascinating. We were learning about wars, about the early settlement, the American Indians, formation of the states, about presidents, events and eventually about the slavery etc. Everything over the 200 plus years of the country existent was available live and I was living it. As is often expressed, history determine the future, this was the case. American's were walking the book. I later took an AP history class prior to graduation to not only satisfy my precollege requirement but because of my undoubtable interest in the subject. I was participating in full discussions, presentations and projects. And despite how easy high school was, it was nevertheless interesting and by the time I got out of high school, I thought I was more knowledgeable of Americans' history than a good percentage of natural born Americans.

In addition to the book, we were also experiencing the daily business of America. On the twenty eighth of February 2001, the next big event in the new land came upon us, the big earthquake. Nisqually Earthquake, named after the epicenter. We were out, just sitting down in the GYM facing the main exit door for our PE class when allover sudden we felt some shaking and trembling. The front main door seems to be banged hard by someone from outside. As we look around, we saw little debris falling from the building and instantly the alarm sounded off, calling everyone to get out of the building. Like fire drill, we all reported to the sport field where the attendant was taken, and we hold off there till it was cleared for us to report back to classes. It was my first experience of an earthquake. I saw the physical destructions including falling parts of our gym and the 4th avenue bridge in Olympia, and of course all the news coverage for few days following. This was a 6.08 magnitude quake, high up there according to history. Unlike Africa, most of the climatic disasters that I later experienced across America were usual in the American life; mostly they were forecast days ahead. Unfortunate, this earthquake just happened with no knowledge and warning. The damages reported were minor, but it was yet another historical experience for us.

We were also welcomed by the athletic department. We were approached leanly to see if we could be interested in sport; running and soccer, two of the best sports Africans were known for. Coaches were always longing for African students, viewing or expecting them as best players in soccer or running. At those time, Kenyan, Morocco, Ethiopian to name few were among the world dominants in the sport world. African players share recognizable world reputation. They sought the same expectations in us. There were also students from our ESL classes who were part taking in soccer, they too requested us to join. In the beginning of the school year 2001-2, that September, I had turned out for soccer. I was a sophomore but playing with mostly freshman kids and not so well 2nd yearers in the C team. I was a junior by age, and seventeen years. Soccer was the only sport I knew back from Kenya, but I was not among the best players. Back in Kakuma and prior, playing soccer was our routine activity and the most available option for sport. It was the activity that kept us engages with time during our hardest time of the refugee camps. We play at our free times and it was very competitive that only few made it to the best of the best or the school teams. I often played as a goalie till Kakuma when I started playing in the field.

My first year as a C team player was very great. We had a blast year, winning all but one match. We lost to Tacoma, Bellarmine preparatory High School on their field ground. Bellarmine Prep was a strong private school, not only recognize at the time in soccer, basketball, other sports success but also academically. Our first match against them played on our field ended in game in draw, two by two. C team was not much of attention to the public and school community. Despite how good our team was, we didn't draw much fans and attention. My foster mom never came for any of my home game, but the caring parents of my teammates were not coming either. Varsity was viewed as the real core soccer team. At every varsity team, not only was the stadium pack with parents and school students, and national anthem played at some games, senior night and championships. Varsity was the dream that every C team or junior team participant always hoping to make by the end of their junior year. As a senior in the varsity, a participant was offered standing ovation at the last game. Seniors were honored in every game of any sport and hence every athlete always looks to seniority status. I never possess or vision that dream of making the varsity or even that proud.

At the end, soccer didn't impress me, but I confirmed one thing, that I could run. This was also what many including my PE teacher, John and his coach wanted, for me to turn out for track and field. Two of us running for North Thurston, was an expected dominant. At our physical education class, we always outrun the other kids. My teacher, Mr. Madison always praises while challenging others as he describes our speed that "we run like the wind". He often asks if I were on the track team and if not, why. At that same time, 2001-2 John and his coach were talking to me about joining track and field instead of soccer. Both suggested I could be better than in soccer. I was embracing their suggestion but reluctantly.

In the beginning of the 2001-2002 school year, I walked on the field and surprised the track coach. As always, I was very reluctant, didn't want to show him that I had made my mind to join. He continued to show that me that they will appreciate having me on the team. I told him that I will try. The coach looked at me, crack a smile with wide open eyes, stretch out his hand to hi-five me, and to share the moment. He called everyone and introduced me, saying, this is Bul, John's cousin" and he will be running with us this year. I started running while John was nursing his ligament. It was a cross country season. Unlike track and field, in cross country, a lot of students even those in non-fall sports turnout to enjoy running in the wood. At that turnout, we had a lot of students that never return for track and field. As a team, without John, we never perform as expected but it was a lot of fun. I lettered or was recognized.

Away from North Thurston school district, ten to fifteen miles northwest of Lacey, in the Yelm school district, my cousin, Gabriel Atem along with his fellow distance cousins; Michael Chuol and Andria Lual were making their names and school heard and in the record book. They run a remarkable year, dominating our conference and eventually making it to state championship and winning it. Primo was playing his favor sport, he was a soccer star at Yelm, sometime teasing as what we were running after.

I ended cross country with a better feeling, and much hopefully. Being part of a team was one thing, contributing individually was more feasible then in soccer. I turned out again a quarter later for track and field. Again, John injured his foot, that time nursing a broken metatarsal. He was disappointed, but his coach saw something to hope for in him. John was only finishing his second year, with couple more years to dominate, which he later did including setting records. I run that year, kangarooing several events in one meet just to collect points. I remember one meet, at Tumwater, I run the two miles, a mile and eight hundred meters. My coach was very surprise, but collecting nine points at the end, finishing first in two miles, third in a mile and I believe also third in eight hundred meters. The disappointing season ended on the Yelm high school field when I failed to qualify for district.

As the track and field concluded, it was a matter of few weeks prior to my last days at North Thurston. I was looking forward to the graduation and a summer afterward. I was finally awarded my home school credits the previous fall and had made my mind to graduate that June 2003. That spring term was the most nervous. I had to finish my college bounce courses and at the same time settle my high school requirement. That also meant graduating from the foster care program and moving out of the house. My foster mother did not feel ease with my urgency to graduate. She saw concern that I was not yet ready to attack the American life by myself. I didn't know much about leaving independently, either but I was excited about graduating and a chance to go further in my educational career. I was ready, I assured her. In March that winter, I received governor scholarship for my college. I also had to apply for college and fill out financial forms to request more money for college. Thanks to a lot of help both from my foster mother, case workers and teachers, everything went as planned. I graduated on June 10th, 2003 from North Thurston High School, the same day as my cousin Gabriel and all the boys at Yelm. This was a great a accomplishment, the first to graduate from high school in my family.

9/11th, 2001

The September 11 attack of New York, the Pentagon, and Pennsylvania was an eyewitness hard to believe attack that changed not only America but the world. Before the day became historical, it started just like any other day, a normal beautiful day as many later recall the New York sky that morning. We woke up that Tuesday morning and we had just made it to our first class of the day, just few minutes before the session was about to conclude. The business around America was usual, Boston and Newark airports where the planes bounced from knew no hidden agenda among their customers that morning, they were ready for safe travelling of their customers.

The facts are what became the attack was years in the making, masterminded by the leader of the Al Qaeda and coordinate by their sympathizers. In the morning of September11th, 2001, the Al Qaeda plan was to run into the American icons four commercial airlines, to break America, to terrorize and get American to rethink over various involvements in the Middle East, obviously by revenging with mass killing. At the end of that dark day, their plan had scored some points and their name heard, and yes terrorizing as their goal was concern. This was unusual act of war, as I heard that term "terrorism" the first time that day.

We were in our first class of the day, English literature. As usually the TV was on CNN live when all over sudden, the marquees reads "breaking news". The volume was down; the teacher was facing the students with his back turned on the TV. At a distance, I saw this tall building trampling with smoke almost submerging the building and people running from and away as the fire tracks run toward the fire. I remember one of my classmates pointing toward the teacher to look at the TV. It was not small to ignore. The class was almost over, but the teacher phoned the administration to ask if the children could see the breaking news. Many students were not paying attention at all, but I was devastated. At 8:45, the first plan from Boston was hijacked and drove into the North Tower, killing all the onboard, many innocents who worked in that building, and first responders. Few minutes later, 19 to be exact, the South tower was hit by another while million around the world watch the unfolding incident on the first tower. Both planes flew out of Boston Logan airport.

As Americans and security turn on the New York, another plane out of Newark, New Jersey was taken over by more hijackers, gearing it toward DC. This flight strikes the side of Pentagon, the headquarters of American military. Because of the delay in one of the flights, the passengers in the fourth plane had learned about the attack and the bravely stopped their plane from killing non- onboard passengers. The passengers wrestled the hijackers of this plane as they drove it onto the empty space near Shanksville, Pennsylvania, killing everyone on board. According to the intense coverage that followed the attack and many writings including the history website where I learned more, there were 19 hijackers who participated, all from the Arab's countries.

The two towers hit were among the tallest of New York and of the world at that time. Made of steel and glass, the weight of the planes, tones of gasoline in them, the buildings and the thousands of live all scrabbled to the basement with the smoke filling the atmosphere of New York. The aftermath and the responses were unbelievable. I never witness the Sudan civil war, never took part in the real army struggle, never hold a gun against our enemies, and I never watched the confrontation of gun fight or any bombardment on TV. But yes, the civil war had cost us to fled, and the destruction of our home plus millions of lives of the fellow Sudanese. However, the 911 attack of the World trade towers, the Pentagon, and the attempt pardoned by patriotic citizens who never feared about rescuing their life were all too much to comprehend.

The period ended; we left the class for the 2nd class of the day. I was heading toward my physic class. In that class, there was a wider screen TV and much closer to the students. While we only saw the 1st building during the last minutes of my English literature, we saw the entire incident and coverage in the 1.30 hr. physic class. The memories of seeing the airplanes penetrating the buildings, the pentagon, and the one that smashed on the PA field at 500 miles per hour were something unimaginable for me. I was scared and couldn't wait to run home and watch the full coverage in it entirely with full understanding. My eyes were stuck on the TV, while my teacher along with the students minding their own business. It felt unreal looking their reaction, or perhaps there was something they could do but continue their immediate agenda, studying. Unlike the highlights and stories of American Embassy booming in Kenya and Tanzania, the Oklahoma booming, Pearl Harbor etc., that I later learned myself; this immediate disaster was not like any other. Well, I was living it. The scale was not comparable, and big commercial airplane into skyscrapers, it was astonishing and heart breaking. About 3,000 died that days excluding thousands more injured or whose lives were changed forever as a result, particularly the millions who later suffered severe lung disease from that smoke. Millions in property value and market all halted for days and of course the impact of the fear.

In the aftermath of that awful day, I came to my own conclusion that Americans were strong people whose lives could not be shaken easily. America's normal business was continuing despite so much of that incident. I saw that right in my physics' class, the second session on that morning of the attack. The kids paid less attention when I pretty much had my eyes glued to the TV. As President Bush summarized the reaction that September night saying, "Terrorist attacks can shake the foundations of our biggest buildings, but they cannot touch the foundation of America". This believe was also captured by the selfless acts that led many firemen to run into the smoke engulfed towers to rescue strangers that morning of the incident. It was the same selfless act or call it bravely that led the passengers to wrestle the hijackers to force the plane down the PA field. A cross America, help was pouring from citizens whether it was the blood drive, comfort, fundraising for the cause or fire fighters driving to New York to help. I remember our own fire fighters, from Washington State, at the time driving thousands of miles to New York to help.

The vast coverage of the aftermath also revealed something I didn't know. I came to learn a lot about Khartoum and the fact that the United States had backed up our own enemy for years. The incident revealed the many unknown. It was the turn of the tide. For many years, the American government, particularly the Regan Administration had helped Sudan against us or our affiliate the so-called rebels, or SPLA/M. Blacklisted or among counties sponsoring terrorism was some else that I learned but this was close to me, it was also about a country that I was calling mine. I was surprised to hear Sudan on the blacklist or their participation in the killing of thousands on the September 11, but I was rather happy then sorry or worried for anything they could do to Sudan. I knew I was a Sudanese, from Sudan and my green card shows, but I could explain myself better then what the piece of paper said, or the name Sudanese implied.

At least I was not a Muslim. In the middle of Sudan and the attack of September 11 was a man who's for couple of years had resided in Sudan and maybe Khartoum had support him against the west. He was Osama Biladen (later killed on 5/1/2011), a Saudi born who was discovered as the leader of the terrorist organization, Al Qaeda, an organization he found, claimed responsibility for the attack. Washington declared the group the terrorist and decreed them as the attackers of America on that September day.

Not many American knew at the time what was going on in Sudan then; the ongoing twenty-one civil war and its consequences includes those that brought the Sudanese Lost boys to America or directly the two million lives lost in the decades of the war. Perhaps there were no reason or the media/government careless. However, the loss of three thousand Americans and disrupted American business, prompted Washington to unveil Sudan. This incident gave the media the green light to excavated more about Sudan. Along with our arrival, the incident of the attack opened the world eyes. The attack completely closed the years of Washington helping Khartoum and opened the doors for Southerners. There was at hand something to pull away the American government backing of the Khartoum government and legitimizing the rebels from the south, I thought. The removed curtain gave ways for individuals and organization to reach out their hands to the Southern Sudanese people and since then, individuals citizen in one way or another got heard and help internationally.

As for my fellow lost boys in the process pipeline, 911 was consequential both in delaying and terminating the process. There were lost boys on the flights to America, many crowded Nairobi, the departures point and many still in their process at Kakuma when the attack happened. For those on the planes, they were never informed while on the plane, instead the pilots and all the crew teams mentioned that they could not go to New York straight because of the weather. My immediate cousin, Barnabas's plane was diverted to Canada. The boys in Nairobi were stagnated in a crowded un health compound, and many future processes placed on un definite hold, ultimately terminating the process altogether.

As mentioned earlier and in many ways, I was scared and brought to thoughts, one of course why I left war in Sudan to encounter another in America. I felt the war was following us as I later heard that same expression from the boys. No Sudanese lost boy of course lost life on that day, but in the revenge, some feared to the opportunity of the draft to participate in the war or that America was not safe after all. We were struggling with all that our minds were saying. I felt that I was going to encounter a lot of people asking me if I know anything about Sudan involvement in the terrorism act. I was not personally afraid when it comes to a point of questions about my Sudanese hood or what I knew about Sudan as related to Osama. I knew that many Americans didn't know anything about Sudanese or Sudan, and with demand of explanation about my knowledge of either Biladen or Sudan, there was an opportunity to distinguish not only my distance from Biladen or Sudan enlarge, but to explain the un heard stories that brought us to the United States or the entire Sudan civil war to the world. My only fear was if someone would just attack me knowing that I was from Sudan. There no direct threats that I remember, but over the years most of the lost boys educated the world about Sudan and the civil wars and what eventually brought them to the far world. The other impact was September attack put an end to the fled of Sudanese boys to America. It probably cut off so many innocent boys or girls who were desperate to join us in the hope of better life America. The other instant impact for the lost boys was the curving of the Sudanese travelling. This was not only the lost boys, but many others could not travel easily even few years after 911.

Having lived many experiences of the twenty-one years of civil war in my country, and the million lives lost, 911 was very unimaginable. The nearly three thousand deaths on that one September day was too much to comprehend. As a refugee for so many years, we never had access to our civil war information, particularly the casualties. Most of the information that reached us in the refugee camps was mostly news of victories. The few defeats were never specified as casualties were concerns. I remember when a war cinema was brought to Kakuma and we were supposed to watch it, but due to the present of children and women among us, it was postponed abruptly. In some capacity, we heard about some confrontation that had left so many deaths including the fight for Kurmuk, Kapoeta, Juba and of course civilian attacks mostly by Khartoum backed allies. We witnessed our own non war deaths especially in Pinyudo and the attack at Gilo, but this magnitude was overwhelming especially when I could see all that at one place, on TV. This day was a worldwide day of terror against freedom, the very same cause we were fighting for in Sudan. For American government, this was the day to take a second look at the world, a day to see who advisories were or who were providing them safe haven. It was this day that the mastermind of the September 11 terror became known to have link with Sudan.

For us, the lost boys of Sudan, many felt sorry carrying that identity of Sudan with them, but for others that was the opportunity to be heard after all. In most cases, I was very terrified by the terror, many suffered random attack just because they were Sudanese. Widely, some Sudanese documentations were confiscated. At end, the aftermath coverage filled off the curtain for the world and southern suffering and stories were heard. Many of us were able to narrate stories against Khartoum and why we were in America. The attack gave some of us the opportunity to get the story straight, distinguish ourselves, the southern region against Khartoum. I had the chances to show them the reasons I came here, and that it was because of such similar terror against the Sudanese in the south of the country.

September 11 attack did not just invigorate the unfinished 1991 American's gulf war, it too gave D.C another looks at Sudan. Over the years especially in the early eighties, DC was in good term with Sudan, who also was in association with Biladen. It was the US oil company, the Chevron that discovered and drilled the first oil reserve in Sudan in the late 70s. The revenue from this drilling of course was used against the Southerners. And until his overthrown from power, Numeri was a friend of Washington, in fact he was on a visit to the US when he was overthrown. While some Christian organizations had already helped in changing Washington view of the rebels; the SPLA, the 911 terror attack on America was the final turn around. This came with many sanctions including a stop on companies that were helping Sudan with the supply of oil revenues. This procedure in turn indirectly helped South Sudan and its road map to independent.

In the years following the US retaliation, the American public was also made aware of the inhuman act of genocide, ethnic cleansing and humanitarians' issues that were taking place in the Darfur region of Sudan. Again, before that dark September, many American or maybe many advocates of peace around the world were not aware of the Sudan crisis or simply where it lied on the map. 911 opened many American eyes and in our case, many learned about us, our arrival and crisis of the Sudan afterward. The American government I believed paused and so were their allies who had participated in their indirect help of Khartoum for so many years. The American petroleum companies pulled out of that business and so did they convinced Canadian companies and other allies to get out of Khartoum's business. The Sudan army was much superior than the SPLA in term of weapon because they for many years had used the oil revenues from the south to buy superior weapons and airplanes to use against the Southern rebellions. This 911 was the turn of the tide for many around the world who finally understood the Sudan civil war and contributed in many ways.

By 2002, just as expected, the world pressure on Khartoum and their alienation through crippling sanctions, in combination with many other situations including the reunion of the SPLA, peace deal was the option. Both parties to the war accepted to come on the table before the Intergovernmental organization called the IGAD, the east Africa block. The president of Kenya, Mwai Kibaki along with his IGAD nominated fellow Kenyan, a retired army general took the initiative to act as the chief mediators. The fate of Sudan peace was in their palm. Khartoum was now on a challenge, with another opportunity for a compromise with the SPLA despite so many attempts in Nigeria and Ethiopia since Bashir took power in the 1989 coup. The process took years, but it was a complete obligation to IGAD, and the SPLA was in a good mood and commitment as in the past.

Unlike the 1972, the chief negotiator for the SPLA, the leader and chairman was looking for nothing short then a peace that would lead to self-determination or a New Sudan in which everyone was to be treated as first class citizen from border to border or religion to religion. He was a man who never agreed to the 1972 deal, as he paraphrased it shortly after that peace, calling it a "shot up deal". As he later unveils the 6 signees of the six protocols called the CPA, the deal was not to be own by one person and surely not by him as was the case with the Lagu 1972 accord. The first five protocols of the CPA were signed by five leaders of the SPLA including Salva Kiir and Pagen Amuom, leaving the final signature to the people of South Sudan in the form of referendum. As he joked while elaborating on the protocol during a speech in Panyagoor, we all got our hands on the deal "if its smell bad, we would all stunk" and via versa.

Unlike the Abuja negotiations, hosted far away from the eyes of stakeholders by Nigerian president in Abuja, Nigeria, the IGAD was an in-house or around the dining table talk. It was at home near Kenya and Sudan, neighbors as was the case with 1972 Addis Ababa talks, but also by a president who was new to his post and who wants to rule a country that is next to a peaceful nation of all Sudanese. More important, there were Southern Sudanese refugees at every corner of Kenya and around the venues of discussions. They were witnessing the sense, and, their desperation was in the atmosphere around the negotiation tables. Kibaki along with his IGAD appointed Chief mediator Mr. Lazaro were now looking in the eyes of these refugees who were desperate for peaceful settlement of the long war. The chief mediator, Lazarus on the other hand was not someone who would political be influenced, he was a former lieutenant who understood the consequences of wars and in fact had travelled to South to taste the people desire of the talk's outcome.

For many of us across the world, we were on a dot by dot concurrent with every protocol in discussion. Thanks to technology, we were getting updates instantly. I remembered the many times I had gone to our school and city libraries only to search on Sudan news, the very first way I learned about what was on the world web. A lot of the refugees from Kakuma and other cities of Kenya were swarming into Machakos, Eldoret, Nakuru and Nairobi where the negotiations were being held either to keep themselves informs instantly, show their desperation for peace, or to witness history in the making. The process was progressive, more hopeful than ever and many people saw Omar and his vice for the first time on TV and in person. Every signatory deal was called protocol and as days went on and on, there were series of protocols signed. Eventually, the peace deal was reach; Comprehensive Peace Agreement (CPA) was signed in Nairobi after a long smooth period of ceased fire. This peace gave six years called the transition period for the Sudanese, especially the Southerners to decide in votes whether they would remain as part of Sudan or succeeded to form a republic themselves. The result six years later was the split of Africa largest country and the birth of the continent fifty fourth nation, the independent republic of South Sudan.

September 11 was an eyewitness awakening to the world, and it started the changes on how the world did business. Several attacks before the 2001 including the 1998 bombing at Nairobi & Tanzania and other closed cases against the so-called Islamic Militants or radicals were now under close review. Travelling became more scrutinized, with intense screening. Instantly after the attack, many possible travelers avoided the air travel including many airlines travelling the world nearly empty following the 911. Since then, a lot of people pay attention to whoever is on board the plane, stereotype spun up. As the fear spun up, categorization in association to terrorist became base on physical looks; dressing style, names, the country of citizenship and more importantly where the flight was bounced to. I encountered that tied insecurity eight years later, October 2008 when I was on my way home to Africa for the first time since my arrival to the USA. Against, since 2001, the word terrorism has come out of the shell in full context and no one ever since then resist; the intense screaming at airports, confiscation and all together the fear of flight.

Dead End!

I never admitted the culture shock at any point during my early years of transitioning to American life. According to the online Oxford Dictionary, culture shock is defined as the *disorientation experienced when suddenly subjected to an unfamiliar culture or way of life.*

I fell into the definition above, of many unfamiliar instances, firsthand experiences that I suddenly was subjected to. America greeted us with overwhelming experiences and opportunities that for sure were first encounters. As a refugee, experiences included the adequate foods, adequate clean water and a big comfortable bed. I expected much in the land I was coming to and for sure there was more that I never had the opportunity. I didn't know the diversity of America, but I knew it was a different country and much richer, hence, a mind blowing for someone who lived a deficiency refugee life for decades.

I was interested to learn and never shy away, constantly conversing with adults, and watching TV, all of which helped me with my transition. Among the early instant variations includes school system, weather, laws, the people, traffic, the language, the do and don't etc. to mention just few. Even today, there are thousands of identities that I would never fully compromise with or would defuse my recognition with as American.

We learned a little about America during our orientation and they started immediately after boarding our flight from Nairobi, Kenya. We were introduced to what we then referred to as "the green thing", salad as we came to know it. Many of us did not eat the salad, while others only tasted it with curiosity. As we later arrived in the state, food was plentiful, unlike what I had lived with in my years of refugee prior to arrival in the US. Here food was not only in abundant but very diverse. We saw a lot food being dumped at home, at schools, and over at places we were invited for dinner, this was new, something we never saw for over a decade. At the refugee camp, especially in Kakuma, we were used to eating one meal a day, sometimes go a day or two without eating. In addition, there was so much sweetness in most foods, also very ironic that we were being picky about what we never had for years.

Unlike many kids who came here and easily adapted to the mainstream, I came to the US as a teenager, seventeen per my papers. Already acquainted with a British African English accent, that mean recognizable enough by anyone that I was indeed a foreigner. In addition, my age made it hard to easily melt into the culture; resistant and being careful. For things I had to learn, I worked hard but the cultural conflict resists identities that were not so normal with my home born culture.

The American educational system was one variation we encountered immediately after arriving in the United States. First, we had to be immunized to get accepted in high school and we had to keep that record later till college. Unlike in Kenya and Sudan and maybe many African countries, here in the US, the students were the ones that leave the class after each class session to attend the next lesson in a different class. You had to meet different people from class to class, sit in a different seat unlike the system we were used to where the teachers come to your class. The system was very easy, with a lot being during the regular life. Unlike in Kenya, we didn't have to study very hard, even during the exams you could open your book to find your answers.

Language was not completely challenging, but significant differences exist. As I later came to learn, the Americans speak English differently from east coast to west coast or north to south. My English background in Kenya was pretty good at least for a form four candidate (high school senior) when I left. However, our English was more of a British or as others may say, African-British mixed. We were using British way of spelling or pronunciations. In this case, organization was not with Z but S, Centre spelled with r before e and some many pronunciations like in the case of water. And then there was the street talk, particularly with many young Americans and those close to the so called the hippies. They young were using a lot of slangs, short forms of word, and spoke quickly in their conversation unlike many adults who spoke something that was familiar to us, formal English.

The first language confusion was a slang that distorted my comfort with English was the use of the ordinary word; chemistry. Yes, I understood chemistry as a subject or disciplinary of science. But during our lunch at high school, my classmates were talking about relationships, about girls and boys. The conversation then turned to me and one Hispanic boy referred to me as a ladies' man. I understood the phrase "ladies' man" base on the context of the conversation. He added that many girls were always crawling around me in the class. I replied that they were just being nice, interested to know about my background, plus I was often assisting them with their class work, I explained. At least, you have some chemistry going on, my friend Jamie insisted. Chemistry! I retorted. I was termed by the word, didn't know what he meant because clearly it was not in the context of the subject. I pretend to have understood the word chemistry just to avoid embarrassing my integrity. I ended that conversation quickly as I left thinking about someone else to ask what that meant. That was clearly an incident of culture shock. Over the years, I came to know American way of talk is very deep and couldn't never be learned complete. American talks in metaphors, in slang, and of course there is variation of spoken English from one part of America to the other.

Cultural variation also came in the high technology that we saw around, from the sense of technology behind the first airplane that I took, to escalators, skyscrapers, to the shocking number of cars on the road. I once admitted telling my cousin that the number of cars was probably high to outnumber the people or that when the cars in one city are lined up, they could reach Kenya. There was a lot new thing to be frank; however, I did not want my annoying young foster brother as he humiliates someone running around telling other people how all everything was so new to us. I had not uses a lot of the new things in my new house prior to my arrival there, things like flashing the toilet, switching on/off the light, using computer, watch TV or shopping at departmental stores in Africa, however all those were there even at Nairobi, not in the refugee camp. The kid was as talkative and mouthy like no one I met before. After all the questions were often about the entire Africa, a continent and he would not understand much of my explanation. He was too little for world history.

As the year came to an end, for the first time we were also celebrating the Christmas differently. Yes, the churches including the one we went to celebrate the birth of Christ with the reading of the bible. However, the whole happy Christmas we were used to in Africa, the one we celebrated like no other over several days at our starving doom days of the refugee, was only a one service celebration here in the rich country. There were no night prayers, there were no dancing, and all we saw everywhere including our own house was Christmas trees, the exchange of gifts and yes, random wishes of happy gestures.

Thanks to Community Youth Service, a not for profit organization that was instrumental in helping us transitioned into the Americans' life. Early in our first year, 2001, we were introduced to the CYS coordinator, her name was Mary Deans. She came to my school to get ESL students informed about the CYS and its programs. At the end of that introduction, my cousin John and I were convinced that it was the right place for us at least to get us transition into the American society instantly and smoothly. Yes, some students were hesitant to join, but we took it quickly. The organization was charted at helping not only recent immigrants, ESL students, but all students who need help transition into American independent life. It was teaching students some computer classes to increases their computer competency, how to approach interviews and organized resumes, how to acquire and hold jobs and to help students understand life beyond. They were also counseling and that was a very big help to a lot of the students in that class.

I remembered our introductory day, we all introduced ourselves, our cultural background and why we chose to attend the class. Unlike me and my cousin Riak, many of the kids were either born in the country or brought into the country when they were young. Nevertheless, it was hard for them to melt into the American melting pot well. Some of the reasons they had joined the program include the opportunity to learn how to find and hold jobs, how to express themselves, to learn how to feel included in the American society. There were instances during that introductory when the teachers would say directly to the student that for all those reasons, you're in the right place and we will make you fit in well, including making you overcome those challenges. Luckily after graduating from the program, I had learned more than expected and my friendship with both the instructors and fellow students later remains for years after the program. In the class, I learned a lot about computers; both typing and using Microsoft programs, Photo shopping, webpage design using HTML, and photo finishing in black and white.

At the end of the program, we had learned how to get along not only with everyone in that class, but how to make friends outside, how to search and hold jobs, and how to overcome challenges or stereotypes or say fitting in to the mainstream. It was from that class that I learned the quote, to always "keep your blues at home". In extra, we learned about taxes, how to files federal income tax returns, and how to buy a car. In fact, I bought my first car, taught how to drive my first manual transmission car by the help of the program connection. This organization in part gave us a key to our life success in America. Yes, I almost landed a girlfriend in that class, but only to find my heart and mine fighting each whether it was ok to have a girlfriend.

We earned our first jobs while in the program. Many of us in that class were assigned to help at department of labor and industries or L & I. Some went to work at the community library. I was placed to work at the department of Labor & Industries, as an office assistant, my first job ever and first executive title. During the summer, we would go to work and, in the afternoon, convened at the class to share our work experience and learned more. The good thing was, we were also paid for attending the class. We were getting paid a minimum wage, $ 6.90 per hour. Overall, the class served its purpose especially to most of the kids that were enrolled. At the end, we were left confident, knowledgeable and brave enough to face the American dream at our own and against odds in one way or the other. The program manager and I remained friend afterward, even helping me financially at some much desperate times, including when they remitted some money while I was in Nairobi during my first visit of Africa since I had been in the U.S.

Adjusting to the American life was not easy especially in our own home. We had to earn trust from our host mom but perhaps that was an America and not her personal. We could not invite a friend, cousin and even the very one she knew were our blood cousins including Gabriel who was responsible for our coming to America. After notching that Simon was frequently stopping bye, she put a rule that no one is coming in her absence. Our counter response was, we wouldn't be going upstairs, meaning, we wouldn't eat anything if that's why you're preventing friends to stop by. We felt like we had to counter response that way knowing she was the mother of the house, but that was the culture conflict we had. We always felt she had to learn from us too, not just a one-way road. Her usual response was because "I said so"

As mentioned in another context, we dinka are like social bees; often gather to chat for long times and as parents later learn too stays on the phone for a while. At that time, we were often in desire to share time together. Simon was always lonely at his place especially after schools or over the weekend. We didn't know any were then, but Simon knew the road to our house. He would ride the 3 miles in the chilly afternoon to our house. Even with her at home, she had to approve his coming, either Simon had to call her, or we walk to her and request if Simon could come over.

As time passes, we let Simon into the house without mom approval and we just hang out down in our basement with him. We avoided going upstairs or eating anything to make sure everything remained as she left them and to show our gathering meant nothing than just companion and Sudanese times. Regular conversation, singing hymnals and traditional songs were very important to us at those time. Eventually, mom learned about us & I would say she just didn't know who we were or the trust she could have in us. But before we went our way to educate her, we had misunderstood that it was a one-way thing for her, just for us to learn about the United States and not the American to learn about us considering us being in the U.S soil. In matter of fact, it was an American culture, as we later learned more. I finally learned that mom favor saying of "because I said so" as she often denies our requests was in fact a universal phrase in most household.

For us, being in the parent care had been something we were not used to, we had been adults and independently cared for our own for a long time. As mentioned earlier, the first thing I asked mom our foster parent was whether I should call her mom or grandma. That statement showed how some of us were unused to. Nevertheless, we were very respectful of our parents. At one point, we tried to leave our mom and be relocated to another host family, so we may get more that we desire or due to have, but it didn't work out. We weighted what we might lose and what to gain including our school and friendship that we had cultivated in our new environment. Despite the differences, we lived at the Dildine and in many ways regarded her as a caring mother. We continued a very great relationship years after the program, in fact she was excited when I brought to her my wife and kid for the first and only time.

Our challenges were our desire to live as adults and not had to ask everything, just like we were used to, whether it was about inviting a friend over, staying late at school or even going on the computer. This was not just in our own house; other boys were encountering such and more issues. During the monthly meetings, we often see other boys and parents talking about all the complaints, including issues of allowances, but I and my cousin just suck it in. We were told in few of our meetings regarding our endless demands that if we work around our houses, doing in house chores, we may get some allowance. Some of us, me included didn't understand that from it face value.

The issues that were money related didn't bother us for long; many of us found their first jobs shortly after those discussions. We also understood that being in America, we wanted to be like those young American friends; with money, own a bank account, buy our own needs, and own a car etc. However, under the host family and maybe in our own program, it wasn't easy even when we use our own money to buy our own. The program at first had laid the policy that we could not be driving, the parents could not teach us, but after long cries during those meetings, the finally easy into their policy, but still restrain partially. But after all, I think they were in ought with their own policy. Their own children like many American teenagers were already driving by sixteen, unlike most of us who were older then sixteen at the time, and so by limiting us away from this fun, they were against American dream, they were showing how they were unrelated to us or even to carry the burden of a foster child "You have to buy insurance before you drive", they finally added another restrain. That was easy, the requirement for an insurance was state required, not them. We didn't know much about what that meant, but we were interested to learn, that didn't hold any of us back.

Among the first few Sudanese from my group in the Puget Sound to taste the American dream of owning a car was my cousin Gabriel Atem, he bought a crafty one, at least today I could say it was crafty, but then, we knew he had a good car. In 2002, I bought my first, a blue Pontiac 1995 Grand am, now we were stepping our feet into the American dream. However, even with this dream still young for, we particularly were in desperate need for the car. We sometime went to sport events or work late and returning home was often late at nights. So often, we would walk a nearly two miles in cool nights and despite other fears.

Despite the status quo and challenges thrown our ways and those about the foster care program we just stepped in, we were unknowingly ready for the challenges. Coming to America was an opportunistic, a reward for so much challenging life we had endured. In another word, we were ready to capitalize on the opportunity. Our past and challenges had taught us much and prepared us.

As our years added up, many of us overcame the early challenges, and in many ways successfully incorporated into the American life. In another way, earning the same share of the American dreams. On my 18th year anniversary since coming to America, I was very grateful to sincerely express my appreciation of America by stating to my coworkers the blessing I have earned with the opportunity to be in America. At that point, I had just finished my graduate school although none of them knew the graduate program I have been taking. Nevertheless, I was thankful for many others including the incredible undergraduate education, the beautiful family; the gorgeous wife and four adorable kids, and of course the American dream of driving a precious vehicle. Like any American, I was living the American's dreams and the publication of this book was something I would have never thought had I not been in America. Also, I obtained the privilege of citizenship in 2005, and with it the opportunity to share the same rights which include but not limited to American only jobs or to participate in elections and not in any better time than to cast vote at the 2008 presidential election for the first black candidate for the United States presidency.

Obama's Election and the History

Ever since his speech as the keynote speaker for John Kerry at the 2004 democratic convention, Obama had been in the spotlight. At that point, I was not vastly into the political watch, I did not know him or his rise from his community organizing to state legislator to US senator at the time. At that same time, I was a regular fox news audience, particularly for Hannity and Coms show, featuring both a republican and liberal host respectively. I was also a fan of George Bush, so I watched the show for that reason. However, it was only years after that speech and just before the 2008 campaign when many showed concerns, at least Sean Hannity of Hannity and Coms show at the time. Hannity in particularly was showing a lot worrisome tone should Obama declared for 2008 presidential candidacy.

This is not and in no way a clip of his biography, but of my own admiration of such an inspiring icon, a family man, a genuine, lovely and humble man whose present in a room is often a smile. I admired both his personal and political qualities. As a politician, he understood his job as a leader of all people, someone whose service and qualities of leadership have sent many unlikely individuals to congress and many after him running for presidency they would have never otherwise imagine. Obama's rise to presidency was not just an American story, his presidency became a way to extend the most needed inspiration to the globe.

At the time, he was a junior senator from Chicago and while many saw his speech as presidential, he was still against odds and many. Inexperience as that later became the campaign slogan against him with his opponents painting him as "not ready for the task or 3am phone call", that presidency was not on the job training, he had no name recognition. Most important, he was black, a first-generation black kid with a funny name as he himself acknowledged. I didn't know America was ready considering the years of history and many candidates before him who never made it most of the campaign season. In addition, some people including Trump who later succeeded him didn't believe he was not even born in America, an obvious disqualifying fact. And although his rise came some six-seven years after the September 11th attack, his name was easily associated with the mastermind of that attack, Osama Biladen. Last but the not the least, Obama's father was a Muslim, which played a lot against Barrack adding to the fact that he himself lived in the Muslim dominated country, Indonesia with his mother after she remarried to a man from that part of the world.

Despite the minor stereotypes and such, he was running against a list of very gifted politicians including Joe Biden who later became his vice, but also against someone with a name recognition, a well-informed and talented candidate; the former white house resident, Hillary Clinton, wife of Bill Clinton, the 42nd president. He won his democratic nomination bid, beating Hillary Clinton and ending a much bitter long campaign. On August 9th, he accepted the party nomination as the democratic candidate for presidency. At that point, history was already made as he declared himself on June 3rd, 2008 after the final primary in Minnesota, stating to his cheering supporters that "Tonight we mark the end of one historic journey with the beginning of another". He became the first black person to win a major party nomination for American presidency. With such a unanimous victory over Clinton, the country in most part saw a high possibility of the first African American president, or black president.

Nevertheless, the road a head was still challenging, it was going to be party against party especially for the die hearts and even those in his party who didn't want a black president yet or who felt bitter for some reasons. But taking nothing away, his opponent, the republican candidate, who also goes by the name maverick was a renounced senator, former war vet and prison of the Vietnam War, also an admirable man was the former 2000 presidential candidate who gave George W. Bush a run for his money. Last but not the least, many people saw Senator McCain with more international policy experienced than Obama. In response and counting on his intelligent and perhaps his admiration for later vice president, his best move following his sealed of the party nomination was selecting that icon, the Delaware Joe Biden as his running mate. This choice, as my fellow African friend Abdul stated it at the time "was it", exactly what he needed to silent the luck of foreign policy noise.

Despite all those challenges, Obama rises was much welcomed by the silent generations, and those that were new or not even yet capable of voting, the technological driven generation. He was inspirational, drawing most of his support from the generations who were ready to part way with the status quo and their parents in choosing their own destiny. I was a college student at the time, and I witnessed that eagerness and the anticipation to cast that historical vote. It was a vote to change the status quo, a vote to place a dent on the ream of racism in America, a vote to be proud about. Many voters crossed the political aisles with republican voting for him and those who never wanted to see black president against him. As I later learned, he was among the few presidents to receive such unanimous votes. I missed my first deserved opportunity to cast that first ever vote as an American and for the first black president because I left for Africa on October 6th, just approximately a month before the general election. However, thanks to the second opportunity, I voted in the 2012 for his second term. He recorded a high turnout as many inactive votes proudly casted their votes in the hope for change or "change we believe in" as Obama campaign slogan read.

From South Sudan - Juba, I was keeping my ears to the states. Over in Juba, South Sudan and with no surprise, Sudanese and most of the world was keeping eyes and ears on America. I had no TV access at that point, but just like years of Mandela's election, I was at the forgotten area, listening through the radio. It was early morning the next day in Africa, late night eastern part of the US and still early night at my home in Seattle when the breaking news emerged from the air waves, announcing the American election of Barrack Hussein Obama as the 44th president of the United States of America. As I came to watched his victory speech at the Grant park in Chicago during the chilly Midwest November night, it was a speech so welcomed around the world as million poured to the parks, and public areas around the country including at the white house and of course Kenya, his dad's home. There were so many tears, so many who had dreamed to see a black president and a chance of history had their prayers heard that night.

Beyond the American shores, the world welcomed the president as a change, a sign of inclusiveness and an aspiration for a new world as he was awarded peace prize before his presidency took it course. He was warmly welcome in any corner he visited, drawing crowds that were only limited by the size of the venues. During his speech in Berlin, Germany, he calls everyone to consider themselves as citizens of the world and in Addis Ababa, Ethiopia acknowledged that human being was one tribe and that the cradle land of human origin as Africa. Throughout his terms, he was admirable welcome at all places, including delivering speeches in places like Westminster Hall where only the Pop and her Majesty the queen were the only most honored invitees

I personally also believe the Arab spring, the political waves that swept off most of the old Arab leaders from their dictatorial seats was in part due to the aspiration from Obama's Cairo speech when he addressed the Arab nations. On his speech, he referenced the age where presidents should rule democratically and to recognize the voice of the citizens who put them to power. Like the young Americans who exercised their citizenship right democratically by voting a black president to power, Obama preferred all voices be respected. The young Arabs were also inspired to change the status quo of their nations, to take back their countries from the dictators although this inspiration was infiltrated by other agendas. With the help of social network, frustrations were easily expressed and shared and in results demonstrations started. Initially, the demonstrations were suppressed, like in the case of Egypt, however they became overwhelming and violent infiltrated against and for the status quo. This sweeping change that became known as the Arab Spring started with the toppling of Zine el-Abidine Ben Ali of Tunisia, Gadhafi of Libya, Mubarak of Egypt, to the election that swept out Iran hardliner, Mahmoud Ahmadinejad to the years of resistant civil wars in Syria and Yemen that resulted in the death of hundreds of thousands and mass immigrations to the European nations all as they fought to earn the same rights and aspiration as the little kid with the fun name that became the US president.

Million perceived the first black president as the turn of page in American history. Without having lived much of the American story at that point, I for sure perceived his election as an American progress toward equality or fair treatment. For me, his election was an affirmation of constitutional guaranteed that all men were created equal and America correctly affirmed the words of the preacher, of Martin Luther King Jr that people should be judged by their character. He was not favored to be president because of his skin but judged by his action and authenticity as someone to do the right things for American. While it's now discriminatory to disregard people base on the color of their skin or nationality, there're still remnants, people whose fears have engulfed their souls only to trigger by another excuse. It was the American progress toward equality that brought me to America, despite how much is yet to be done. America have come long way and people experience discrimination and rays of racism differently. Many of us, the lost boys experienced racism differently during our short days/years in America. I personally recall many on the street incidents when people said go back to Africa, at work when my new coworker didn't believe I had an accounting degree hence questioned if I had one and of course in pay variation. Nevertheless, America has change and I only could count less as compare to so much welcome and love that I have received. There is never a society where people don't hate one another for one reason or another so long it's not condoned.

I thought of his story and presidency as a vivid mark, a fulfilment of what Martin Luther King predicted, the mountain top story and that the son of slaves would one day sit on the same table or that people should be judged by the content of their character. That part of American history was on the mind of those who teared up that November night around America when he became the first black president. For me, his election carried much weight then I could express but for sure an audacity of hope. It was that history that caused me to hesitate about coming to America and although his election was not the final saying, as a young American at the time and listening to many coverages and views about his election in relation to the history of racism, his election was an affirmation of the progress toward the promises and vision expressed by many including Martin Luther King Jr. Thanks America, for bring him to the spotlight.

Nevertheless, Washington was not at ease with his election. The politic of the American political parties or Washington as many calls it devoted itself to the causes to make him a one term unmemorable president, including undermining his achievements. There were few republicans who met immediately after his election, pledging to make his presidency hard and a one term president. His later successor never accepted him as a legitimate president, at least early on. He was promoting his theory that Obama was not born in America. Others believe Trump rises to presidency was a response to Obama election. Upon becoming the successor, Trump committed himself to deleting Obama's or American's achievements under Obama administration in that matter. This was evidenced in Trump exiting the Iran Nuclear agreement, taking every effort to killing the Obama care and of course other executive actions that reversed Obamas' action. On American streets, police brutalities especially against black rose since that election as if it was a response to Obama election. The white supremacist voices rose, and some intruders attempts to get to his first family.

However, America grassroot never abandon him in the face of animosity. Thanks to millions of American, he was re-elected in 2012, despite what was called "shellacking", when he lost both houses of representative to the republicans. Nevertheless, his election did not eliminate racism, and not an affirmation of it either, but a sign that nothing could not happen in America. He opened doors to many minorities who saw the same opportunities.

Family
An Identity of us (I)

In the Dinka tribe that I belong to, family is just the lower and simple level of the larger' extended ancestral line. Like many African communities, a personal identity is a lineage that runs through generations. A simple dinka family of healthy couple poor or rich often long for a child, few lively hood assets including cattle, sheep, goats, chickens and a farm. In the modern world, our Identity added another name, that is from the republic of South Sudan.

Prior to my birth and the resumption of the second Sudan civil war in 1983, many dinkas or particularly then Upper Nile province, there were high instabilities and families moves from place to place in search of better life and in avoiding the direct impacts of the war. That migration took my parents, their siblings and relatives along with my elder siblings had lived at several places including Melut, a town north of Malakal; in fact, it was at the outskirt of this city where my sister was born. While there was no record of her birth, she might have been born there in between 1970-1972. Then the family moved down south to Abuorom, near the Duk County just before finally moving back to Kongor area, to my birthplace in Payoom village.

My father, Reec Nyuop Bul, came from a medium size family. He was one of the three brothers (Bul, Deng) and two sisters (Akoi & Achol), among those that died at infancy and their biological siblings; Kuir Nyuop and Reec-Gutbut, or Reec Thon. Nyuop Bul was married to Ahou Deng Tong, from Kongor.

Genealogically, we're a dinka from Jonglei state, sub-section Twi and from the biggest clan of Twi people, the Kongor. Kongor is further subdivided into sub-clans and I am from Palek linage. The Palek people stemmed from twelve-thirteen generations of two brothers: Aliap and Nyok. The two sons categorized as Palek pan de Aliap and Palek pan de Nyok. The father of these two boys, Leek is attributed to be among the first people who migrated to the area of Kongor and people consider him as a founder of not only Palek but in part Kongor's people. Aliap grand grandkid Aweec's fathered the three sons whom we're further categorized into: Akol Aweec, Atem Aweec and Ajak Aweec extended families. At the time of this publication, these brothers had brought forth lines and my grand grandfather Bul Ajak is the father of the most immediate classification that I fall into either as families of Ajang Bul or Nyuop Bul. My parents stemmed from Nyuop who had my father. I am already married and because of my father's two wives, some people have already separated the children of Reec Nyuop by our mothers. As widely known, human race does not trace daughters and sisters, but yes like my aunties mentioned earlier, my grandfather was also blessed with sisters and daughters.

On the maternity side, my mother Akon Mayom Bol was the second among the five siblings, with two younger brothers (Atem & Dhieu) & older and younger sisters Yaar & Angeer respectively. My grandfather, mom dad died before I was born and I know not any identity of him and I could remember, I never had the time with my parents including my mother to talk about him, to learn the kind of person he was, physically and spiritually. He is also from Kongor, the dinka subsection where I held from.

My maternal grandmother Achok Ajok Bior Wach on the other hand is a granddaughter of a famous man from *Adhiok* community, a subsection of Twi. She was a live when I left for Ethiopia in 1987. She was a very dearly and caring grandmother. While she might have shrugged when I was born, she was of same built as my mother, medium high. In fact, all my uncles and aunties from my mother's side were of similar statute, medium and very strong built, perhaps she contributed genetically. She rarely came to our house, but I used to stop by at her house near Panyagoor and at many times at my Auntie Yaar Mayom's house. Grandmother Achok. According to my sister and other accounts, was very old to run during the 1991 ethnic attack on our village, perhaps she was killed in that inhuman killing orchestrated by Riek Machar white army.

My parents were not alive at the time of this publication, but they are jointly survived by four children: older brother Nyuop, Younger brother Akoi and our exquisite sister, Ahou. According to my older brother and sister, my parents lost the first child, the one immediately before me and the last born, all before their toddler years. So many lost, that eventually my parents were forced to give up their traditional spiritual gods during the early 80s and turned to God, they became Christians. Early on just like many other dinkas, they were animist or believers of faults gods. Those gods never helped, never response to their cries and instead take more than give. My parents disowned him and were born into Christ with their repent and baptism lastly when their last born died.

He was a boy I knew well enough, a boy I had taken care of so dearly. He was number two behind me and I was old enough when he passed.

In addition to our mother, and because of polygamy as part of our culture, my father proudly married his second wife just before my mother passed and he was blessed to bring forth five more half siblings namely, Ahou, Nyuop, Kuir, Bul, and Nyandeeng. As in the dinka culture, my mother, the older wife was still the foundation of my father family, the position of the elder wife in the dinka culture. In fact, most husbands marry second or more wives in the approval of their first wives.

Prior to writing this book, I learned that my father was a very outgoing, authentic, and well-known with high reputation among his age mates. For many years, he was a cattle camp leader and most of those cattle camps were referred to by his name. Many described him as an energetic and very fashionable with traditional dancing festivals. He was very involved in the dances well into his late forties and his sister Akoi Nyuop remembered Reecdit when he went to the dancing right at the birth of his child. He was one that was always expected at dancing festivals or else there was an issue with him. One of his best friends was Deu (Madok) Maketh Deu. They both composed a lot of songs together. His celebrity lifestyle can also be understood through his many nicknames. For his agemate and generation afterward, he is *Ajing, loth e Machuuk, Wandit, Agutmachar, Wanajok* etc. He also scored five kills of cattle and in so memory, he also took the name *Gut- Dhiec* but because his so many nicknames had occupied many minds, that last nickname never stuck like others. This ceremonial killing of the cattle was the dinka cultural rite of passage, from boy hood to adult hood. However, my dad last killing was unusual, it came much later when he by then had passed the age of his youth. He was already settled, already several years a married man, a dad. Oddly the victimized cow was from his maternal relatives, something very unusual

Another memorable event was when he exchanged nine of his long horn cattle for only one bull. As his sister, my aunt Akoi Nyuop later recalled the incident, she was so prideful that she stated that her brother should be known as a person who cared so much about his energetic sportsmanship pride. He was a very adventurous human being, at least for luck of better word to describe his youth hood. I wish I had witness or had more opportunity to learn from his childhood friends.

As for their physical look and well-being, like his brothers, they were all tall, with the shortest among them being uncle Bul Nyuop at about 6 feet. My aunties were at least 5.8 feet tall. Ironically my paternal grandfather was a very short man as I heard from sister. A childhood friend of my father and my sister both recently described dad as an energetic dancing enthusiastic loving manic. He couldn't miss any dancing or young hood activities of his youth, I guess that say a lot to the many nicknames. My sister said about my father "even at the birth of his children"; he would go out to the dance and had time of his young blood.

My mother on the other hand, who was about five plus feet, was younger than my dad, an obvious situation among the dinka. She was well built, strong enough that she not once but twice stopped the aggression including a gazelle that was trying to enter the cattle barn. She was very caring, very industrious, loving and a good storyteller. With her love for me, she took the three-four weeks escorting me when I left for Pinyudo. She carried my luggage those three weeks and making me strong throughout. I also witness her strength not only in all the housework as a mother, she was always toeing to toe with my father including her hard work hard in the building of our barn while she was pregnant with me. At another instance of her strength, she stopped a young gazelle that once was trying to enter the barn. My aunty, her sister once told me how energetic my mother was as a girl considering being courted by the energetic young Reec.

She was a good storyteller, knowledgeable of many riddles, and tongue twisting. My mother was an example of a community wife, lovable by many. She was unifier, an example of a very discipline woman, very honest and outgoing. Today, I look at my sister as a carbon copy of my mother especially as a caring sister, mother and industrious wife herself. I can say she was raised very well.

My mother fateful death was a result of her hard work. She was pierced in the stomach by a cow in 1988 and due to luck of healthcare facilities and our village disconnection with the cities or outside world, she almost died from internal bleeding. She was rescued almost a little too late. She was airlifted to Kenya and for three months, she was treated at Lokichioggio. During her release, she was commanded to stay away from hard labor especially heavy lifting. However, she could not hold that recommendation for long. As a result, six months after returning to the village, the stiches were stretched, and the wound reopened. She passed sometime between April and June, before September 1991, just before Riek Machar led attack on the Kongor and entire

Bor area. As her age was concern, she might have been at her late forties if not early fifties. As my sister later told me about her death, my mother last's words before she passed was regrettably dying not knowing what ever happened to her Bul-Manyuon as she often referred me. She was probably in her late-forties or early fifties. This is indeed the hardest part of the story, but yes since we separated as she returned home after escorting me during my journey to Ethiopia, she never knew, never heard what had happened to me and I never heard from them or about her since we parted in Machabol in 1987.

My fraternal grandparents passed before I was born according to verbal history from my parents and siblings. I never knew their physical look, not even a picture of them. I don't know among my uncles, father, and aunts who resemble or look like whom between my grandparents. My grandfather as I have heard was a very short man. And although I could not attribute their heights to my grandmother, she was not very tall as I would guess because dinka men don't usually married tall women than them. As for my granddaddy, many members of the extended family used to say that when a visitor come looking for my grandfather especially those who didn't know him, they would have stood in disbelief when he tell them that he was in fact the person they were looking for. At time, he would just joke by sending them on their way, saying he didn't know where Nyuop Bul was. However, like many males among the dinka especially of his dinka Bor from Twic, he had few nicknames that he was called. My sister recently told me that one of his nicknames was *Mabior e weer*, meaning the moon. This nickname was however not his character, but a white Bull of a cow.

I left my parents at a very young age that I could only express less of them. But I know they were very industrious farmers, very loving and caring parents. All the way till I parted with them, they had always provided all we needed. Yes, growing up at those times and at such short time with them, I had never learned from them how they got married or where, their dinka youth hood which defined who the person become, their challenges as youngsters and the sweeties they saw in one another during their courting. But as parents, they raise us with a promising future. They taught us the spirit of commitment and hardworking.

There was much I could have learnt from my family and extended or the community entirely, but my separation from the family plus their early death all had weaned me from that history. They were born and live in what would be called today as Stone Age. They grew up away from any civilize world. Among many that I would know include how they look, there is no record of any picture of them. As young children that never had those grandparents, we missed very important not just their being, but their wisdoms and the opportunity to lie on grandmother's lab or walking with grandfather holding our hands. I am sure too that my parents felt bad that their parents never lived enough to see most of their grandchildren let alone their grand grandchildren. However as for me, the sad history did not stop with me, it repeated itself for us and our children again. Unlike my brother and sister, some of their children have seen grandpa, my own children never have fraternal grandparents in their life and that love toward grandparents is something they will never buy from anyone. I never say the word grandpa and sadly my children will never say it too. And at this writing, I had already witnessed that love of grandparents, obviously with my kids who have none. My daughter since she learns to talk and seeing us putting phone on our ears, she imitates us and from nowhere she picks up the object or sometime real phone and pretends she is talking to grandma on the phone. She would say "hi grandma, how are you and then she put the fake phone on our ears and said, talk to grandma". And passing this moment forward, at time when she will know what grandma or grandpa mean or latter when she will ask where grandparents are.

Like many African communities, in dinka culture, history is verbally passed on from generation to generation via cultural activities, and stories. The child school was always at home and with all the extended family members. For me, the war weaned me and so many boys from South Sudan so early that it weaned us from the history and culture. The many years away from culture took away even the desire to learn when opportunity came around during the later reunion. The challenges and cultures of the new place had already occupied our mind, plus some cultural identities such as the language or dancing were in most cases partially lost. At many instances, I tend to distance myself from what should have been normal, with feeling that I might be wrongdoing or getting involved in cultural norms. Thanks to my sister, because she grew up at home next to my parents and the entire community; she is quite with our culture and our birth numbers and now she is my source of that cultural knowledge. Since our reunion twenty-one years later, I had learned much about my mom, our relative and about us as a family all from my sister. I regarded her as my library and big part of the contributor to this book. Unfortunately, we cannot learn so much while we are physically disconnected from the community or past certain age of our life. This will not only hunt us, but it will create a lost culture. I fear that all I am trying to learn would not be forwarded to my kids in the right way especially when they're already engulf in the mixed American culture they're born into.

The dinka are among thousands of African communities with significances Identified and unique culture including language, family tree, family and community responsibilities, rite of passage just to express few. And for many of us, and the generation that we will raise, there is much challenge a head. As the result of not only separation but growing up in a world where we constantly had to fight to survive and while run from place to place in search of safety and basic needs in the refugee camps, it was easy to pay less attention to the culture and it traits. Like many of the Sudanese in the south, I was forced to live with strangers, to learn from them, and at time forget about my own identity. You had to compromise and that mean, giving up some in exchange to gain some so that you coexist symbiotically with those friends who once were strangers.

As the largest tribe of the South Sudan sixty plus tribes, each with its unique language, dinka dialect as the dinka or monyjang refers to their language is also very dissimilar across the vast dinka settlements. The language varies greatly in relation to the geographical habitant. There are variation and challenges across all the dinka subtribes and clan, yet movement from one part of dinka territory or intermarriage or any other aspect of their life is not limited by language variation or other short comes. Yes, there is no standardized dinka language due to variation in the dinka dialect in corresponding to multi sub-tribal dinka and due to effortless modernization in the dinka land to promote the identity of the large tribe in the country.

Other unique identity is for a dinka to know his or her genealogy. Before I got separated from the parents, my mother use to sit with us and read out our relationship with the neighbors and other people we knew. She uses to count ancestral line or family tree. It was a very important part of our life growing up, but that memory disappeared during my hard years of struggle. I could still count my family tree to the ninth or eleventh generations, but that is line I know only goes through a single person. I could not say who the brother(s), the sister(s), the niece(s), the nephew(s), the uncle(s) were in the line to the ninth or eleventh of my family ancestors. This is like a tree with no brunches in a sense. Sometime my sister act as the library of cultural inquiry, just like how my mother would have been. Culturally, blood relationship is very important for any child to know for one reason or the other and it worth a cultural completeness to have the knowledge. The knowledge of a family tree or blood relationship is also very important when young adult start to pursue relationship. You can't never knowingly get married to someone of a blood relationship, it's consequential.

Like many of the world tribes, we dinka are social being. We live as a community, a clan, or as a tribe. In dinka like many African communities, you could live with any relative for no cost. There are rarely homeless or outcast as we often take in one another and share every little we have. Our social being is also demonstrated in our communal activities, festivities and work. Dinka helps one another during farming and harvesting.

Cultural expression of excitement and norms is another very important aspect of any culture. For the dinka, our cultural dances carry burden in the advancement of our dinka identity. Just like the language variation base on territory, the dances also vary, and each community expresses their culture through dancing. Like many other missed opportunities due to the early separation from the community, I never had the opportunity to know much about the dinka dancing and relevant. However, over the years in the refugee camps even at the very sour years of our struggles, the dinka never disown their dancing celebrations and I had my opportunity to learn some. The dinka Bor traditional dance could generally be taken as easy, just a matter of jumping up and down continuously. It could be easy if one dance alone. However, it's harder when you must dance with others and uniformly be correlating. Besides our cultural dances are never perform solely. In addition, there are various styles of dances that are fading, and I have not had the opportunity to those one. Much worse, the next generation is at a great disadvantage for an identity that they would seek with no opportunity to find it. Also, there are things that accompanied dancing such as singing or composing songs and you must know how they're both use particularly in the past when courting a young woman. Some time back in the refugee camp, I had one occasion in which I was very excited to participate in the dancing ceremony, but I was very shy doing it due to lucking confident or enough practice in doing what should have been obvious to me.

The years of separation, the years of trying to get civilized in other cultures had washed to the blink of extinction the culture that is so important in the community life of the so call the dinka. Many of the diaspora tried to carry on the culture in one way or another. In 2008, like others, I took my initiative to return home and got marriage to a dinka girl to raise a dinka family. Like many communities in the diasporas, we often come together to forward those cultures and insistently speaking the dialect or calling off those that seem astray. Thank to technology, many are leaving behind recorded traditional marks on record for next generations.

In the greatest scheme of things, dinka as people and its unique cultures are essentially going through cultural erosion, a change we could at introspect call "when we were dinka". As one of the most devastated tribe by the decade of Sudan civil war, with million lost in that effort and currently dispersed around the world, inheriting foreign culture in exchange of our own, and much of the homeland deserted, we're heading into a change that is un reversible.

Homecoming & Marriage

And as I close in on my college graduation, already set for June 15th, 2007, I started saving for the expensive long journey back to Sudan. To that point, I was yet to travel back home since arriving in the US late in 2000 and yet to see my sister since I left her in 1987. At that same point in time, South Sudan was still a part of the Sudan. My plan was to visit in December, a very great time of the year especially for Christmas and families together. I graduated as scheduled, moved to Seattle, joining the Sudanese community there and particularly Kongor brothers. However, just five months before the planned journey, my car broke down and could not be repair, at least cheaply. It was a 1995 Pontiac coupe with still got good mileage on. I paid about $ 2,500 for it back in 2002. The estimate to repair it was not worth the value seven years later. The next three months were my toughest time yet. I was jerking two jobs in which I had to catch a bus from point to point, mostly sleeping on the bus between jobs and sleepy during my desk job. I never used the bus system prior to that, so it was a tough experience, mostly time consuming between jobs.

Besides travelling from job to job, my cousin's child was born by C section at that same time and in the absence of my cousin, I took charge. The C section happened at one hospital, but then the baby got transferred to another hospital where extensive care was given, and mother was left at the first hospital. Although there was no needed care from the parent at the hospital, we all of course needed to check on the baby and have updates for the parents. I solely and tirelessly devoted my responsibility and time on visiting him despite my commute challenges amid the two jobs. I managed about a week of visit. Thankfully, his mother recovered quickly or at least with her dire need to see her child, she was released by the end of the week period. The baby also did good at the hospital, again thank to the un waving care of the hospital. Both the baby and mother were reunited and shortly the baby was discharged to the mother. In the short time, I learned the difficulties of not having a reliable car while kangarooing two jobs. At that exhausting experience, I could not continue the challenging bus commute, but to postpone my plans and invested the money to buy myself a car. The year came to an end, we celebrated the Christmas, the New Year and again we reset our resolutions. For me, going back home was still my number one resolution.

Before March 2008, the plan was still that simple; solely to visit my sick dad, my sister that I had not seen or heard in over a decade and of course the rest of my relative since 1987. In April, I got promoted from my fulltime job to the accounting, the job I was hired for and a new warehouse person was hired. That also meant few more dollars. At that same time, my boss, the controller somehow made a comment from nowhere, saying to me that I look responsible and I should start a family. I didn't have a girl friend and I wasn't talking about girls. I didn't know how that comment came about, but instead I took it as a compliment that I could start a family. At my part time job, my unique scheduled was discovered by the HR and I was notified of the new schedule. Nearly everyone had something like 8am to 5pm, 5pm to 8am with minor accommodations. I was something like 7pm to 6am and only 3 days, very irregular schedule. The new schedule could not work with me and they couldn't accommodate me with my own schedule. I introduced myself to the HR and she learned about me but there was there was nothing she could offer me. But upon hearing about my educational background, she suggested an accounting job only if I would go to Dallas, their corporate office. After few in touch emails with the HR, I resigned due to look for another job, only to be documented as the only no quit or fired employee at the time.

Soon, I got another part time, a security job for a weekend. It was in Bellevue, same city as my other job and with a fitting schedule. It was while working here, mostly by myself at night, very sleepy at time that I recalled the years when my father and brother used to persuade me to get marriage. Yes, this is a dinka culture; you don't solely decide your future especially when it comes to getting marriage. Since I arrived in the USA, I had tirelessly remitted money to assist all my parents and in so doing, there was a feeling I could do something for myself, get marriage at least. So, this reminder resurfaced and yes due to arrange marriage option, which would be a successful visit; to kill two birds with one shot and particularly in the present of my father. I started thinking about getting marriage. Of course, there was no girl where I was and that was not what they were thinking too, to get marriage to a girl over here in America. They knew it was their job to find me a wife, to get marriage to a girl of their choosing unless I came and spend many months to get my own. This was a possibility of an arranged marriage.

Like many Asian's cultures and just like my boss and another co-worker too from India, they were married off by their parents to men that were in America, men they barely knew, but thanks to the culture. My parents could choose a wife for me or in this respect honored by suggestion even in my absence. I started recalling all the suggestions from people I knew, friends and relative back in Kakuma whom I had communication with at the time and the roommates I just joined after my graduation. I was always laughing it off, retorting that I wasn't ready and too that I will see my own when times come. But then, my memories came to a communication I had with a childhood friend, a cousin and even in unimaginable way, a cousin on the other side to the girl I was thinking about. Of course, he never noticed what he once said while he was only describing his own role in her upbringing, a description that kept this information in my mind some years later. My friend was just narrating his responsibility in my future wife when he went back from Kakuma to Sudan to get her and later placed her in Kenyan school and how she was such a responsible girl. She just finished her high school few months before my graduated from College.

The descriptions matched some of my preferences in choosing a wife. I never promised or made a quest for her identity; I never disclosed loving that description of her educational accomplishment. He wasn't directly describing the girl to me, but that would be a good choice if I wasn't related to her. So, when my option to seek a wife came into my mind, I started the process to find out about the girl. I went back to the friends and relative from Kakuma, who were at the time were in Nairobi. I asked them separately and showing not much intention about the girl (s) they were thinking. I jot the name down, her family background and again I showed no seriousness that their suggestions were taken. Both guys had the same girl in mine, they knew her from Kakuma, was a neighbor, and coincident, she was related to them; their mothers came from the same sub-section of our Kongor community.

Still I didn't know whether she would be related to me or not, until the most surprising call came to me, this time from her own relative who like her cousin whom I got the description from. This was from a sister already married to us, a clan's mate and have met her before I left Kakuma. Well, she called me as my own relative; her maternity grandmother and my mother came from the same section of our community and this was a very strong relationship. She said nothing at that initial conversation, but eventually she would suggest her. Just as part of my quest for her background, I asked her why she wouldn't be related to me if she was her uncle's daughter, her cousin. As these quests were in my favor, this matrix was getting exciting, and it was like all these were coming from the same house, a join effort.

My next step was to go to my brother, and too not disclose to him that I was in the mind set to get marriage. I only asked him about the girl I was told if he knew. First, I asked him if we were related and after the no answer, which I asked with figures crossed. The second request I made was for him to look at her physically and just watch her moves, her work, her relationship with others and if all that seem ok, get a phone number from her. At this point, I didn't share my communication and my mind thinking with anyone. I had to dig further. I then called my cousin, the first who described the girl. I didn't tell him that I was into her, but somehow, I lured him back to that one-time communication. I figured out from him describing their relationship and where I come in and not her. As I mentioned earlier, dinka culture like most avoided marriage one's blood relative.

One more step, I called my uncle Bol Atem Deng, he was well informed about our genealogy. At this point, I had enough evidence that she wasn't related to me. Also, I was counting on the fact so many people had thought of her as a good match for me. What was left is me to contact the girl and from there see how things go. Whether she would even imagine a relationship with a man he couldn't see. Thanks to digital age, that was possible. The solutions to that were; 1st, I had a picture and she could confirm how I look, 2nd the idea of an arranged marriage was familiar to both of us. 3rd, she would have a chance to see my family; dad and brothers and last but not the least; I had all the people who suggested her to counted on as her trust. I had to start the process, as girls were getting married quickly with many lost boys at the time getting marriage.

Now that I have heard everything and prior to initiating the relationship, I called my brother back, asked what he think if I wanted a meaningful communication with her. He knew the girl very well; his approval of her was very instantly. My brother at one point as a radio operator had helped both her and her sister when they had come to use the radio to talk to their family members back in Sudan. In addition, my brother knew her people, very respectful parents and uncles. As I suggested before, I was going to take it lightly and see what happened before I would request him to throw in some pitches for me.

I got her phone number, contact her and the conversation began. At the time, she was in Nairobi, but mostly between Kakuma, the refugee camp and Nairobi. Her family was back in Kakuma but there in Nairobi she was at her cousin's. My first call was a little shaky, I wasn't sure what to expect but I had a plan on what to say. Prior to this encounter, I had never courted any girl. I never had a dinka kind of a relationship with a girl; a relationship that is often more about knowing one another through intense talks over a lengthy time. However, in the Kakuma refugee camp, I had gained a little confidence and experiences listening to my friends who were courting at the time and where often chatting about their experiences. I had jumped into their conversations few times and at time they commended me that I was good, and I should go with them sometime. However, I had been away from those conversations and from the culture for a while, I had been in America for over eight years, and although I had several chances hanging out with girls and being in the team and class with a lot of them, these were Americans and presumably a different talk. However, I was on a mission here. At least it would be just two of us and nothing to shy about. After purchasing my ten-dollar calling card and there alone at the part time night security job that first night, I made my call and hoped she picked it up. After couple of rings, and luckily as I wished, she picked up the phone. Hello? a very girly sweet sound came through. I responded, yes hello. How're you? I went further. I then asked whom I was talking to and after she responded just as I wished. She asked who I was looking for,

Just like a dinka girl. I introduced myself, well with a fake name. She asked if I called the right person, where I was calling from and in fact where I got her telephone number. She insists not talking to a ghost man. She asked all that with a very calm voice, very natural and they were legitimate questions, exactly the kind of dinka girl I was looking for, not opening to unknown. I made it clear that I was calling her and somewhere within Kenya. She quickly questioned why I was talking to her and not in person if I was in fact in Kenya and if the call was intended for her. I felt bad not disclosing myself, making her to ask so many questions. However, this was my plan, an introductory call. The other reason for hiding my identity especially where I was calling from was what I learned from the Andy Murphy movie, coming to America.

Early upon my arrival in the USA, I came across "Coming to America", the movie and I had watched so many times that I remembered every next play. The movie is funny, Andy Murphy of course, but I always saw the same scenario in me when time come. The movie is about this prince played by Murphy, who refuse an arrange marriage to a beautiful lady chosen to him by his parents, just for the prince. Both couples never spoke and knew not each other prior but the bride had accepted to marriage him, to a prince. As for the groom, he wanted a girl who will accept him not because of his family status or for what he possessed, but out of love. The weeding was brought forth, but at the end, he talked his parents out of the weeding, at least putting if off for a while. Following his and bride family submission, he then asked his father to go to America but never told him he was going to look for a wife there. In

America, he made himself a simple man, found a janitorial job and portrayed himself to a girl as a simple person where in fact he was from a rich family, he was a prince. As he wished, he wanted the girl to love him for who he is not for what he owns or his family success. As a janitor at her father's kitchen, she married him.

As for my case, I had nothing to compare myself with the prince, but being in America at my time was valued highly. In a sense, a lost boy or for that matter a dinka man from America was regarded like a prince. He could get any girl he wanted. Parents were also giving their daughters sometime forcing them to marriage men they didn't like or while some were still young, just to bring wealth in exchange of their daughter. At the same time, more girls were falling even for those whose personalities were not known or wouldn't marriage to otherwise. I didn't want a future wife to accept me for being from America with the assumption that I had money.

At the time, this was unusual process, courting over the phone, and through others. In another word, this was not the dinka way, but it was a new thing and quickly became embraceable. Nevertheless, I was excited, felt like I had seen her in person. I told her that we will talk again. I didn't make an appointment, but she left it up to me just like I initiated the first call. We say by to one another. Yes, it was a promising opportunity. She had met few of my qualities, especially the personalities.

The next call didn't take many days, I called right away the next day and there we picked up from where we left off. As our conversation resume and greeting got sweeter, felt at ease, my confidence grew, and I felt the need to un mass my identity and eventually my mission. I had to be honest. I started with an apology to her, saying that I didn't give her my real name and with some excuses. Shortly after some ooh moment from her, I formerly introduced myself, where I was calling from and all the questions that I didn't answered in the first call. It was too early as we both would expect to say the reason of my call, but we went on to just know one another. I asked a lot of questions I already knew about her, just to show I didn't hear her from anyone else or that I knew anyone she knew. I believe it was the third call that I revealed to her why I have been calling and what my intentions were especially considering where I was, thousands of miles away. I revealed to her my family and what draw me to her while I was that far from her. At this point, we had no picture of one another; we were beginning to recognize one another voice and personalities. In my own feeling, my confidence of her was growing each day and as some people might say, I was getting to love her. She didn't oppose, but there was another chapter.

As in most African communities, a wife belongs to the community, you don't bring the wife home alone. And as we felt committed to the relationship, we felt obligated to bring in witness and other voices that would cement our relationship. She introduced me to some people that were with her and we got acquainted of one another my message was well received. Few weeks later, I got some of my boyhood cousins including the two who suggested her to visit her make a pitch on my behalf. They both were glad I had made that choice if in fact I was going to make it happen. They both knew each other, and I believe both did not even talk the way unfamiliar people would, they were related after all. After their meeting, they saw something promising too, her acceptance, but again, slowly. He recommended her as a great choice if I will of course make it happen. The "if" was emphasis because some of us had not kept their promises and others did not. At that time, people were often skeptical of the distance relationship and commitment on our side. I was different, a trustworthy kind of person, and I told them to count on me if she will in fact also be patience considering the distance between us and other competitions. In another word, I was putting it on her and showing my guys that I was in completely.

Few months went by and the conversations were more promising, learning from one another's relatives, friends and personalities. I came to know her more as a daughter of Mathiang Gak Chol and Adut Kuir Aguer, from Kongor, Pawiir. She was a sibling to other five sisters: the older two and the younger three. As a girl with no brothers, she had taken hard choice to help her family, something often the boy responsibility in Dinka. With the help of her cousin, she left her family at Kakuma refugee camp, a commitment she solely made for her family to pursue education. She graduated in 2007 from St Michael girl only high school in Nakuru, the same year I finished my bachelors at Western. Obviously leaving home was a tough choice for a dinka girl let alone for a reason that was often seen as boys or husband obligation, going to school. In the short time we courted, Yom demonstrated her humble heart and layback patience. She was always poise in her conversation, with consistent and speaking eloquently. Luckily, her big extended family include people that I was related to all assured me of who she was. I felt completely informed of her. It was often a great experience chatting with her; we were making a lot of progress.

In May 2008, just two months since our first conversation, she had to make a tough decision for both of us. She was planning on going back to Sudan, back to our area probably for the first time since she fled in 1991, to see her mother and sisters. Ever since the culmination of the CPA, thousands of Southern Sudanese had returned home and at it was then when her mother repatriated to Kongor despite all the challenges that existed. Yom was going to visit them and see if she could find a job to help her family. As someone who cares about family too, that was a great decision. Unfortunately, she was going to a remote area where contact would be very limited if not impossible altogether for both of us. I didn't object to her decision nor could I make any suggestion when I was not yet marriage to her. That was a big test toward this young relationship. On the other part, it was a decision that could be regretful in my part for not at least voicing my objection to her trip home. The bad scenario was, she gets forced to a marriage arrangement without my knowledge and against her choice. That was a possibility as was always the case in the dinka community. As someone who respects her family, she might not say no again as she did the first time, when she spoiled her first forced marriage attempt for reason to finish her high school.

I was keeping my fingers crossed, that she was going to keep her promise and would find a way to get in contact with me again. I was also hoping that she will make convincing argument to her family if any man comes via the family instead of directly via her. There was nothing I could do, and although she was heading to the remote area, she was heading home. The only option at that time was if I were someone else, I would have committed to sending her something she could then forward to her family, but I didn't want to do that before marriage and I also didn't want her to be questioned about where she got the money. Whether she was going to accept it, I didn't know. My only option was to strongly promise her that I was coming that year, that if she could wait, I would make it happen. I committed to her that I was totally in love with her.

I sent her two hundred dollars and few words to remind her of the relationship. I reintegrate how devoting I was to the relationship and my intentions where to come true if she waits for a little while. She left Nairobi, stopped in Kakuma and when she got to Lokichogio few days later, she showed me why I should be trustful of the relationship. She made the last call while at the border, just the last time before crossing into the Sudan land and into areas that had few chances of phone communication. We said the last word including interchanging our first show of love when I referred to her as "honey" and her retorting, "Sweetie".

For the rest of few months, which at that point felt like a long time, I was always hopeful and in the spirit of anticipating a call. At home, she met her mother and sisters again after the former returned home during the repatriation after the CPA culmination. However, there was not much to do at home. There were no jobs and she didn't see any way to help her family. She decided to head back south, to Bortown where her sister live. At Bor, she reunited with her sister and her sister's husband helped her found a job with the state of Jonglei. Now back in area with communication access, she waited not long. She surprisingly overwhelmed me with her faith and commitment toward our relationship, when her phone call found me again. At those times, any phone call with the 249-area code was an anticipated call, or obviously from Sudan. Her phone rang one night and as I said hello, she responded," It's me", the voice said just as sweet as before. I had waited for this moment. Immediately after we exchanged our greeting, I confirm the phone to make sure I got the number in case it abruptly disconnects. There was often an expectation to receive such call, so my phone card was often available. I told her to hang up and I reached into my wallet for a phone card. My call went through and the sweetest conversations resume and forever remained. My brother was in Juba at the time. He had come to Juba shortly after some refugees from Kakuma repatriated to Sudan upon the signing of comprehensive peace agreement. He had no idea this conversation and relationship was in fact really and proceeding. It has been four – five months since I told him to check out the girl. He knew I was a very committed guy to anything I put my mine and interest around at least he had seen my commitment to my school during the challenging years of Kakuma.

The donning thing at the time was keeping such a distance relationship. Like my cousins who commenced me at the initial pursued, both had witnessed instances were some of the lost boys had made commitments and never followed through. Those instances had created some doubts in such unorthodox relationship and us. Meanwhile, me and the wife to be continued to call one another, learning more about one another while strengthening our relationship as time went by. It was at that time that we I felt it was time to get relatives and friends into the informal discussion. I first reached out to my brother, resurfaced what I had mentioned to him 5-6 months earlier. He was surprise to hearing it but as a person who knew me well, there was no doubt. At her side, she her told her cousins and sisters. Like I mentioned, this was a very odd relationship. Traditionally, when a girl is in her age of marriage, potential grooms come by and ladies or sisters in particularly were usually aware. A respected girl often handles this openly, she brings home a guy that relative will see and make their own judgement on. In this case, it was very hard her sister to believe this misery, a ghost man. Where is he, was probably her first question. They were both the same thoughts, none of them had seen me in person. It was a tough case to make. But it was about faith and the very goal she had set for herself.

However, it was my responsibility to talk to my future sister-in-law and to win her approval. By then, I had already shown my interest to Yom's cousin who lived with her. For my sister-in-law Akuol Mathiang, she knew one man already and the news about the ultimate man was in adequate, perhaps due to my reluctant approach to contact her. At the time, a lot of people had changed the culture of courting. Many grooms had been making some bribing, huge ones to convince relatives. I chose not to adopt the approach. I thought I was going to be true to the culture and follow my intention the regular way, not paying anything under the table till in dowries or afterward. This placed Yom in a tough situation, her ultimate man was not talking or still in the old culture. Luckily, time was on our side, it was getting closer to my planned time. Besides, she was always working, and people were coming home at her absence and too seeing her sister late in the day, all help avoided potential challenging conversations. By this time, it was August and I was finally in the preparation mood. I had tapped my right-hand man to start thinking about coming to Uganda to meet me. It was finally at this state, then with so much sure and so few days that I finally told my younger brother about it, gave him the green light to come by and see her. I knew my father was not going to be objective of my marriage proposal, so I didn't tell him about the marriage, but I sent the information through my younger brothers that I was coming. I had also been thinking about how this would happen or what approach should I propose to her.

In early September 2008, I booked my ticket for October and since that booking day, it was just one day at a time. I was getting excited as hope soar to finally see my sister, my father, my brother's second wife, and eventually get marry to this sweet person. As the weeks became days and days run to hours, I was thinking of the modern marriage, about her ring, clothes, and necklace. I visited some ring shops, but there was no conclusion, I didn't have a clue of the ring and clothes' size. Besides the decision to buy a ring was not an easy to jump to. The culture of rings was so foreign when I left the refugee camp, in Kenya and I didn't even know if this was something widely expected or necessary. I ended up buying nothing altogether. We made the final agreement with my wife to be and she also went through her plan. I told my elder brother and he took his role including receiving the guest. His family was in Nimule, South Sudan just across the border from Uganda.

As my friend drove me to the airport that October the 6th at around ten thirty in the morning hour for a 1pm flight, I was overwhelmingly thinking ahead of my trip. Yes, the trip to Europe was scheduled for ten hours in the sky with three to five more hours of lay over and then six to eight more in the sky on the way to Uganda, Entebbe international airport. There were probably twenty plus hours before I crossed the world to the African soil, yet there I was procrastinating. After several hours of waiting the final departure and last calls to friends, surprising them that I was leaving for African, the hour came; we were in line boarding the KLM over at SEA-TAC. The long flight was underway, there were no worries of the fear of flight especially after the horrible September 2001, my heart was already out there in Sudan, already thinking about this or that. After hours in the air, rounds of pre-prepared foods, long forced sleep and the dawn sky of Europe approaching, I was about halfway on the trip. As we came out of that first flight, my ears were plugged, barely could hear anything, but I was stamping my foot trying to relief my ears, that didn't help very much. However, what proceeded as I emerged at the airport made my ears' problem nothing.

I exited the plane like everyone, walking toward my next gate. I was very reluctant because the flight was few hours away. I spent my hours walking and taking short reading including a page about Obama's book that I found at the airport. There was so much about Obama from magazine, on cups etc. I was stopped by an undercover airport security when I was just trolling about. At first, I didn't trust who they were, hence I didn't give them my passport when they first asked for it. I told them that if they were security, they should show me their ID. At that time, my mind was still fresh about the movie Taken, featuring a kid that was abducted during her European vacation. I walked with them to my gate before I could give them my passport just to make sure someone at the gate would be knowledgeable of my whereabout. When I left the U.S, I was proud to have the American passport in hand, and in my own little full capacity thinking, I had conceived my oneself that the American given passport was not questionable, and even after that initial confrontation, I thought it would be quick especially if they learned that I was an American and coming from America. That didn't go smoothly as anticipated. It became an investigation, and I became more furious in my feeling. The questions were as stupid as I could imagine, or silly to say. I was in no worry or hurry of missing my flight, it was couple hours away; hence I answered their questionings and waited for their research. I belief it was stupid to ask why I was going to Africa, obviously my passport was showing that I was a Sudan national before becoming U.S citizen. But not only were that, questions like how much I paid for the ticket, or where I worked, to the reasons for my trip, a little absurd.

After an hour from office to office, and from security personnel to the other checking my passport ID against my physical look, they came to convince themselves that it was me, just that I might have shaded some founds since the picture was taken or perhaps had nothing but jealousy. But there was some truth to the passport picture vs my then physical look if they had asked why I looked a little soiled. I had lost a lot of weights since graduating and for sure I was looking a little skinner. The worse was, they were not questioning me directly, maybe I would have explained well before we could take that hour of nonsense. They were trying to prove themselves why they were security guards.

With no finding or reason to further detention, they released me. I walked to my gate and in just short wait was set for my final flight. There were more questions, but this time, there was nothing exceptional. We proceeded. I met some Sudanese, follow lost boys as we boarded. One of them was my acquaintance at the refugee camp. As the flight geared out of the airport, I knew it was just another landing but with less anticipated interrogation. The six-seven-hour flight went by quickly. We arrived on time at the Entebbe airport, located on the slight of land just between Lake Victoria and Lake Entebbe. It was around eight o'clock in the evening when we arrived. We went through the immigration quickly with excitement building. As I approached the baggage claim, I was expecting my cousin to pick me up. He already arranged for transportation from the airport to the hotel. He was anxiously waiting there to receive me. It was nine years since the last time I saw him at that point. As we met, he had the same look, a little more bearded and but with his eyeglasses. We had a big Sudanese style greeting. He got my bag, called the driver that he booked the car and we were on our way to Kampala. I was tired, so we got to the hotel, dropped my bag, and with my carry on my side, we had few conversations to catch up and how my travelling went, then we went to bed.

We spent a day and half in Uganda, did some shopping, and on Wednesday at midnight, we got on the Sudanese owned bus, named *Nationdit* to South Sudan. My first destination was Nimule, the first South Sudan town just across the border from Uganda. Nimule was one of the historical cities to the SPLA in the fight for independent. It was one of the biggest outposts of Juba, a SPLA/M strong hold during the war. A long with few other cities such as Buma as mentioned earlier, they were never recaptured by the Sudan Army forces. My brother's family was in Nimule along with my uncle's, aunt, and many other relatives. I was also expecting my wife to be in Nimule. She came to Nimule from Bortown that same night when I left Kampala. I was very anxious to get to Nimule. But, the hurdle of that long road with its history was still worrisome to me. However, for many Sudanese who had travelled that road since the SPLA and civilians moved to Juba upon the CPA agreement, there have been no incidents of LRA or at least, the fear had not stop them. The travelling between Juba and Sudan was at its safest. We only had a small un enemy related incident just half an hour after departing Kampala. Our buses' rear tire blew out just as we were about to exit the Kampala territory. I travelled not necessarily that same road before, but in 1997-8 when I visited my father and his family in Labone. At that time, any road through Equatoria was not safe especially for civilians. My travelled in 1997-8 was a very dangerous trek, we lost people on the way in barbaric ambush. In addition to the LRA killings in most of that territory, the communities in that same areas were not friendly to the SPLA and particularly the communities that fueled the movement.

South Sudan was not a country at this point, but the war has ended, SAF has pulled out from the southern region and in correlation, the local hatred and LRA were totally at their lowest level. Travelling was much safer. People were travelling by bus and in huge numbers. We stopped twice before we got to the Uganda-South Sudan border, near Nimule. One stop was at the junction as the bus drop off some people and picking up replacements. The other stop came later in the middle of nowhere, a stop for rest and for those who wanted to relieve themselves. The road was obviously unpaved, crooked, with water at some place forcing the bus to swerve and nearly disastrous. After dazzling for hours, we arrived at the Uganda side of the border at around 2-3pm. We had to go through the border immigration as we exit Uganda to Sudan. After that immigration process, it was only few minutes before we get to Nimule, South Sudan. The Southern Sudan border point of entry or immigration was at Nimule. However, we were citizens and Nimule was my first destination, so we jumped out and walked home, people were waiting for me there.

I came to Nimule on the ninth, warmly welcomed by the family and relative. It was there that I met my brother's 2nd wife, my wife to be at the time and all the relatives including my aunt for the first time. I was not properly dressed, yet I was very excited to see everyone again, I was home. It was a great feeling to see that group of people in my first return home since I left Kakuma in the late 2000. My brother's kids were already grown, not the little cutes that I left, plus there were four more born in my absence. I also met his second wife that I helped him married. It was a great day to reunite with the family and relative.

Shortly, I was escorted to the hotel where I met my wife to be for the first time. She was there with her companion, my future in-laws. She might have figured out me among the few members of my family in the room, unfortunate I was not up to the standard of expectation for a person coming from America, let alone the man who needs the first-person impression. I was not well dressed and of course looked much skinny as I personally knew.

The next day as expected, the first leg of the marriage process took its course. Both families, with extended members and anyone related to both families came for what became a brief discussion in which my family made it officials the intention to marriage the bride and bride family being recognize with a request to marriage their daughter. At that point, our agreement as couple had led to that moment, and the next was up to the families. They were to response either to agree or totally reject us as a family or me individually. However, there were many immediate family members missing. The best part was, both of us came from families who knew one another, very knowledgeable of each other. The bride family allowed us to stay with our wife. On the 11th, it was concluded to adjourn and transferred the process to Bortown or further to Kongor were the bride's mother lived. We left Nimule the following morning together with my wife, two sisters in law, and my younger brother, my childhood cousin who in fact recommended my choice for this girl, and then the driver also my cousin. We travelled to Juba on the 12th of October 2008.

As interesting as I was meeting all the people I had not seen in years and now my wife in the hopeful agreeable conclusion of the wedding, I was also fascinated about our new-found freedom, about Southern Sudan as an autonomous region. According to the CPA, South Sudan was still a region, just part of the whole Sudan like other parts of Sudan, but with own autonomous government at the time called GOSS, its own president, own army force, borders, and above all, its own freedom. The agreement brought the war to an end for the first time since the days before the 1950s. The Southern President was also the first vice president of the entire Sudan. He was Mr. Salva Kiir, the former member of the SPLA/M Military High Command, a man who ascended to power after the sudden death of the former SPLA/M chairman, and first vice president, Dr. John Garang de Mabior.

As we travelled to Juba, there were historical sites and military posts that I first came to witness firsthand during this trip. During the fought for the independent, Juba was the big fish that the SPLA had their eyes on the entire twenty plus years of second civil war. Most of the SPLA leadership believed that capturing Juba would be a quick downfall of the regime in the south. This town was the center of the administration and right at the heart of all the southern provinces, though geographically a little south of the region. As expected, it was the hardest and SPLA/M only had few shots at capturing it. The big assaults and operations against Juba came from different directions around Juba, but Nimule was among the big bases for those plans. As the SPLA plans were to attack Juba, the enemy inside Juba counter plan was to topple the SPLA aspiration for Juba by capturing Nimule and other posts or town such as Bortown on the opposite end. However, those plans were not easy for both sides, which was why the outposts on our way to Juba were very historical. We had heard quite a lot about the fight for Juba and the road to it. Now I was travelling on that road and ready for the rehearsal from the insider, a former childhood friend, turned SPLA soldier in 1994, and others who had travelled on that road since coming to Juba after the CPA in 2005.

The story started right when we drove the long curved, the uphill drive from Nimule to the first outpost toward Juba, the Achuar. There is a small tributary between Achuar and Nimule, this was a very deep fast flowing tributary, and as a result it was the biggest obstacle for both armies to cross particularly the Arab forces from Juba in their attempts to capture Nimule. I believe the SPLA slogan as the enemy attempts to cross was "we rise together or die together", before the enemy crosses.

My childhood cousin who himself was an SPLA veteran was very knowledgeable of the history of dozens of fights along that river or the entire road to Juba. They call the river, Achuar's river. We in the refugee camp had also heard a lot about the wars along this pass to Juba. As we passed through Achuar and its history narrowed, we caught on to the next post and the other. Along these thick tall trees with deep forest on both sides zigzagging along the unpaved road, we came to Moli and then Pageeri. These two posts were once temporary displaces camps for the many civilians who fled the 1991 Riek Machar led SPLA Nasir attack of the Bor-dinka civilians in his plan to topple the SPLA chairman. Since these posts were temporary stops, they were only known by few structures, stones and familiarity of the area. I remember some of the other cousins in the car were also pointing out a spot where Kuol Manyang Juuk, then SPLA/M commander responsible for the displaced once had a compound on.

As we left Pageeri behind, we also left the heavy tall forest and a head the boys could point to a clear direction were Juba lies. Still too far away and with no tall buildings in Juba to help spot it at a distance, we couldn't estimate our arrivals. A long the road to Juba, I spotted some cattle camps. They were dinkas' as I came to learn. This was very surprising for me, considering the area was Equatorians' territory and very far from the dinka's. This was the first time I came close to the cattle camp since the days I left for Ethiopia in 1987.

We finally arrived in Juba at around 7 pm, having travelled nearly an entire day. It was already dark, I didn't see if there were any welcoming signs or other specials, but we saw the glare of light at a distance. The city was still young, very undeveloped and the few tall buildings constructed during the peaceful time of Sudan were shelled down by the SPLA, plus the enemy brought some down when it exited Juba following CPA demands. We drove over a narrow one lane bridge that linked the Juba city with its outskirt. I had heard of how dirty, how overpopulated, and how windy the city was prior to my coming, but despite all those, it was the base of South Sudan autonomy, I was very pleased to have made it there for the first time.

Coming into the city that night, I was mindful of the SPLA 2005 first time triumphant entry when the Southern army officially enter the city immediately after the Sudan army pull out. The video clip, thanks to the u-tube was a breath taking and impressive procession. It was a musical experience of joy and demonstration of strength and determination with moral, a reminder of our own experiences in the refugee camp of Pinyudo. For people in South Sudan, Juba was the likely place to find any person you dream of meeting. My sister was there. For urgency due the wedding, we only stayed for a day and half there to draw some money and wife's needs. Our next destination was Bortown in our long journey home.

As mentioned previously, Bortown is also a historical site in the context of the Sudan 2nd civil war. It was at Bortown where the first shots of the 2nd Sudan civil war were fired, just at the outskirt of the city, few miles from the town center, off the Juba-Bortown's road. We passed by Bortown on our walk to Ethiopia in 1987, at the time occupied by the enemy. We were ducking and trying all efforts to get no notice. This was not just the next destination; it was my state headquarter, Jonglei State at the time.

On our journey to Bortown, my wife and sister's in-law along with my brother took off early while I larked behind that day to collect fund for the wedding. There was much a head of me, but the road to Bor brought much to mind. That journey brought memoirs of the 1991 Bor people's massacre as was written in the Emma War. In the book, Scroggins described rescuers account of the civilians suffering and killing by the SPLA Nassir along that road. The book brought to live the horrible suffering and skunk smell at the time, with corps randomly hanging and lying on the ground every short distance. While there was no vision of such evident as I travelled at that point, there was so much emotional feeling for me. Nobody on the bus knew what I was going through, but I was quietly paying my respect to the lost who might have included anyone of my blood.

As we got close to Bor, our bus stuck on the muddy road. This was common incident on that road and in fact in most parts of Southern region at the time, there were no paved roads. We had to get out, roll our sleeves, pants and shoes off to push the bus out of the dirt. I did not take part in the effort, only watching and taking pictures. Just in front, there was another small bus stuck and passengers were scattered around waiting for any luck. It was a new thing for me, having experienced the very smooth roads in the United State for eight years at that point. However, as a Sudanese, it was easy for me to understand as I quickly adapted my mind completely to my poor country. After a passage of time, and mostly dirty passengers, we made it to Bor that same evening.

The news to my coming quickly spread and that evening, we received a swam of visitors and relatives that I had not seen in over twenty years and many that were born after my departure to Ethiopia. In the same way, my in-laws heard about our coming and while some were ready to visit us, the main part of the marriage process had to conclude, the discussion on the dowries. Initially, this proceeding was heading to Kongor, where my father, mother in-law and the bride uncle were, but soon we came to know that the road to Kongor had flooded very badly and no one was going through, at least no commercial vehicles. My brother had called my dad and briefed him on the first phase or how the arrangement was going. They also discussed the dimming possibilities of the second phase heading to him because of the road inaccessibility. My father agreed, telling my brother to handle whatever the in-laws agreed to.

In the first meeting between the families at Bor, there was unanimous conclusion that going to Kongor was impossible and marriage settlement was to conclude there. They both agreed on summoning families and relatives. This was the second phase. The immediate family members at the time the bride's cousin, the son of his elder uncle and of course my brother on my side. The message was sent home back to Kongor to mother in-law and her maternal uncle. Despite all the challenges of the road, the maternal uncle, Bul Kuir Aguer made it before any deal could be struck. As always with most Dinka's marriage arrangements, the talks were really about wealth bargaining. The bride's family and relatives were bargaining hard to capitalize on their daughter, to obtain as much dowries as possible and for people leading the bargain to get a share. During this gathering, the husband of the elder sister, Makeer Chol not only attended because of him being a brother to the bride, but because the bride was at his care before this marriage proceeding started, at least since coming to Bortown earlier in the year and in that case, father figure for her.

On my side, my brother was leading the talk along with my cousins and other relatives. After two days of long and intense talks and deliberations, there were agreements and dowries were settled, exchanged and on the last day of that October, both families concluded the marriage as they pronounced us as husband and wife in a feast ceremony. There were blessings and words of good wishes passed on to us. This conclusion was not only the dowries finale, it was a conclusion that placed both of us members of one another's family. The last part, un negotiation ceremonial part was still left for to be finalized by my father and mother in law once we made it home.

Unfortunately, this happily celebration of a union was followed at conclusion by hard breaking incidents. The long discussions with restless preparation with mostly empty stomach all took a toll on my brother. Perhaps he was holding up the entire time, but immediately after the conclusion of the marriage, right before the last guest leave; he felt sick and seriously that he was rushed to the hospital. A day that was so wonderful yet ended so sadly. It was a very nervous night. Thank God, even with no good treatment at the hospital, he recovered so quickly that he pulled himself up and told the doctor to be release the next day. Of course, there was really no care at the hospital. There was a lot lacking; qualified physicians and medical supplies among many.

As he came home, we were yet to learn more heartbreaking news. Before the wedding process was concluded, some people in my community had left for Kongor where my father and other relatives were living. I was later told that my dad was very excited that the roads were again open and possibility that I was soon coming. He had been looking forward to seeing me for years and it was just about time and in fact a great time since I was coming home with a newly wedded wife.

However, the road to Kongor was still very bad, very flooded and muddy. Small cars could not make it. A truck or a four wheels drive like the land rover were rare and even if they attempt to go, it could take many hours if not over a night to get home. Somehow, he was mistakenly told that I was not on the way, probably not going to make it home. This was too hard for my father to hear, not what he was expecting regardless of the flooded road. Everyone at his house was excited about me coming home or reuniting for the first time since 1997 short visit. In fact, my little brother, half-brother to be specific couldn't wait. He came to Bortown sometime before my arrival there. This expected reunion perhaps was very personal for my dad. Immediately after receiving the unexpected news, that I wasn't coming, perhaps returning to the US, he changed as I was later told. There was no quick way to get a hold of me. At the time, communication was mainly by long range radio satellite and too, they were rare, always booked and crowded. Besides, it was late in the day and perhaps it was overwhelming that he couldn't even imagine. The following morning, he woke up early, sat outside his house, and started murmuring words to himself as my stepmother recalled.

Across from my father house was my uncle, Bul, his older brother who that morning had early visitors was sitting outside as they face the direction toward my father. Per his account, my father sat there till he slips down to the floor. He had no idea what my father was going through till late when he could not believe what he just saw. So often, both brothers join one another, this further explain they had lived near since before I was born. As my stepmother later added, my father was stressed out by the news of my not coming. Buldit couldn't make a reason why his brother would be lying on the floor like he saw. It was unusual for him. He often comes to his brother and both started the day together. My uncle along with the visitors were concerned and both started questioned one another, before they found someone to send. When they sent someone to call Reecdit over, or at least sit him up right, he could not wake up, he was gone, right on his seat. He died of broken heart. He fainted. He could not imagine or understood why I had made it all the way so close and not see him after all. He was to see me second time since we parted in 1987 and first since my short visit in 1998.

As for me, I knew I was coming to him; there was no way I would return to the United States without seeing him and many relative. My initial reasons for coming to Africa was to see him not about getting marriage. However, getting married was something he always wanted for me. He was knowledgeable of the girl. Of course, he knew her parents, both grew up together and at the time, the bride mother lived just across from him. As my brother later emphasized to me, my dad long sickness too so much toll on him. What kept him was his constant thought to see you. "He is only waiting for you", that is what keeps his hope, he said. It was in my heart to make all commitment to see him, but I did not directly communicate that to him, personally failing to assure him.

My father was still strong; at least I had always found that on his voice. He had never spoken to me like a person who could leave me or his kids behind sooner. It was just sickness, after all his older brother was living next to him, still stronger at the time. He was at least on his late seventies. There was no record of his birthday as it's was obvious to many dinka. However, his older brother and some of his age mates estimated him to be in his early seventies.

We came to know about this fetal news the following morning after we received my bother Nyuop back from the hospital. I went to see him that early morning before he was later released shortly after nine am. We were all relieved that he got better quickly after stomach flu that scarily rushed him to the hospital. At that instance, family members had ploughed my brother's house were his younger wife and children all had gathered around. On the other room were my wife and my sister in law. My younger brother was just around outside. Everyone was in to comfort him.

However, there was bad news in the air and the adults who knew about it didn't want to wait for too long, a chance that someone could hear it somewhere. Some of us tried to give room to the elders by stepping outside, but they wanted all of us inside. We didn't know what was coming and of course had no other concern at the time but for my brother. They were hesitant on how to start it, but they were against the patience of some like my restless young brother plus the room was hot too, less oxygen to share. But sometime a body language tells and as from the way they went about, something had happened. We have lost Reechdit and no clear understanding of what had happened, but we had been call from Kongor, they said. Upon hearing that, the wives and children just spiked up in flame of cry. I didn't know what to do at that point, didn't make any sense. However, somehow, we had to be adult, therefore me, younger brother and elder brother held our breath. The sound of cry however exploded.

My wife was on the other room, was sick herself. She knew we were gathering at the other room and knew nothing about what was happening. She heard cry when my brother's wife and the kids burst out in cry and her as a very emotional person didn't wait to be told what happened, she broke down too upon hearing cry. One of the elders had called upon that my wife be reveal the bad news quickly and carefully. But before someone would walk out, we heard the noise of cry from the bride's room; they had assumed that something had gone wrong especially with our brother being sick. I could not cry though I along with my wife seem to deserve the most to see our father. All of us boys had wives and kids around us, we could not fall in too in the cry regardless how painful, we soak it in. My wife felt in faint immediately, passing out. There were just a lot that could come to mind at that so hopeful days, and why could such incident intervene, no one could understand.

It took her couple of days before she recovers, and even after then we all were devastated. I was questioning my thoughts. Why, and why. My father had long wanted me to get married, and here he couldn't see my wife first, he couldn't see me walk into his lawn side by side with her. She knew the girl well, I was told. And I heard that she was very pleased upon hearing that I eloped her. I finally had done his will and particularly to a girl whose parents were highly known and respected. He knew the girl himself as her mother resided just across the street from him and her dad was his former youth mate. Both fathers knew each other at their upbringing. I learned later from one of my uncle's wife that both talked at Kakuma about the girl as a potential wife for me, not even knowing how that would happen since I had silent the proposal every time they brought up the marriage talk. I was making a lot of questions in my mind, and maybe my wife too was rebuking herself.

At that point, the important thing for me was to console the new member of our family, the one greeted at the door by such a fatal incident, my wife. I presumed, perhaps she misinterpreted why those two incidents happened right after the conclusion of her marriage. I didn't want to go back and ask the elders who revealed to us what they know happened or the cost of death, I didn't want explanation or assumption, I knew that would hurt us more especially if I would have questioned much. It was hard to get that behind, especially the way it happens, we were just four hours away from home and if the roads were not blooded, we would have been there on his side long before the misfortune. It was just the bad time for something so planned not to go right. Yes, I had spent decade away from him, yes, I had grown to be a man away from him, yes, I didn't need any physical support from him, yes, I was used to life without immediate parents, yes, I could handle my individual life alone as it had been, yet I was born by him till my early departure, but if there was one time I was to have him in my life, this was the time I need him the most. I was now a family man just got married. I had taken someone's daughter to be part of me, to be companion for the rest of the life, and I wanted to present her to Reecdit's family. This was the moment I thought my dad could tell me one thing he remembered about his young bride, Akon Mayom Bol and how I could be him in that instant situation and of course my wife fitting into my mother's chose. I was thirsted to be with my dad for so many reasons including making up the decades of time away from him. All those dreams were resting on one night I owed to my father, one night that he was going to teach me about holding a family. It was going to be my moment, just one moment for me and him.

At those difficult times, we were factored by the situation that brought more prayers between us and throughout our travels. By early December 2008, we started our long journey, and in opposite direction from home. We left for Kampala and then later to Kenya as we couple travelled together and alone for the first time. This was what is call the honeymoon in a sense. It was usual for young couple to take their honeymoon somewhere. This trip was also meant to get the wife her first clothes as a wife. We visited the two countries as I tried to dress her first as a wife. On the way to Kenya, we went through like nothing had happened to us. This doesn't mean we forgot about it, but we at least hide our emotions. I really credited my wife for not showing so much of that sadness in her face. She never asks me anything if there were doubts in her mind or anything, she got asked of why such things had happened at that conclusion of the weeding. We had good time in Uganda and even much in Kenya. We were welcomed every we went and perhaps we both were showing up one another. At our short stay in Nairobi, we got most of what we needed and still visited Nakuru, the near-by city where she went to school as high schooler.

On the 15th, we started back to South Sudan as we left Nairobi to Kampala and finally to Bortown. This time, we were determined to travel all the way home, to Kongor in only five days from Kenya. My days were running down; I had to return to the United States on the 31st, flying out from Kampala. On December 21st, we finally made it home, met siblings and relatives, saw my father's grave, learned a lot of what led to his death, met my mother in law and above returned to the very last place I left my feet on when I left Pawer in 1987.

My home was not as I left it two decades earlier. It had changed. The topography looked different; the landscape was bare. The forest that was often dense and green was gone. I could see distance without barriers. At other place, the once human residents were abundant to wild. The very place I was born at, village which was at most three miles from the Kongor Head quarter, Pawel was not accessible.

Since the 1991 Riek Machar's SPLA Nasir, attack on my village, the area was never reoccupied. The villagers never returned to the villages accepts settlements around the municipal centers such as the Pawel, Panyagoor and the nearby court centers. In fact, the whole dinka-Bor land was deserted at some point and many fled to the displace camp near Uganda-Southern Sudan borders. Few people who run to hide in the swamp areas along the Nile were the first to return home, but they never return to their own villages or their own plots, these were the first settlements around the municipal centers. As more returned after the CPA adoption, the settlements spilled over to nearby villages and tribal centers. Upon his repatriation, my dad settled at Pawel, just outside the town center.

My home was never the same in many ways, perhaps the 1991 attack had casted the area. Over the years even after the end of the Civil war, the village I knew I had remained as a killing field. There has been a lot of tribal fighting especially over cattle raiding and many people had been killed including children and people lived in fear. The fear of cattle raiders that in so many occasions had turn to kids and women abductions and random killing had driven many people to cities, had discourage the moral my people had to grow crops for themselves, and even rearing cattle had become a big risk to take. Thankfully, the will of the people had not changed, people are not only living through all those challenges, but they're in fact trying their very best to keep cattle and to defense their way of life in any way possible.

Bul Nyuop

I returned home with a mindset to visit my mother grave to pay her my last respect, however, my birth village was abandoned, left as a jungle and the road that used to pass by use no more. I couldn't see my mother's grave for just a moment of reunion and to answer her regret of dying without knowing whatever happened to her Bul-Manyuon. I was totally left with nothing, no parent and no village.

Family
An Identity of me (II)

Before I got married, I never favored raising a family in America. For me, raising up a dinka family was the reason of marrying a dinka girl thousands of miles away. Despite the greatness of America, I saw the huge cultural differences, particularly those contrary to the dinka, and the best way was to keep my family at home where dinka culture would be the only center of their thrive. However, love was different and could make decision regardless of preconditions. I felt the love to be near my wife even before I parted with her, the short time after we got married. Nevertheless, I came back to America. The decision was also made easy especially due to the sickness that she went through after I left her. She was very sick and I couldn't be there due to our distance. Thankfully, she was with our people both hers and mine, everyone took good care of her.

Six months after marriage, with wife thousands of miles away, yet to have a kid, future of the job on the line, and all the daily thoughts of a distance relation, I hesitate not but immediately initiated the process to bring her to the United States and ultimately start a family in America. It was a long process, but much chorological, in that I knew every step of the way. I was prepared and active as the process took it course, providing all the necessarily documents and timely ready before the next step. Thanks to the wife's educational background, she was instrumental in getting all needed documentation at quicker phase. I returned to Nairobi on

February 15th, 2009 to complete the process with a medical check and final interview. It was a great reunion after more than a year of separation. However, with the successful process on the 19th of March 2009, it was just a matter of time for a permanent reunion.

I returned to the States and shortly after a quick visit back home to farewell the families, she arrived on American's soil on April 28th, 2010. By then, we were expecting a baby. We were grateful and too anxious for the first baby. Thanks to technology, we found out the baby sex prior to birth. The MRI revealed a daughter, our mother to be. It was not a total surprise forthcoming for us to have a first-born baby daughter. My brothers including my younger brothers who had his kid before me started their families with first born daughters and obviously, they all took our mother's name. On November 17, 2010, just a week before Thanksgiving Day, she was born at 2:30pm, a cute 7.5 pound at the Valley Medical Center in Renton, WA. We could not be so thankful. Minutes later while we couldn't get our eyes off her, the registration came in with paperwork and we had to put the name down, and with no hesitate nor consultation, she was Akon. We spelled the name out, informed the nurse that the name was our mother's, a tribute, a reminder of our biological mom. We were now a complete family, parents and a kid. As Akon grew especially in her baby years, we often called her mama, heartily resembling my biological mother that she had no clue, not an image of how she looks like. However, with such naming, I never felt so motherless as before. Akon had her own mother, and she was often confused and in disbelief every time I called her mama. At some instances she asked where my mother was and of course I had only responded to her that she was in fact my mother. Akon since the first time she had a smile, had been a satisfaction, a joy, a blessing and more like a rebirth of my own mother.

As our mother was remembered and growing by the day, we were hoping for another God bless, with an opportunity to for a boy to name as Reech after my father. Shortly after, God answered the hope as planned, my own plan. My wife conceived. We never openly spoke about the wish; we just had our first baby and there was a wishful future ahead of us. In dinka like with many other African cultures, wives often wish for number of boys outnumbering girls. We were just starting up our family and it was a blessing with Akon just like my brothers have had. For this next baby, we never openly felt the need to know the sex. I personally hoped for him. We had told the nurses and midwives that this would be a surprising baby.

On the same facility, Valley Medical Center on July 28th, Sunday evening at 7.54pm, Reech was born, just a couple of days pass the estimated delivery date. He was too a seven pounder, 7.15 to be exact, however, the nurse somehow told us that he was almost eight; hence his birth record showed eight pounds. It was a quick delivery. My wife had hold on to a long labor until the last hour. We run to the hospital which was only a mile from our residency. As she sat in and the nurses started to add up with all the preparation, I excused myself and told mama Akon that I was going to run home to get few clothes for Akon and to return in few minutes. In approximately fifteen minutes that I was gone, she had Reech. I came back to my surprise of the baby first cry as I entered the room. As another surprise, we both came to know the sex at birth. During the pregnancy, we had the opportunity to see the sex of the baby, a free MIR unlike at Akon, but we turn it down, I told her that I didn't want to know the gender. I was not just denying her to not find out the baby sex, I just didn't want a bad feel while still pregnant especially if the baby was another girl. In fact, she later told me that she never thought it that way. I was ok with a surprise baby. Culturally there was a belief that expectants mother behavior differs for different kids during pregnancy. I didn't not recognize any of that and specifically never paid attention. This was only a second kid, and any sex was highly a blessing.

Unlike Akon before birth, we were not quite with his name. Yes, we want to name him after our father, but my sister and brother during the pregnancy were not on the same page as to what the name would be in the hope of a son. So, once he was born, I called my brother and sister and although they were hundreds of miles apart, they all waste no hesitation, he was in fact taking our father's name, they both agreed. Like Akon, we also refer to our son as our father, calling him by so many of my father's nick names. Of course, both got their own nicknames; initially Akon was willed the name Sandra by her mother's friend before she was even married. Reech, as his mother used to sing lullaby referencing Ajingdit, Akon started calling him *Anyinyiwawa*.

Two plus years later, we were blessed to welcome another boy into the family. Nyuop was born on the 8th of March 2015 at the same facility as his older siblings, at the Valley Medical Center. To be real, I wasn't sure of the name to give him unlike the other two and this could have been the advantage in having the elders in naming the children.

250

While my first gad was to go with Nyuop, I was thinking about naming him after my father-in-law or any name the in-laws provide. But this child was only number 3, a little early according to my knowledge of the culture to give the name to the wife's family. Usually, the wife's side of the family is named after 4-5th birth, a good time to signal the last of wife's giving birth. However, this was not usual with my parents. My mother's father was the child before me, unfortunately he couldn't live long. This mean it could have sent a mixed message to relative on both sides. Before the registration came into get the name of the newborn, I asked my wife what the name would be, and she delivered with no hesitation, saying Nyuop of course as she looks at my face. This was the end of my daydream, and I believe this was what my siblings were thinking. This was what live with no parents was like, you take all responsibilities on your shoulder.

As Nyuop grew, he went through the same childhood as his siblings. Named after our grandfather; we nicknamed him kuakua, a short for Kuarkuar in the dinka Bor section. Unlike my father whose I knew his many youth hood nick names, I didn't know much about my grandfather. My sister again recalled when she knew about grandfather, his nickname was Mabior e weer, after the moon.

Nyuop too brought a lot of joy into the family. If I recall the early years of Akon while she crawls, she uses to know the time I return from work and would always be waiting by the door. This was the case with Nyuop; he was often excited hearing the door crack in anticipation of my arrival from work. He was so a sweet boy, never wanted to go to bed unless I go. Like Akon, both started walking months before their first birthday. Reech on the other hand was a little slow in term of doing things independently. We never really trained Akon and so we thought Reech was going to follow easily especially seeing Akon doing a lot by herself. Nevertheless, he showed early signs of brightness. Before his first preschool, he knew all the alphabets and was counting numeric; competing with his sister who already was in preschool. I was so overwhelmed when his teacher ranked Reech among the top student in her class and of course he showed so much of that at home, reading halfway his kindergarten year. I used to tell them how I started my first school when I was around 10.

Our fourth child, Mathiang or as baby kuakua use to call him, Sabit-Mathiang or baby Mathiang was born three years and six months after Nyuop. Born at the same hospital as his siblings, he was 7.13 founds when he arrived on 10/20/2018, Saturday at 2:35pm. Yes, another 2pm as Akon. Soon after the nurse wiped and wrapped him in his first earth's closes, she allowed me to hold him. Unlike the other kids, somehow, I felt very emotional holding him and I couldn't take my eyes off staring at him while he was of course crying in response to his new world atmosphere. Perhaps that emotion was attributed to the hard pregnancy his mother had of him or perhaps the naming he was soon to undertake, after my father-in-law. He finally got the blessing from his only living grandparent at the time, the maternal grandmother who named him Mathiang after her own husband. The naming, like the other kids brought to live, a father I had not met and referring to him was a way to create that link. Like all the kids before him, Mathiang too added much love in our family.

Left; Me and children; Akon, Reech and Nyuop   Right; Wife Yom M Gak & our little Mathiang

Brother Nyuop Reech and children; from right to Left: Bul-Malaat (11/19/1995), Ahou-Monday (2/4/1998), Awur-Madul (12/2000), and Akon Nyuop (2/2/1993).

Left: sister Ahou Reec Nyuop, a mother of 5. Right: Aunty Akoi Nyuop Bul

Left; wife -Yom Mathiang Gak. Right; Bul Nyuop, as a runner at WWU

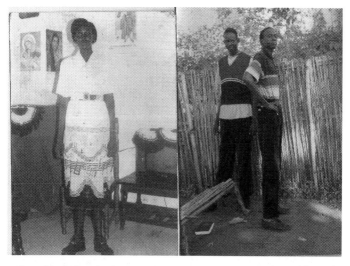

Left; Elder's brother's 1ˢᵗ wife, Abul Gak Akech. Right; younger brother; Akoi Reec Nyuop, and nephew Deng Adieu Bul Nyuop

In memory of fellow collegemate, Rhoda Bec

Having just walked our longest journey, approaching Kapoeta, 1992, we met the future South Sudan, 1ˢᵗ president Kiir, picture at left.

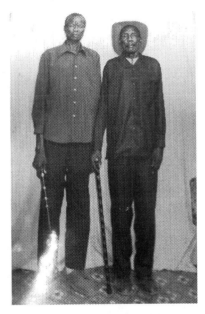

Mother- in-law; Adut Kuir Aguer. with uncle Deng Monychol Deng

Right: my father Reech Nyuop

Western Washington University

On Jan 31ˢᵗ,2003, I finally dropped in the mail my college application for Western Washington University. It was a certified mail, to guaranteed safe, trackable and confidential delivery. It was a local mail; hence expected delivery no later than three days from posting. I was finally relived that my application was done and the next step for me was to start my university education. I had zero negative expectation such as not being accepted or even a worry of financial to pay my education.

After decades of continuous wandering from refugee camp to the other, with disrupted schooling as we constantly move from place to place, country to the other in pursued of safety, and even with stable educational years of Kakuma, Kenya, there was never a hope for higher education then high school graduate degree. College was out of reach. As some used to say, a refugee cannot obtain free education beyond high school. This was one opportunity that brought me to the US and I saw the possibility immediately. I was keeping my fingers crossed, very determined to capitalize on it.

Sometime in the spring of 2001, my ESL teacher, Miss Edward arranged for many of us who hard interest in post high school a field trip to visit the biggest university in Washington State, the University of Washington. We spent the day there going around the campus, visiting the stadium, the admission office, the university dining hall, student center, and even entering some empty lecture halls. It was overwhelming for me, so many students, a huge campus, and possibly crowded lecture halls. As a foreign student, I viewed myself like a special need student, meaning that I was going to be constantly visiting the professor and at such crowded classes, I couldn't image the professor available time. Because of the school population, it was bothering to reason how many of the student could be assigned to one counselor and how could he/she find time to meet the needs of all the students. How could the professor help high lecture class, how could a student go from class to class on time especially in that very wide campus? Those were few of the numerous questions I remembered asking my field trip teacher. It was a lot of wow for me. I never been to college campus prior. The huge buildings, restless students, and so much I couldn't comprehend. It was all new, a culture shock

Western was the only choice I made instantly upon hearing about it and before I even know where it was. Western Washington University, a medium size school north of Seattle, located in one of the Pacific Northwest old cities, called Bellingham was just thirty minutes' drive to & from the Canadian border. I was only few months in America when I immediately heard the name of Western Washington University. I didn't know where it was, whether it was a university or college and in matter of fact, I was not as quite clear with the different between a university or college and how I will make it there. However, I got sold by the name and immediately dream about going there.

As time passes, other teachers and knowledgeable individuals educated me more on the universities in Washington States. My best teacher, the computer teacher Mr. Wally DeBord taught me well about colleges/

universities; private and public universities and colleges as he introduced me to university of Washington, Washington state university, eastern university, and central Washington university in addition to Western. Hearing his counting of the universities, I heard western Washington as a university for the first time. Immediately, I extorted that I want to go to western. I then learned from him were western was, how far it was from my high school, the detail such as the student attendant, and what the reputation for that school was. Because he was a technology teacher, he brought on the screen, the map and sketch of the campus. He later mentioned to me that his son too went Western Washington University.

In the Autumn of 2002, some months prior to when college applications were accepted. My high school teacher and I wrote a letter declaring an only unequitable interest in the university. We also requested a day off from school in order to visit Western. We had a good tour of the school and at the end met some people in the admission. The response was not an initial acceptance, but it wasn't discouraging either. The response prompted me in accordance with the law to summit my application the next year before the application deadline, i.e. any time between January first and April 15th for fall quarter enrollment.

Like many college bounces, I waited to be accepted, and obviously from only one school. There was no doubt that I was going to get in. I was counting on my early commitment, the connection already established in addition to my grades, an A student. However, as I later learned more about America, college bounces submit applications to many schools with favors, second choice, third choice and so forth just to make sure they get at least one acceptance. With my only application in one school, I certainly had counted my eggs before they hatched. I received my acceptance, very recognizable special letter. But again, unlike other college bounces, I solely celebrated my big movement of acceptance. I didn't have anyone to share it with.

Life was just going as planned. I felt then that nothing was to get me worried; my dream for post high school graduation was on the right track. I just had to wait for few more months before I call myself a college student. And as that first summer out of foster care rolled on, I was much looking ahead for the fall to start rather sooner to start being a college student. But not so far, summer was busy as I work hard to get myself ready financially. I had two jobs that summer and while I was now paying rent for the first time and buying my basic needs out of my pocket. Unlike many teens, I wasn't excited to live by myself to get away from parents; I was excited to get ready to experience the American life solely few months prior to college. Besides, I had lived for a decade without parents let alone that I was only exiting a non-biological parent's custody. I moved in that summer with Simon, thanks to CYS connection and my high school teacher, Mr DeBord who helped me that summer moving in the apartment.

However, the road to college was not that easy, there was more to do during that summer. There were the financial aids and scholarship paperwork to be finalized. The Students Aid Report, also known as SAR, was yet to be review, edited, and then to resubmit. In the editing process, I had to accept or reject the offers listed. I was not quite clear about FAFSA process besides the initial application which I had submitted early that year. It was the first time I saw the FAFSA award and different kinds of loans, the term work study, the state and federal grants. They were all new to me and I had to seek help. I went to Mr. Debord once more time.

When the fall came around, it was a different quarter, unlike the past two and half years of high school. Stepping on the college camp was like reaching a promise land for me. For many years since landing in Pinyudo, leaders often wished education, to go to universities and be educated citizen of the New Sudan. In Kakuma, people spoke a lot especially about those who never went to college and those who failed to complete their degree or drop out. This is where I had always wanted to be and my mostly reason for coming to America was to achieve university degree. This was a different environment from high school. College campus of course was larger, more complex and easier to get lost but very independent of the community and I was expecting students to be more responsible on their own affairs, no parents to lie on. Of course, this was where degree matters.

Stepping on college campus in another was a change as I expected it. As a higher education, I expected more adult-like students. For only two and half years in high school I was tired seeing student leaving their food plate on their dining tables, and other silly acting including noise in the class. This was college, the start of a career, independent living and better decision and plans. I came to college few days early for student's orientation and to start my first on-campus job. The orientation was a very helpful experience, I later volunteered in two of the occasions, welcoming the new students and showing them around campus, setting up their networks and creating friends. I was also able to familiarize myself with classes, recreational center, dining halls, and off course the Old Main, the main office.

At the dorm, the ridge, I met many cool friends though the first roommate left me with a memorable bad experience. He used weeds. He was smoking in the room in my absence and that room smelt so bad for hours, something I never experienced prior. But my doom was lovely, at least I can admit years later. I was a beloved guy, unique in status and outgoing, often greeted nicely by many girls that some later perceived me as a pimp, the ladies' man. There as a tall Brazilian guy that use to be part of the basketball team. He was funny and often calling out my name. In fact, he contributed to the quite hour song that was coined in my name. We used to sing the song before the quite hours, a designated studying time. I stayed at the ridge for two years.

Academically, I came to Western with my mind made. I knew what I wanted to career in, and I never wasted time on deciding. Agriculture and accounting were always my interest, but I learned something about macroeconomic a summer before my freshmen year and I decided to tag it along as a minor. My plan was clear and well thought out, to graduate in exactly four years. At summer start, the first summer before the freshmen year, I registered for thirteen credits and on the waiting list for one more. Through the four years even later when I also took part in sport, I maintained at least fourteen credits.

I was a member of the scholarship association, formerly known as the achievers, the recipients of the gate foundation and governor scholarships. We had a class together, a very important class that used to bring us together, coaching us into our success and college experiences. This class kept us together and it brought us to share our college experiences. Of course, the instructors were our peer mentors, they knew everyone. In addition, our association also made it uniquely affordable for us to share a formal dinner with the university president. This came twice. The first I got the invitation and reference a dinner with the president, I could never belief. It was a big deal and I called my mentor right away to confirm the validity of the mail and soon after, I jumped in to confirm my reservation. I was later seated on the middle table, with Dr. Moore, the university president and Jiguvut, the student's president advisor. I never saw that coming, but I was dressed very nicely. They were so welcoming, and very exceptionally nice to me. I felt rewarded beyond my scholarship. We had a good chat and particularly with Dr. Jiguvut, who was an African himself.

As the first year came to conclusion, this was the first time that I had not participated in the extra-curriculum since I came to the US. Previously in high school, I played soccer in my freshman year and then in Track and Field and cross country for the last year and half. Here, I was always a very loaded full-time student, but athleticism was missing as I previously planned. But while I tried to disassociate myself from the extracurricular activities, my cousin John Riak back in high school was having a great athletic year. He started the year to the finish, with school setting record performances in track and field and cross country. He dominates his high school conference and district and end up going to state in two events in which he finishes in the top five on both. Those were John performance, never had such good performances when I was running as the star of that same school, but that start to motivate me again here at Western. I came to Western considering no running at all at least in the first year. My goal was to come there and to make sure I succeed academically. The unshakeable dream I had was to solely pursue and achieve a college degree.

I didn't participate in the direct combat for the South Sudan freedom, hence I thought to owe myself and the nation the opportunity of education, one that million never had. I didn't want anything that I would put as an excuse for any failure. In addition, running especially at college level needs a lot of training and time to put in and I never thought to afford that time. I didn't want that participation to limit my hours of study or work. At the same time, I had the obligation to support my parents back home by sending them some money that I had to work for. Besides, I was providing the sole support of myself, so I needed an undivided time to working and school. I had been working since high school, sometime even holding two jobs to support my own needs. My financial aid was at last sending me a check after all the tuitions and all the programs were paid for, but I was not to rely on that net pay, but because at least I had to buy my books early before the classes starts, and all my other basic needs had to fulfill some personal needs prior, so working was a right mind set for me.

Just before the year ended, my college mates and particularly my dorm mates came to learn more about me and that I was not just African American from my look, but in fact a Sudanese, a recent immigrant to the United States. Most of my dorm mates knew nothing about Sudan or the civil war's impact that brought me from that corner of the world, but many runners in fact knew that students from

African were always good runners. In this pursued, I met and created best friendship with Dustin who at the time was a freshman who lived in my 3rd floor dorm and he started talking me into running. He asked if I had run before and that it would be feverous to be teammate with him. As time passes, he finally asked me to come and checkout or watches them running during one of their home meets. He was not a distance runner himself, but he enjoys and took his running seriously with pride. Although, he wasn't the sole factor that finally geared me into running again, his encouragement and motivation were in part among the reasons that finally got me on the team.

I ended up running for the team for two years both in track and field and cross country. I didn't run to my potential due to my reluctance and work, but it would be mistaking to say I wasn't serious with my running and even the teammates would dispute that if mentioned to them, but I was always among the top best considering my limited devotion. I had to keep my work and fulltime student status a priority. My goal was to graduate in four years. However, running at the college level was an opportunity to not past by at least for fun and friendship. On my first turn out, on the first day of practice, the plan was to run ten kilometers work out. I never run that distance prior to that practice and my teammates where amazed at the end of that day when I told them that I just run my first ever ten k. Like John and our former coach, they were delight that I would be enough asset to the team. However, it was a competitive team especially the top five. However, running in that atmosphere with the best assistance coach, the friendly most motivating assistant coach, and the friendliest committed teammates, it was worth turning out for that team despite the shuffling for the positioning for the top five. There were high time and low performances in my two years of participation, but I will remain cherishing those performances and acquainted friendship.

Among the few memorable meets include the 2005 Spike invitational 10k that I run at Central University track and field, the 2005 University of Washington invite in which our team ended at 2nd just behind 2nd team of Chico state, and finally my only and last cross country regional at Chico State, California 2006. The Spike Invitational 10k was my only won event in College. I finished the long 25 rounds with a time of 33.32 minutes.

As for the cross country, my best performances were numerous, some better than expected, but my 2006 Chico state regional conference performance stood out though also disappointing. As a team, we came into that race ranking eleven nationally with a potential to advance to National championship. However, this was the last meet and every team wanted a spot. The meet was won by Chico, the best team coming in. They had four runners in the top ten including second and third finisher. We finished in 4th place, narrowly missing the 3rd place by two points to University of Alaska Anchorage who were led by an all American, a Kenyan runner, David Kiplagat who finished 5th overall. I paced my team with the 17th place finish, covering the 10-kilometers course in 33.25, just before our best runner who came 18th, just 2 seconds behind me. In fact, four of us were less than five seconds apart. This was the first time I led the team. Nevertheless, it was a disappointing finish overall for the team.

I went into that meet with more in mind than to help the team. I had in mind to show my coach and everyone that I was disappointed for not being selected a year prior. In 2005, I had a very bad finishing in the conference race, placing number 7 on the team, but with eight runners to pick for the regional, I was not even chosen. I was never consulted or asked any opinion whether I wanted to go, or should they pick someone else. Our team captain run badly in that 2005 conference meet, he finished in tenth place, supper tied, but still he was our best runner and yes, he could replace me with no question. However, a lack of communicating the selection disappointed me and I had that in mind coming to Chico.

As always, I was very reluctantly approaching the startup but with the mindset to run conservatively and finish strongly. As a team, we finished our warmup with a short prayer and a sendoff cheer. Our owns line up placed the top runners first followed by the rest of us. The time was up, few instructions, and the gun went off, fired into the air sending us on the 10k course. As expected, everyone was fighting to get to the front. In the process, so many started out quicker, perhaps faster than planned. Some people fell, and others got bummed or stepped on foot at the start. I expected that fight at the beginning, hence I started slow, among the last starters to get on the course. As we went around the first loop, the runners were not tied yet, hence there were no hard breathing and whizzing, but all you could hear was the hissing sound between the clit contacts with the gravel. There was a long narrow line of runners formed. For us behind, it was a long way to get to the top and slowly, I was moving to the front, passing my

competitors and teammates one by one. It was at the end
of the first loop, not far from the starting point that I got a
cheering boost from my coaches. TJ, the assistant coach was
doing what he knew best at, running a long side; giving us
splits, shouting to every Viking to pick up speed and spot.
We could hear him, but the legs were not pleased, and the
thin atmosphere was doing us no favor, we were getting
tired against our will. As we went third, four, fifth and
approaching sixth miles, many were losing it, and many
tried to finish strong. As I saw the finish line, I tried to put
on the last energy, but every runner was thinking the same
and some passed me while the distance was diminishing. By
the time we finish, I didn't know my position, all I cared
was if we would make the national.

After few minutes of rest, while many teammates were
finding one another, and coaches busy trying to figure out
our position as a team, my cousin and teammate came to
congratulate me. John had earned 4th place individually. I
was told about my 17th place overall in the race, and just
seconds in front of my team best runner. At that instant, I
knew that it was not good for us as a team, especially me
finishing a head of our best runner let's alone his position.
At the end, the results came out and we had finished 2
points shy behind Anchorage for fourth place. We didn't
make it to National, only 3 team advanced. It was very
disappointing for us. And despite finishing first in the team,
I started blaming myself. A Chico 7th finisher just passed me
at the last one hundred meters, taking a point away from us.
We would have headed to National had I sprinted the last
hundred meters in beating the him or the Pomona if not

Alaskan who finished just before me. My teammates had a bad day and that was an overall bad performance for us.

The course was rather flat and not in any comparison with our own course that we just won the conference the weeks prior, nevertheless, the weather was sunny, a little hot for us if that was an excuse. It was a disheartened final race for us, seniors. There was so much expectation of us.

Western campus didn't receive us with the same good reception as we left. We had failed and many students who knew the graduating seniors knew that most of us were going to be no runners the year to come. In my case, I became the men athlete of the week and honored with front website page picture and another big picture hanging in the GYM for every bye passer to appreciate. That became my last run and final participation as a Viking athlete and with that concluded my final records as;

2.03 minutes for 800 meters,

4.34 minutes for the mile and

33.24 minutes in the ten thousand meters, or 6 miles.

Those stats added to my best wining moments going back to high school track and field and one six-mile race at the college level. However, I clearly knew that all my Personal Records (PR) at that time did not depicted my potential and capability; they were my personal best for the limited effort and participation I had been part of.

As my extra curriculum athleticism came to an end, my college years were also coming to conclusion as planned, graduating in four years. In March shortly after winter quarter finals and just before our final years of college fun time, we planned a team outing, this time not far off running, but running was going to be our second agenda;

we were going to Mexico. Coincidently, it was spring and unlike many who heads out to Cancun or any other exotic college gone wild's Mexican destinations at spring break, we headed out for Christian mission, to help at the orphanage. Our trip was sponsored by Cornwall church in Bellingham.

We flew to San Diego and then drove for six hours pass Tijuana and spent the next nine days of our spring break at Mexicali. It was a different country, different rules, different culture and much a conservative place for college kids like us, but we had to turn it down. Our mission was to volunteer in helping and share some of our donations with the orphanage and the needy. It was a great experience, helping in the community that was needy just like where I had come from. Personally, the trip experiences took me a back to my years of the refugee life, particularly the years of Panyidu. There, I was handing out the clothes and the fact that I was on the giving end was an emotional personal reminder. For most of my refugee life, I was always in need, not only for food, but also for clothes. We used to get clothes from the UNHCR, and they were distributed to us just like we were doing then to the poor Mexicans who buy no mean were not even at my position, they were living their happy life at home. We used to fight over one another to get such second-hand clothes. That history was revisited here as I saw those Mexican fighting over our second-hand clothes. I remember standing emotional about the experience. No one in my group knew my personal story, especially in relation to what we were doing. Most of them grew up receiving more and giving some as we were doing. My teammates were white, many of them still young that they had never been to poor countries or experienced any such lifestyle.

On the last day of our trip, we visited the prisons and we listen to some of the stories that led the prisoners into those prisons. Prior to that moment, I had never been near the prison or jail and it was heart breaking listening to their stories and feeling helpless. The prison was big and there were section including a section for women, we also visited. We returned to the USA and to Western with world experiences that changed some of us to prompted them returning to that orphanage years later.

Back in Bellingham, we were student again. Spring was my last quarter. Prior to the trip, I had put in my college graduation evaluation with my academic mentor, Mr. Antonio Esqueda. He had looked over my college academic requirement in my absence. I thought I was all set and that only three classes were yet to take in the final quarter to graduate that spring. His evaluation reveals to me that I had taken one too many classes in one science department and so I had to take one more in another department. That was kind of bad news. Now, to graduate that spring, I had to enroll for twenty credit quarter to end my plan and to graduate at the end of the 2007 school year. With twenty credits, I optioned out of track and field season to focus academically and became a tough quarter.

Our graduation date was set to June 15, just few days before the mid of the summer 2007. Unlike my high school post-graduation which was consumed by college paperwork and trips for WWU summer start, dormitory visit and selection, this time I was preparing to join the working world professionally. It was time to look ahead, to put resume together, to attend career/job fairs, and much to put in applications for jobs. That spring, I was also testing the water with the future accounting dream job as tax preparer. I enrolled in the AARP tax preparation class and voluntarily, I participated in the tax preparation at the Bellingham city library. At the same time, I was getting myself ready with the requirements for the big day, the graduation. I had ordered my cap and gown, my tickets for few cousins and friends, had bought a new shirt for the big day, and I was consulting my teachers for advice as I prepared to exit Western. Senior anxieties had kicked in that quarter and combined with all the other preparations; I was just ready for any passing grade. I would mention that the professors helped a lot that quarter with not only great advices to seniors, but with the most of all, the grading.

As some of us felt overwhelmed by the milestone achievement in the making, the best four years of continuous friendship was becoming a history and soon to be miss campus and many friends. I was ready for a party. On the last night prior to our big day, my roommates also graduating threw a big graduation party. There was beer everywhere and yes, a lot of unknown people mostly girls in our apartment. The graduating students were under pressure. You had to do something, and that include some intimate relationship. I particularly was in a tough situation, everyone was drinking but not me, everyone exchanging phone numbers as I pretended to be un sociable, and yes, my response to unavoidable question, "what are you doing tonight?" was disappointing, "I am going to bed and get ready for tomorrow". And despite our early plan to bet to bed early as advised to get up fresh and not be late for the graduation, the party and my anxious for the final day preparation didn't let me sleep easily. I found myself thinking so much about this and that and what I have left undone and the future after graduation. It wasn't until three in the morning when I finally caught some dizziness.

On the morning of June 15th, 2007 exactly four years and 5 days from my high school graduation, I was just few hours to stand tall on the podium for my college degree. We assembled early that morning all with our attires in Western Washington University purple and white, just like four years earlier. We were in black gowns, different tassels for different departments. Few minutes later, we matched into the auditorium, already filled with parents, friends, schoolmates, faculties and so many other guesses. We matched in college by college and then major by major. I happened to sit between two of my best friends, whom we met and lived on the same dormitory in the first year. I felt so comfortable around them just taking that moment that we started together when we moved in four years earlier in September 2003, we had several classes together and we also worked together, now we were about to finish it together, it was unbelievable.

The ceremony proceeded with the valedictorian, the head of the alumni, the university president and finally with the chair of the board of trustees giving the final authority to the president that we the seated students have completed the school requirement and with the power invested in him by the state, declared us as graduates. Those words were gold, and even emotional for me. The moment was coming real, and it was taking the hold of me. There was so much final words of encouragement and blessing, there was so much flash back but still we had to walk to the podium, shake hand, grasp the diploma, turn with a quickly smiling for a camera with the University president, and wave to cousins, friends, classmates who had come to share the joy. For me, it was a dream accomplished and timely, a self-endorsement of some though.

I was grateful to the people who gave me the opportunity of a life time; which includes the two fraternities who awarded me the two scholarships, the American tax payers who gave me the opportunity in the state and federal fell grants, my friends who believe in me, particularly those who travelled that morning to my graduation all caught on camera, and finally but not the least, the SPLA freedom fighters who protected us during the intense pierced revolution and who always encouraged us to school for the future of the new nation. I was overwhelmed and as many of my friends would later understand, I was the first in my family to reach high school level of education, let alone that college degree.

It wasn't until ten years later when I decided to return to school for another leap of a step, toward my masters. Again, the spirit to enriching my educational value drove me. My graduate programs, the MBA degree was for me to satisfy my bachelor's degree, to increasing my value and what I could provide to the community. This came in the summer of 2016 when I finally took the first class of many, a start of what I had dream of since the days when me and Roda last spoke about it in 2005. I was accepted into Southern New Hampshire University, again like Western, this was the only graduate program I placed my application with and immediately got accepted in. I concluded my program on December 2018, earning a specialty in finance.

The Promise Land!
The Republic of South Sudan

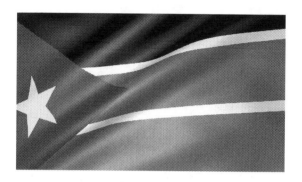

Then the fade of a half-century Southern Sudanese struggle came down to July 9th, 2011, the day of destiny, the day of achievement, the day of peace or as the tireless voice of the Government of South Sudan 1st Speaker of the Legislative Assembly read during the inaugural celebration, the "independent day of the Republic of South Sudan".

This day was a long dreamed of for many brave veterans. 2011 was an overdue year for the Southern Sudanese. I had often hope for our success in defeating the enemy and ultimately succeeding in ending the war. I never imagined our success to come as it came in 2011, in a choice of vote let alone with nearly 100% unanimous vote of secession from Sudan and in creation of a separate nation of our own. There. Like so many victories and defeats that were announced over the Radio SPLA or BBC during the struggle, many had believed the news of SPLA victory for New Sudan were going to come the same way, over the wires.

For southern Sudanese, Khartoum peaceful settlement was never something to believe in. As in the writing of Abel Alier, the former president of the Southern Regional Council, "too many agreements dishonored" proved why Southerners never believed in Khartoum peaceful settlement of the decades of war. And for sure never on handing over self-determination to the southerners. Yes, there was the Addis Ababa accord that ended the first 17 years civil war and perhaps handed what was known the peaceful years of Sudan. However, the agreement never endured and more importantly, it never delivered the substances that were agreed upon, which in fact led to the second civil war. In the SPLA war or second civil war, southerners never had any reason to believe in Khartoum peaceful deals. In addition to many broken agreements, other never saw the ray of day light. Examples include the Cairo agreement, the 2-3 Abuja's and 1989 Koka dam agreement. In fact, Bashir overthrew Sadiq's government on the heel of much expected signatories.

Nevertheless, this time was different. No doubt both parties to the war were warried and had exhausted resources and human lives or for many other reasons. There was no winning by either side. This peace was embraceable and it worth the hope. Southerners were confident in what the chairman had bargained and signed. For most cases, he had always impressed his people, and many believe in him. After all, he was a former Anyanya officer who never felt the truce of the Addis Ababa. As the chief architect of this peace process on the side of the SPLA/M, his vision was in every section. Unlike the many small peace accords that never saw the light of day, many Southerners saw the light with the

CPA. Southerners were at every corner of Kenya, witnessed every step and stoke of the process. In addition, the SPLA negotiators were very knowledgeable of the many broken promises on the side of the Khartoum, hence they very well were complete in their negotiations and reservations. The SPLA was not taking any offer or protocol literally but with more deliberation and if possibilities. This was evidenced in the reservations such as the two armies, the sharing of power with separate governments, sharing of resources, and the ultimatum following sixth year. The last protocol was left to be sign by the Southerners at the conclusion of six-year interim period. However, the protocol gave the opportunity to the people of Southern region to decide in a referendum vote to decide if to remain in the unity of Sudan or decide their own fate in splitting the country. In addition, the southerners were to play internal role in the central government with the SPLA chairman taking the spot of the first vice president, and the creation of Joint Integrated army.

The end to the negotiations were culminated in joyful celebrations and dignitaries around the world witnessing the first step toward the next phase of ending Sudan then long running civil war. Garang and his counterparts in the Khartoum administration for the first time publicly joined hands not only in the photo opt but also in the speeches that demonstrated the need to make the CPA a lasting stone. Signed on Jan 9th, 2005, at Nairobi, the CPA became the road map to the next phase toward the fade of the Sudanese quest for lasting peace. It was at this conclusion that Garang showed much of his desire for an independent South Sudan.

At his long address to the Southern Sudanese, he laid a clear future, a sign of separation that he never witnessed.

I was a second-year student at Western Washington University and like many fellow Southerners, we could not wait to celebrate the first May 16th especially with the hope laid by the newly signed comprehensive peace agreement. It was a special first May 16th as Dr Garang personally referenced it when he marked the same occasion in Rumbek. On May 27th, the Friday before the day we were ready in Seattle to celebrate our adjourned May 16th celebration, we arrived that evening from Western Washington University; me and my fellow Sudanese Rhoda Bec. This became one of the darkest days for our Sudanese community in Seattle and for me and her family. Roda Bec became sadly the sacrificial lamb of that celebration. A murderer was awaiting her, and he took her precious life away from us that day, the 28th of May 2005 when all the Sudanese were very drawn in celebration of May 16th that was the happiest of all. This not only did it derailed the party, but of course her own chance of seeing what she had suffered for.

I came to the party, met my fellow Sudanese including Roda's brothers, John and Jima. In fact, I almost asked them were Roda was, but somehow, I held back, knowing I can call her anytime. It was Saturday and we were heading back to school Monday night. But after a short hanging out, I left for my home city, Lacey Washington, to my friend Mary Deans house to do some yard work for money. I turned my phone off immediately after starting the work and by the time I turned it on, there were desperate tone of messages including ones that requested me to call back. Some people were not aware where I was knowing that I was schooling with Roda. I came to learn about her death from the calls and it devastated me for weeks. I couldn't believe and for that entire evening while crying silently in the yard, I was praying, asking God that the incident was not fatal as was mentioned. Some friends told me to watch the local news and I waited just with the hope that it confirms my wish. At 11 o'clock, I was flipping from channel to the other hoping to find one that was presenting the hopeful scenario. To no avail, she was indeed gone.

For a while, I blamed myself, stating if I had not brought her back, perhaps she could be a life. The news of her death reached Western campus, her roommate and so many who adored her. It was a very sad lost even for many who knew her barely. The candle visual was hosted at the red square and I remember the amazing grace song came out of my lips without my thought. It was not until I saw her body when she was presented before taken back to South Sudan and in the present of her mother that I finally let's my thoughts of Roda go.

Roda was a special person and for only a year of our acquaintance, I came to know her as a happy person, likeable by many. I was very excited of having her and for most time, enjoyed her companions as the other dinka to share our unique dinka culture on Western campus. We were always dinning and hanging out at her dormitory. She was a fan of *Everybody loves Raymond*, a comedy show. She was always amused by the show. She was often heard laughing like there was another person in the room with her during that show. I was also happy that for the 2nd time in my educational life, I had a Sudanese girl in my class. I was looking forward to seeing Roda graduate from college and she had my silently committing to helping her every way I could.

As for the road to referendum, we never hope for the bad scenario; however, the six years to 2011 were long way to go and it proved bump. The interim period started on the 9th of January 2005, the day of the last signature, but the next big step was the SPLA chairman coming to Khartoum to be sworn in as first vice president of Sudan. This was an oh moment for many southerners. This was where many of us had the doubt even while knowing it as a key achievement for the Southerners and the SPLA. According to Sudan history, a Southerner had never officially held high office in Khartoum let alone the next in line to the president.

As was preplanned, the SPLA Chairman arrived in Khartoum with few of his own bodyguards, wife and some SPLA top commanders. He was awaited not only by the Sudan president, world dignitaries including Kofi Anan, but also by millions of Sudanese, most of which had never seen him but heard of him. We were watching his arrival live as this was a worldwide must see return to Khartoum. Even at the former enemy house, this city was receiving the most hated now turned important guest and festivities were on all corners of the Sudan biggest city. The inauguration went marvelously, but that was not a pay for us in the South, our paycheck was still five plus years away.

On the 30th of July, just twenty-one days after he was sworn in, the unexpected thing happened, the South Sudan hero died on a plane crashed near New Cush, South Sudan as he returned from Uganda. This was the last thing Southern Sudanese would expect, we were not yet at the promise land. It was a quiet moment. Everyone held his/

her breathe in hope the news was just in accurate, just like previous rumors in the 1990s. At the confirmation of the accident through worldwide coverage, riots broke out and particularly in Khartoum where the protesters burned up cars, turning them over, touching structures and crowding streets and government buildings. Over a dozen people died. The figures were pointing at Khartoum, yet there was no proof. It was not only Southerners who were outrage; most of the Sudanese saw such incidents as provocations against the CPA. At the South, and with all Southerners worldwide, our doubts about Khartoum just jumped up again. As of what was next especially with the short-term position of the vice president and president of the South, we were less concern about vice presidency, but felt a hold back on the next president of GOSS going to Khartoum again. This incident placed a deep hollow on the next six years just started. Although there was no wide concern about who was going to be the next president of GOSS, those who were acquainted with the history of the SPLA were concern on how the president would be chosen. There was no doubt the next top SPLA general would replace the late beloved hero, but there was fear of the uninvited takeover. In a process many of the Southerners never questioned, General Salva, the vice of Garang was nominated the successor.

However, and while Khartoum seems shocked of what had just happened to the vice president of Sudan, followed by speech regarding their commitment to CPA, southern were doubtful of the survival of the CPA and indeed the road to 2011 proves bumpy. There were often sporadic confrontations here and there particular with Sudan backed militia attacking civilians at the borders.

There was the fourteen-mile incident were incident of aerial attack occurred. There were other bombardments inside the Southern region that Sudan never admits carrying them out nor knowing. The incident of Helig of course was the top of all. This was an incident like no other, almost a resumption to war. It was the master confrontation between then most equipped armies. Within hours and days, the world turned it eyes and hears toward it and was of a grave concern. There were artilleries used that were never used before or that SPLA never had hand on during the entire twenty plus years of war. There were even incidents when the officials were detained at Khartoum, there was famous of all, when the SPLA general secretary Pagan Amuom was detained. The growing concerns left the SPLA to minimize top SPLA generals from travelling to Khartoum. However, Southerners were committed in what they want and many including Kiir were careful in holding the fragile plate. The South shooting off oil drillings to revenge unfair deals, luck of corporation and commitment on the side of Khartoum did not help but confiscated the relationship further.

Prior to his death, Garang took the message on tour visiting many areas of South Sudan and region of Abiei. He also made it to North America informing Southerners what he just signed, the CPA and the important protocol yet to be sign by the Southern Sudanese, the vote on referendum. He was crystal clear on what he was selling, but he wanted the people to decide their fate. He wanted people to use it as he called it, "for their own good and benefit". And while he could well be remembered as one who fought for the unity of Sudan, a Sudan for all the people, were all people are treated equally and were religion play no part in government(secular government), he too left memorable quotes and phrases that clearly could be interpreted as his call for succession. Those memorable expressions include the call that he had brought peace to the people "in a Golden plate" and it was up to them to take care of it. From his Panyagoor speech, he said, "I bought back 50% of our oil, the next 50% is for you to bring". To the audience at the greater Equatoria gathering in Canada, in the context of the final protocol, the referendum, he said "who want to be call *abid* in his own country" signaling perhaps a clear choice for separation. On the day of CPA signing, he said "Sudan will never be the same again". In these regards, Garang was personally pointing to total separation from the Khartoum regime if no future demonstrated in the years leading to referendum.

Garang was not the only voice calling for secession; many Southerners were directly preaching separation. In fact, this has always been what the Southern Sudanese wanted, always fought for and many embraced that protocol more than the others. I remember urging a congregation at Nairobi during my first return home three years before the 2011 referendum to return home and make their voice heard. I reminded them to do it for us, those who were far away and with uncertain to vote. In that speech, I told them about what Gerang's meant when he said people should use the CPA "for their own good".

Over in the US, many lost boys and girls were frequent making rallies at Washington DC and UN in New York for such purposes; first to make their voices heard, while also calling for international to observation and ensure fair and open referendum in the Sudan. In our case, there were only a handful of locations in the entire continental USA and it took us hearts to drove far There were campaigns advocating that we Southerners in the diaspora also excise our rights to vote. Thousands drove hundreds of miles to cast their vote in the center assigned to them. But first, we were keeping our hope to make it to January 9th, 2011 for the referendum vote. Others were returning home from far corners of the globe to register and eventually to vote. In the states,

Inside the country, there were many attempts to allow voting only within the Sudan borders, inside the country. Many Northerners were optimistic about Southerners choosing separation and bad apple particularly in the Government were always taking steps to halt it. However, CPA had tied in international view and participation and in many cases; their hands were tied behind their backs.

Besides Khartoum, there were few voices including our brothers within the SPLA/M who preferred Southerners not to break away. These voices include Eastern Sudan and Kordufan who in fact were SPLA, but unfortunately geographically outside the Southern region territory. Others who favored the resources from the South to remain on the control of Khartoum argued that Southerners were never going to rule themselves.

On January 9th, Southerners went to the voting sites to cast their first and the only vote in the history of Sudan. We voted here in America, and Seattle where we live was one of the Northwest voting centers. Across Sudan and the refugee camps, Southerners poured to the centers to cast their votes. The votes count was unanimously with 98% for succession. It was anticipated, but the joy of the celebration that followed was even a great demonstration of unity among Southerners. At this point, we were done, the world had already had it in their book, and it was just a matter of six months prior to crowning a new nation. Still, there was fear, we were not yet a country and perhaps anything could happen, but at least our voices were heard. We were walking away.

As the world got ready with all paperwork and delegations to represent their country at the birth of South Sudan, Southerners were never preparing on anything but just for the day to come and the flag be raised first time among the world countries. July ninth was coming quickly. In Seattle, I was consulting my friends to find those who had South Sudan TV or Al Jazeera. On the morning of the July 9th, 2011, as millions of Southerners from far corners of the world and from far cities and villages inside South Sudan flocked into Juba to take part in the celebration, the world dignitaries and leaders crowded the narrow newly paved Juba airport to officiated and witnessed history. We were trying our best here in Seattle to be part of it live. I was asking my friends if there were get together parties to watch the celebration live. At that time, some of us had purchased South Sudan TV cable and yes people even without one gathering, there several houses most of us gathered to watch the celebration live. We went to our friend James Akot's house to watch the celebration. I barely turn away my eyes off as I watch more than five hours of energetic festivities. It was a very emotional achievement and a joy to have witness the conclusion of the long struggle. With many empty stomachs and shaky legs, there was no hold back to not celebrate at the naming of that new baby. It was a worldwide endless exhausting day of festivities.

This was a day that reminded us of all that we had gone through for half a century, the very reason why million died for, the day to appreciate so much, and of much emotional reflections. This was the day why I had been called "the lost boy of Sudan", named so because of my early separation from parents for the sake of that day and freedom. This was a very joyful welcome. It was a very emotional day, made worse by so much memories and revelations including the many revolutionary songs rehearsed that day and, seeing veterans walking the long stage, the unveil of John Garang statute by the president, the singing of the national anthem and ultimately the raising of our own flag for the first time among the world flags. We felt born and recognized as the world crowded our house for the first time that July 9th, 2011. In the clear day light, in the eyewitness of the world dignitaries and those watching around the world, me included, our nation was born, the Republic of South Sudan was added on the map. And in paraphrasing the words of Martin Luther King Jr. we were free at last.

Printed in the United States
By Bookmasters